Social Entrepreneurship

Meng Zhao · Jiye Mao
Editors

Social Entrepreneurship

An Innovative Solution to Social Problems

Editors
Meng Zhao
Business School
Renmin University of China
Beijing, China

Jiye Mao
Business School
Renmin University of China
Beijing, China

ISBN 978-981-15-9883-8 ISBN 978-981-15-9881-4 (eBook)
https://doi.org/10.1007/978-981-15-9881-4

Jointly published with China Renmin University Press
The print edition is not for sale in China Mainland. Customers from China Mainland please order the print book from: China Renmin University Press

This Springer imprint is published by the registered company Springer Nature Singapore Pte Ltd.
The registered company address is: 152 Beach Road, #21-01/04 Gateway East, Singapore 189721, Singapore

Foreword by Muhammad Yunus

I am pleased to see the release of this important scholarly work on social enterprise. I appreciate the hard and timely work by my colleagues at the Yunus Center for Social Business & Microfinance, Renmin University of China (YCRUC). This book makes an excellent effort to answer questions that I believe are critical for the current stage of social enterprise and social business development in China.

This book provides an appropriate and useful way of looking at what a social enterprise is fundamentally about. As I put 27 dollars in the hands of the poor people in rural Bangladesh more than 40 years ago, I was not offering financial support or teaching a business model, I was delivering my confidence in their inherent potential of pursuing an independent and better life. I was igniting their entrepreneurship.

Social enterprise is a broad umbrella concept within which there are many specific concepts. This book helpfully clarifies the differences and connections among these various concepts. I am sure this will help the readers in avoiding the confusion sometimes created by careless use of these terms, such as social enterprise, social business, corporate social responsibility, B Corp, and so forth. I see very often people use terms like social business and social enterprise interchangeably because of lack of understanding of both. This book will be helpful in clarifying the differences and making readers appreciate what they are, and what they are not.

Enormous possibilities wait for us to guide the national and the global economy in social direction by applying these concepts in appropriate ways. There is overwhelming concurrence that the present personal profit centric economic structure is leading the world to massive social problems, particularly the problem of high-speed concentration of wealth in fewer and fewer hands. In order to undo this trend quickly we have to shift the economy in the social direction as fast as we can. This book presents the options we have to achieve this.

This work has become especially attractive because it is among the first of its kind to conduct in-depth case studies of outstanding Chinese social enterprises. It offers its views on their strengths and weaknesses, breakthroughs and struggles, convictions, and concerns. This kind of knowledge is in great need both in China and worldwide.

I would like to applaud my academic colleagues at Renmin Business School for their contribution through this book in helping understand the updated landscape of social innovation in China. I give my best wishes to YCRUC and its partners in China for fixing their mission to substantially contribute in improving the capabilities, and social impact of the social enterprise and social business communities.

I hope social enterprises and social businesses will continue to grow in importance in the Chinese economy and become a major source of Chinese solutions for social problems in China and the world.

June 2018

Professor Muhammad Yunus
Founder, Grameen Bank
Nobel Peace Prize Laureate 2006
Dhaka, Bangladesh

Foreword by Zhenyao Wang

Let Enterprise be the Source of Benevolence

In today's economic world, three important trends are growing fast and starting to converge. They are business for social good, social enterprise, and social finance. These trends have been isolated from and even opposite to each other. They are now forming an in-depth integration of businesses, philanthropy, and finance, where the development of business and finance are driven by benevolence. I call this trend the new era of benevolence economy.

In this era, the most important task is the promotion of social entrepreneurship. Social entrepreneurship refers to the spirit of social enterprise practitioners who are dedicated to improving social welfare and promoting social progress by using commercial tools. This spirit can not only improve the efficiency of philanthropy by adopting commercial tools, but also can transform businesses into a force for social good and thus improve commercial civilization.

This book is a record of the best practices of Chinese social enterprise. These practices show that on the one hand, charity activities in China are rapidly merging with international trends and present innovation, and on the other hand the development of Chinese social enterprise has its unique features in structure and trend.

The development of Chinese social enterprise has four important features:

First, Chinese social enterprises have a solid social and cultural foundation. In Chinese culture, "philanthropy fortune" is a proper term with a long history. The link between philanthropy and fortune has deep cultural roots in China. A typical example is the "Boy of philanthropy fortune," a popular figure in Chinese mythology.

Second, Chinese social enterprises have early precursors. Back when the reform and opening up policies were implemented the government was challenged with many urgent social problems. One was employment for poor and disabled people. With limited funds, the government had no other choices but to encourage the development of private enterprise and state-owned social welfare enterprise to help vulnerable populations. Indeed, solving urgent social problems via enterprise is the essence of social enterprises.

Third, social enterprises in China grow relatively slow. Although the social enterprises listed in this book are successful, social enterprise is not the focus of the country's policy, and therefore this organizational form is still quite new to the public. Even social welfare enterprises run by the government today are less active for various reasons. Poverty alleviation by private companies or nonprofit organizations is not part of the policy support framework.

Finally, the support system for Chinese social enterprise is weak. A nationwide social enterprise certification system started a few years ago. Only seven enterprises were certified. A dozen were certified in the following year. The total number exceeded one-hundred in 2017. In contrast, when the UK started social enterprise certification, more than 70,000 enterprises were certified. We can say that at the beginning of certification, the gap between China and the UK was 10,000 fold. This difference does not reflect a gap in social enterprise practices, but a gap in our understanding of the certification itself.

What should we do to change this situation? I think the fundamental solution is to transform our mindset. The publication of this book is an important pushing hand for this transformation. When the whole society is still quite unfamiliar with social enterprise, the most effective solution is to introduce real cases of social enterprises with related theories to the public. The public can gain intuitive knowledge and can eventually reach a consensus on social enterprise.

Thanks to all the authors of this book. They worked hard and collected these exemplary cases, many of which are famous in the philanthropy community. I hope these cases can help carry forward social entrepreneurship in China.

Professor Zhenyao Wang
President of China Global Philanthropy Institute
Beijing Normal University
Beijing, China

Preface by Meng Zhao

Dear readers, by opening this book you have demonstrated an interest in social enterprise. Through vivid case studies and a rigorous theoretical framework, this book offers a panorama of flourishing Chinese social enterprises, social entrepreneurs, and their entrepreneurial spirit. It was coauthored and compiled by a dozen faculty members from the Yunus Center for Social Business and Microfinance, Renmin University of China and the Business School of Renmin University of China (hereinafter referred to as YCRUC and RMBS, respectively). Over a span of 10 months, we visited ten social enterprises that play a leading role in their respective fields, while collecting a large amount of data from more than 70 hours of both formal and informal interviews. We look to address two fundamental questions about social enterprise in China that have been very controversial over the years.

First, what is a social enterprise? This book proposes a framework that defines and categorizes Chinese social enterprises based on social entrepreneurship, and includes ten case studies to support this framework. Second, what are well-performed social enterprise startups like in China? This book portrays the key features of leading Chinese social enterprises through detailed cases.

On June 11, 2017, YCRUC and RMBS, along with 15 main institutions that promote social enterprise in China, released the Beijing Initiative on China Social Enterprise Development. These institutions include the Center for Civil Society Studies at Peking University, China Philanthropy Research Institute at Beijing Normal University, Social Governance & Communications Institute at Beijing Normal University, China Global Philanthropy Institute, China Charity Fair, China Alliance of Social Value Investment, China Association of Microfinance, Youchange China Social Entrepreneur Foundation, Yifang Foundation, Beijing Pro Bono Foundation, Non-Profit Incubator, Youthink Center, Social Entrepreneurs Star, Shenzhen Social Innovation Center, and Shanda960.com. The Initiative calls for the formation of a professional network that is dedicated to enhancing the development of Chinese social enterprises in such areas as certification, education, research, capacity building, branding, investment, and policy support. This network should work for shaping a necessary consensus about the concept and practice of social enterprises among relevant stakeholders, and developing a road map for the growth of a social enterprise field. This book is an action taken in response to this Initiative.

It is our hope that readers would be intrigued and prompted to explore and engage in social enterprises. We do not intend to thoroughly review the history and the concept of social enterprise, describe the status quo of social enterprise development, or resolving debates in the field. Rather, we propose a framework for defining and categorizing social enterprises on the basis of researches and case studies. The purpose is to provide a more rigorous cognitive foundation for deepening the discussion, research, and practice of social enterprise in China. The development of social enterprise in China is still in its early stage where people have different understandings of the connotation and boundaries of social enterprise. We shall review existing literature, clarify research findings, and find out these implications to Chinese social enterprises. On this basis, we try to propose a view of social enterprise that can both have a conversation with existing researches and also fit with unique realities in China.

This book proposes a defining framework of social enterprise that provides standards for deciding what a social enterprise is and for categorizing different types of social enterprises. This framework draws on 144 papers in leading international journals, domestic and foreign case studies, and our observation and studies of Chinese social enterprises. Our team analyzed the organizational features of dozens of social enterprises recognized by major international supporting agencies, including Asoka Foundation, the Schwab Foundation for Social Entrepreneurship, and the Skull Foundation. We also studied the features of 46 widely recognized social enterprises in China. Our analysis suggests that, first, the dichotomy of social and commercial elements fails to capture the diversity of social enterprise practices. This challenges the conventional and popular approach of relying on this dichotomy to define social enterprise. Second, there is no universally accepted definition of social enterprise. Some scholars argue that as social enterprise is diverse and complicated in nature, a universal definition of social enterprise does not necessarily contribute to research and practice. But we found there are already several schools of defining social enterprise. Third, in addition to social and commercial elements, current theories have all factored in other elements for the definition of social enterprise. The dichotomy view of social and commercial elements will only lead to a partial understanding of existing research findings. Based on these points, we propose to adopt an entrepreneurship view to replace the dichotomy view in defining and categorizing social enterprise. Specifically, a defining framework on social enterprise should not be limited to evaluating whether or not an organization with a social goal has a viable business model or is financially sustainable through generating revenue. A more plausible framework should help people understand how an organization combines a variety of entrepreneurial elements, including but not limited to social and commercial elements, to solve social problems.

This book, for the first time in China, integrates a theoretical framework with rich management cases in the discussion on social enterprise. It is targeted at various audiences. Practitioners can learn experience and lessons from the case studies. Scholars can use the cases in teaching, and gain inspirations for research. Policy makers, certification agencies, professional service providers, and investors use this book to identify and evaluate promising social enterprises.

The ten social enterprises included in the book were all founded in the past decade and are all located in five cities—Beijing, Shanghai, Shenzhen, Chengdu, and Hangzhou; each city a witness to flourishing social enterprises. Most of them registered with industrial and commercial administrations, and the majority of their founders have substantial business experience. The background information of the ten social enterprises can be found in Table 1. The enterprises are each dedicated to solving a different social problem. Having reviewed over a hundred Chinese social enterprises, we believe that the ten selected enterprises are leaders in their respective fields featuring better operations and faster growth. We fully understand the complications of social enterprise development, and do not intend to, nor can we, predict the ten enterprises' future. However, we believe that over years of exploration, the enterprises have formed or are forming promising business models with the potential to solve social problems on a sustained basis. In addition, we have found some clues in these enterprises to prevent them from shifting away from their social missions or, in other words, from going back on their social mission in pursuit of financial revenue and profit. These clues include institutional design, decision-making, organizational culture, and behavioral pattern.

The social enterprises included in this book provide innovative solutions to widespread and intractable social problems. Most of them are pioneers in their respective fields. CarbonStop developed China's first carbon management software and online low-carbon education system. Be Better launched the first financial quotient (FQ) training program series in China that target financially disadvantaged children. 123langlang.Com developed innovative educational products that can improve the reading and writing skills of children who suffer from dyslexia. Shared Harvest CSA was the first in China to put forth the "new generation of farmers" mission and push forward "community supported agriculture" by forming a national alliance. DaddyLab was the first in China to supervise product safety and push industrial progress based on a model that combines independent product testing and online sales of qualified products. RiceDonate designed the first model of its kind that combines online games with charity to encourage enterprises to participate in large-scale donations by demonstrating healthy ways of life. Chengdu Langli launched China's first platform for communities and individual families providing services include senior care, social work, and senior adapting. DreamCycling was the first to have launched an integral service system that provides first-aid, insurance, food and lodging, and welfare to ensure the safety and satisfaction of cyclists going to Tibet. Xihaner set up a full set of standards, processes, and training modules for intellectually disabled people to offer car wash services. Lastly, 0Fenbei launched big data information service to facilitate targeted poverty alleviation.

Good social enterprises both in China and overseas are committed to shaping a better society by aligning themselves with clear social missions. If the aforementioned ten social enterprises are able to fulfill their missions, then we can imagine the picture of a future Chinese society like this—consumers trust food safety and product quality. Many youngsters from rural families voluntarily return to their hometowns to start their own businesses and become "the new generation of farmers." The public trust charity projects often participate in activities for social capital. Senior

Table 1 Basic information of the social enterprises in case studies

Social enterprises	Year Founded	Location	Area of social impact	Founders' professional background
Xihaner Carwash	2015	Shenzhen	Intellectually disabled	Commercial investment, commercial venture
Shared Harvest	2012	Beijing	Agriculture pollution, food safety, rural construction	Started business venture after receiving doctorate
Chengdu Langli	2011	Chengdu	Senior care	Commercial venture
Be Better Education	2009	Shanghai	Economic citizenship education	Commercial enterprises, non-profit organizations
DaddyLab	2015	Hangzhou	Product safety, Health	Civil service, commercial venture
Rice Donate	2014	Beijing	Public welfare and charity	Started business venture after getting master's degree
123langlang	2009	Beijing	Dyslexia	Commercial enterprise
CarbonStop	2011	Beijing	Environmental protection	Commercial enterprise
0Fenbei	2016	Beijing	Poverty alleviation	Commercial enterprise, commercial venture
Dream Cycling	2013	Chengdu	Cyclists' safety and psychotherapy	Civil service

citizens feel free to walk around at home or outside with adequate safety facilities. Children who lack financial and educational resources have access to educational opportunities to improve their qualifications. People are aware of the importance of carbon reduction, and take active measures to supervise and reduce carbon emissions. Parents of intellectually disabled children or children troubled with dyslexia do not have to worry about their children's ability to support themselves and fit into society. Governments and private institutions are able to identify, track, and assist the poorest people. People who travel in Tibet feel safe when cycling around.

This book is the first of a series of books of case studies on Chinese social enterprises. By sharing the cases of various social enterprises in China, we hope to expect a bright future and keep the public informed of social entrepreneurs' endeavors to tackle daunting social problems. For social entrepreneurs, social problems are not cause for depression and anxiety, but rather motivation for change.

Associate Professor Meng Zhao
Founding Director of Yunus Center for Social
Business and Microfinance
Beijing, China

Preface by Jiye Mao

This book is the collective wisdom and hard work of more than a dozen faculty members from the Business School of Renmin University of China, who are devoted to promoting the development of Chinese social enterprises. I'd like to share three of my viewpoints on social enterprises and about this book.

First of all, why should we pay attention to social enterprises? The year 2018 is a historic time. It is the 40th anniversary of the reform and opening up policy, and also a good time for us to reflect on the past and plan for the future. In the past 40 years, Chinese society has experienced enormous changes, made remarkable achievements developed at a pace rarely experienced in human history. However, numerous complex and serious social problems have manifested in the wake of such a phenomenon. These include poverty, food safety, environmental pollution, protection of the interests of vulnerable groups, underserved elderly, and other historical and new problems. Some problems didn't disappear during the process of social reform and development, and instead tend to worsen.

In fact, no matter how highly developed a society is, inequality cannot be eliminated, and there will still be vulnerable people who are not benefited by social progress. The more advanced a society is, the more people are likely to care about social problems, and are willing to take action to find solutions.

Who's responsible for all these social problems? The government, enterprise, or the individual? It has been proven that any single part is not enough. It requires the whole society, including government, and all the people who have realized these problems and are willing to enact the labor to solve them. How to solve social problems effectively? In this fast-changing society, existing social organizations, charities, and other traditional methods are facing challenges. When economic development reaches its bottleneck, the opportunity for social transformation and upgrade is coming, and society is calling for new forces and innovations to address these challenges. Yet, no matter what solutions they are, sustainable development will be an important feature of them. Sustainable development is also the theme of today's global development. Social enterprises that come into being at this age are just in line with the concept of sustainable development, while being effective in solving social problems.

What is a social enterprise? The common interpretation is that it is an enterprise that uses business solutions to solve social problems. However, there are also other interpretations in academic and practical fields. A social enterprise research team from the Business School of Renmin University of China (RMBS) led by Dr. Meng ZHAO, puts forward a more accurate and inclusive definition: a social enterprise is an organization that uses entrepreneurship to solve social problems. One core of this definition is "entrepreneurship," which refers to entrepreneurial characteristics such as opportunity identification, innovation, risk-taking, and perseverance.

Second, why would RMBS study social enterprises? This is because our vision is "to become a world-class business school that knows Chinese management best." Since the object of any management study is organization, this new form of organization, China's social enterprises, naturally draws our attention. World-class business schools should have world-class practices to guide social development and the ambition to change the whole world and benefit mankind. In the first half of 2017, I visited two universities in the UK. One of them took sustainable development and social responsibility as the research subjects of their business school and the whole university. The other business school requires all the research to denote social responsibility and sustainable development, giving priority to recruit teachers of these fields. Today social responsibility and sustainable development are among the most popular topics in business education worldwide. In order to fulfill its social responsibility, RMBS hopes to play a leading role in the development of China's social enterprises. Therefore, in early 2017, in collaboration with China Institute of Inclusive Finance, RMBS and the Yunus Center of Bangladesh cofounded YCRUC. The team led by Meng ZHAO and Jianying WANG also worked together with 15 main institutions that promote social enterprises and released the Beijing Initiative on China Social Enterprise Development, furthering the development of China's social enterprises.

Some researchers at RMBS formed a force to study social problems and enter social enterprises. They are dedicated to the development of social enterprises in China. A group of young and middle-aged researchers organized themselves to conduct field research in many social enterprises. They came up with the enlightening case studies of this book based on their findings.

Thirdly, the feature of this book is that Dr. Meng ZHAO, one of its chief editors and main promoters, elaborated on the definition of social enterprise in the foreword, hoping to help define social enterprise and promote its development. This book includes ten of the latest cases that are quite representative. For practitioners, the power of role models is unlimited. These cases demonstrate different entrepreneurs' paths to solving social problems in various fields using different models, which can encourage more people to join in the social enterprise movement. For researchers, case study is a bridge between theory and practice. Case study is an effective and scientific way to summarize theories based on practice. Based on research and analysis of these cases, we can find the general rules that lie behind them. Our expertise in the fields of business research and case study enable us to summarize the theory based on the study of typical cases of Chinese social enterprises.

What this book lacks is the cross analysis and comparison of these cases, as well as references to existing literature. I hope that in the follow-up study, the team can focus on in-depth cross case comparison, and come up with more theoretical findings to guide practitioners and make more contributions to the research. Through our efforts in teaching, research, and social practice, we hope to promote the development of Chinese social enterprises.

Thanks to Meng ZHAO and Jianying WANG for their leadership and efforts in writing this book. Without their perseverance, the book would not have come out. They are passionate in the research of social enterprise, and have done a lot of organization and coordination for the development of the case studies in the book. Thanks to all fellow colleagues for your exploration and hard work. Thanks to all the social entrepreneurs who have accepted our interviews and investigations. They are the real leaders who kept on exploring and persevering in darkness and uncertainty. They pointed out the direction for the future of Chinese social enterprises.

I sincerely hope that this book will contribute to the development of social enterprise in China. I'm fully confident that the future for Chinese social enterprise is bright. The most difficult phase has been conquered and future steps will be steady.

Beijing, China

Professor Jiye Mao
Dean of RMBS

Acknowledgments

Many thanks to the following organizations and individuals for their pertinent suggestions on the theoretical framework and case selection of this book:

Ruijun Yuan, director of Center for Civil Society Studies at Peking University and his research team

Chunli Dian, Secretary General of China Charity Fair

Xuan Xia, Director General of Shenzhen Star of Social Innovation

Beiwei Li, Secretary General of Yifang Foundation

Hui Ling, Secretary General of Youchange China Social Entrepreneur Foundation

Yingwei Chen, Secretary General of Social Entrepreneurs Star

Ai You Foundation Venture Philanthropy Project Team

Hua Ju, Professor, School of Government, Peking University

Yongjun Li, Director of Department of Public Policy, School of Government, Peking University

Xiaomeng Zhang, Associate Professor, School of Marxism, Renmin University of China

Xiaohong Zhu, Professor, School of Humanities, North China Electric Power University

Renxian Jin, Associate Professor, School of Public Administration, University of International Business and Economics

Jian Li, Associate Professor, School of Management, Minzu University of China

Chao Guo, Professor, School of Social Policy and Practice, University of Pennsylvania in the US; editor in chief of the magazine *Nonprofit and Voluntary Sector Quarterly*

We would like to thank China Social Enterprise and Social Investment Forum 2017 for the opportunity to release the definition framework of China's social enterprises.

Thanks to graduate student Guo Xinnan of Renmin Business School of Renmin University of China, for her contribution for writing part of the chapter of "Social Enterprise Theoretical Framework." And thanks to graduate student Yujia Zhai, undergraduate student Zhuang Mi and Shuo Zhan, and MBA student Jinfeng Cai, of Renmin Business School of Renmin University of China, for their contributions for writing the cases of this book.

Contents

Social Enterprise Theoretical Framework

Meng Zhao

What Do We See When We Adopt a Dichotomic View?

Nowadays, it is a common practice to judge whether an organization is a social enterprise by the interrelationship between its social and commercial elements. This is called the dichotomic view. A popular definition of social enterprise is that social enterprise is the one which can solve social problems through business solutions. However, when we take a closer look at their social and commercial elements, we find that organizations can be of various forms, such as commercial enterprises undertaking social responsibilities, social organizations or institutions conducting commercial activities, welfare enterprises, and state-owned enterprises. We can find attributes of social enterprises in all of them. All of these organizations use certain commercial methods to solve social problems. Are they all social enterprises? Is social enterprise a new organizational form with unique attributes, or is it just a collective term for all business practices that can solve social problems through business solutions? This may be the first confusion caused by the dichotomic view. Further, we believe that there are other larger confusions, which will be demonstrated later in this chapter. First of all however, we'd like to discuss where this dichotomic view will lead us when we use it to understand mainstream literature. We find that current research can be classified into three major schools: Social Objective Priority, Social-Business Balance and Exclusive Social Objective.

Social Objective Priority believes that it is necessary for social enterprises to have commercial goals, but their social goals should be prioritized over commercial goals. Their commercial activities should serve their social goals. Typical expressions in current literature include: Social enterprises solve social problems through business solutions, but the focus of these enterprises are always social problems; Social enterprises are those that conduct commercial activities to achieve their major social

M. Zhao (✉)
Business School, Renmin University of China, Beijing, China
e-mail: mengzhao521@yahoo.com

M. Zhao and J. Mao (eds.), *Social Entrepreneurship*,
https://doi.org/10.1007/978-981-15-9881-4_1

goals, rather than to maximize profits; Social enterprise is a social innovation to solve social problems; it can conduct economic activities to provide goods or services, but these economic activities must serve for their social activities. Organizational forms of social enterprises recognized by Social Objective Priority theory include co-operatives, associations, trading non-profit organizations, community enterprises, development trusts, and fair trade organizations.

The school of Social-Business Balance believes that the social and commercial goals of social enterprises are in an equally important strategic position and together they constitute the core objective of social enterprises. Typical expressions of this school include: Social enterprises are those who combine and balance their commercial and social capital, and whose economic and social activities are equally important; Social enterprises are those who can balance between social value creation and project sustainability, and pursue a sustainable and balanced development; In social enterprises, social goals and commercial goals should possess equal footing. This opinion is based primarily on the research of B Corporation (B-Corp), Low Profit LLC (L3C), and flexible purpose corporations in the US, and community interest companies in the UK. For example, B Corporation is considered to be in line with the definition of social enterprise because it integrates social logic and commercial logic. A few scholars from the Social-Business Balance believe that projects with corporate social responsibilities can also be considered as a form of social enterprises. They believe that corporate social responsibility can be carried out by applying blended value in specific projects and achieve social goals, which means traditional enterprises can also achieve social goals by setting up social ventures within itself or cooperating with other institutions. In this sense, corporate social responsibility can create both commercial and social values equally, and thus make the enterprise a social enterprise.

The school of Exclusive Social Objective considers that the social goal should be the only organizational goal, and the definition of social enterprises should weaken or completely exclude the element of commercial goals. This school believes that social enterprises may not need to use any commercial methods, nor engage in any commercial activities to achieve social goals. Instead, they can achieve financial sustainability through stable donations or external funding. Social enterprises can sell products or services to support themselves, and they can also depend on external funds from government projects, foundations, or their parent non-profit organizations. The school of Exclusive Social Objective believes that a non-profit corporation can also be a form of social enterprise. Social organizations in the US include both charitable organizations and non-profit corporations. In the US, both non-profit corporations and for-profit corporations are certified and administered by their respective departments at the state and federal levels. A non-profit corporation must have a clear set of operating mechanisms, management system, and corporate governance structure, just like a for-profit corporation. However, a non-profit corporation does not pursue profit and the profit cannot be distributed either. How the asset should be divided after its dissolution should be clearly defined in advance. It enjoys tax incentives and special government funding in some social fields. Compared to traditional non-profit corporations, social enterprises are significantly innovative.

It is obvious that even when we just analyze from social and commercial aspects, scholars' understanding of social enterprises is diverse and even contradictory. The schools of Social Objective Priority and the Exclusive Social Objective believe that some enterprises can use corporate social responsibility just as a way to maximize their profits, so these enterprises cannot be regarded as social enterprises. The school of Social-Business Balance do not mind taking projects with corporate social responsibilities as social enterprises that can blend social and commercial values. The school of Social Objective Priority and Social-Business Balance emphasize the importance of commercial models and commercial activities; however the school of Exclusive Social Objective does not agree that pursuing market operating income is necessary for a social enterprise. So the question is: When people say that social enterprises solve social problems through business solutions, what exactly does it mean? Does it mean that business solutions should always be used to pursue social goals, or are they equally important so that a balance should be maintained? Do social enterprises have to operate while relying on their own operating income, or they can rely on other funding but still need to adopt an operation and management model similar to that of commercial enterprises? Can we count corporate social responsibility projects, commercial enterprises that create significant social values or non-profit organizations that rely on stable external funding as social enterprises? The answer given by the dichotomic view is "yes and no." So this perspective may seem simple and straightforward, but it actually leaves too much room for people to interpret according to their own experience and interests.

The Limitation of Dichotomic View

In addition to the confusions listed above, dichotomic view has four limitations.

First of all, dichotomic approach leads to excessive simplification of existing research findings. Dichotomic approach can help us understand the scholars' fundamental propositions, but when we explore the logic of existing research findings deeper, we will find that the most theoretical and practical enlightening statements actually contain elements other than social and commercial ones, such as the capabilities and assurance elements, which will be discussed later. Even on social and commercial elements, the three schools have different understandings. In terms of the social element, the school of Exclusive Social Objective focuses on the non-profit and public interest attributes of social enterprises, while the schools of Social Objective Priority and Social-Business Balance emphasize solving specific social problems and having clear social missions. While in terms of the commercial element, the school of Social Objective Priority requires social enterprises to carry out specific commercial activities and earn operating income. The school of Social-Business Balance on the other hand, emphasizes that social enterprise should have clear commercial modeling and a competitive operating strategy like traditional enterprise. These meticulous differences lead to difficulty in defining social enterprise, which cannot be solved by the dichotomic view.

Second, dichotomic view seems to have provided a simple and clear definition of social enterprises, but in fact it leads to divergent interpretation on social enterprises. People are obsessed with the relationship between social and commercial elements. Do social enterprises have to earn a profit in the market? Is an organization that seems "too commercialized" still a social enterprise? When most social enterprises have not yet made profits, and even if they do, they normally won't share dividends, people are still arguing about the proportion of the dividends they should share. The attempt to define social enterprise by the criterion of "solving social problems through business solutions" won't help us distinguish real social enterprises from other enterprises. The obsession with the relationship between social and commercial elements hinders us from interpretation other elements that are equally important when defining social enterprise, and from forming more detailed and complete interpretation of social enterprise.

Third, dichotomic view won't help us in interpretation the different forms social enterprise takes. These forms are complicated and diverse. For example, different social enterprises in the same social sector may differ significantly in their models and effects of promoting social transformation. The dichotomic view is not helpful in interpretation the fine differences between these forms. In other words, dichotomic approach is ineffective when differentiating between various social enterprises. We need a framework that can define social enterprises in multiple dimensions, which requires the introduction of elements other than social and commercial.

Finally, dichotomic approach attempts to define social enterprise completely with some elements in the connotation of social enterprise, which may not be helpful to the ecological diversity of the practice of social enterprise. For example, it may lead to the exclusion of some types of social enterprise and the imbalance of resources allocated to different types of social enterprise, and may limit the identification and support of diversified social enterprise development patterns and social innovation patterns. The only way by which we can effectively push the development of something so complicated and diverse is through a multi-dimensional defining framework.

What Do We See When We Adopt Entrepreneurship Perspective?

Due to these limitations of dichotomic approach, we propose the entrepreneurship perspective to define social enterprises. We believe that in addition to social and commercial elements, it is necessary to consider the element of social entrepreneurship when defining social enterprises. Compared with "solving social problems through business solutions," defining by "solving social problems by entrepreneurial means" is more line with the original concept of social enterprise put forward by the early scholars. Our definition of social enterprises in China just needs to return to entrepreneurship, which is promoted originally as the core of social enterprises. In 2006, Greg Dee in his *Framing a theory of social entrepreneurship: Building on two schools of practice and thought* mentioned that social entrepreneurship is the core of social enterprise which differentiates itself from the traditional enterprises solving social problems. A social enterprise is an organization that uses entrepreneurship to solve social problems and create social values. The application of entrepreneurship in solving social problems created the concept of social entrepreneurship. Social entrepreneurship refers to an innovative organizing process to identify and find opportunities to solve social problems. Research holds that connotations of social entrepreneurship include innovation, opportunity identification, problem-solving ability, resource utilization ability, and risk-taking, as well as other measures to prevent social missions from drifting, including governance structure, profit distribution models, and identity recognition. We categorize all these elements related to social entrepreneurship into capabilities and assurance elements. The former includes the various abilities of an organization to solve social problems, while the latter refers to the behaviors and mechanisms of an organization to guarantee its social missions do not drift easily.

The perspective of entrepreneurship is different from that of solving social problems through business solutions. Commercial means can be understood as the means to earn operating income and apply market-based business strategies in order to ensure the sustainable development of the organization. Social entrepreneurship does not necessarily require an organization to earn operating income. The sustainable development of an organization can be achieved through stable external donation or funding, as while as its ability to solve problems, such as opportunity identification, innovation, and risk management. So many elements of social entrepreneurship may make it too complicated to define social enterprises. Therefore, we need a balanced perspective, which can be used to better explain the complexity of facts than the dichotomic view, and is easier to understand and use at the same time. The perspective of entrepreneurship attempts not to deny the scholars' or practitioners' attempt to describe social enterprises with social and commercial elements, but to understand the complex phenomenon of social enterprises more accurately and comprehensively.

From the perspective of entrepreneurship, the core elements of social enterprises are combined together to determine its connotation and identify its type. Compared with the dichotomic view, defining social enterprises by this perspective ensures the connotation is consistent, all the organizational types can be included, and their individual differences can be distinguished. From the perspective of entrepreneurship, practitioners can explore social enterprises of various types, and can find the right path to create their own business that fits their value and ability. Third-party support organizations can use it to identify the right types of enterprises that they can help, and evaluate their development level by their performance of these entrepreneurship elements. Meanwhile, the inclusiveness of the entrepreneurship perspective allows various existing forms of organizations (e.g. private enterprises, state-owned enterprises, institutions, etc.) to see their potential to transform to social enterprises and know where to begin, and therefore can carry out the transformation selectively and gradually. We hope that the definition framework of social enterprises based on the perspective of entrepreneurship can provide a theoretical basis for the sustainable and stable development of social enterprises in China.

Different scholars may emphasize different elements of entrepreneurship when defining social enterprises. We extract the keywords used to describe the concept of social enterprise in each paper, and after categorizing and abstraction, we categories them into four core element types and 13 sub-factor types. Table 1 summarizes these element types. Table 2 summarizes the ratio of different entrepreneurship elements used in the literature of each social enterprise definition school. For example, "social and commercial elements" ratio refers to the proportion of papers that define social enterprises using only social and commercial elements among all the papers of the school. It can be observed that 50% or more of all the three schools used other entrepreneurship elements besides social and commercial elements to define social enterprises. The school of Social Objective Priority is more inclined to define social enterprises with "social, commercial and assurance elements" than other schools. The school of Social-Business Balance is more inclined to use "social, commercial and capabilities elements", while the school of Exclusive Social Objective is more inclined to define social enterprises with "social-ability element combination." Compared with the dichotomic view, the perspective of entrepreneurship can identify the essential differences between different schools more comprehensively.

Table 1 Entrepreneurship elements of social enterprises defined in existing literature

Types of entrepreneurship core elements	Types of entrepreneurship sub-factors
Social elements	Social mission/value
	Social goal/influence
	Non-profit attribute
Commercial elements	Source of income
	Commercial logic/value
	Commercial goal/influence
	Financial sustainability
	Commercial activity and model
(Entrepreneurship) assurance elements	Governance structure
	Profit distribution model
	Identity recognition
(Entrepreneurship) capabilities elements	Innovation
	Opportunity identification

Table 2 Multi-element analysis of different schools defining social enterprises

Different schools defining social enterprises	Social and commercial elements	Social and ability elements	Social, commercial and guarantee elements	Social, commercial and and ability elements	Social, commercial and guarantee and ability elements
Social Objective Priority	43.9%	0	28.4%	21.6%	6.1%
Social-Business Balance	50%	0	19.2%	30.8%	0
Exclusive Social Objective	50%	50%	0	0	0

Definition Framework of Chinese Social Enterprises from an Entrepreneurship View

We studied the main social enterprises certification criteria overseas, including Social Enterprise Badge, SE Mark and Community Interest Company in UK. The certification criteria of UK Social Enterprise Badge include: Social or environmental objectives, the state of independent operation, the proportion of commercial income, the proportion of profit distribution, and the nature of certification agencies. Those of UK SE Mark include: Social or environmental objectives, the state of independent operation, the proportion of commercial income, the proportion of profit distribution, asset lock and the nature of certification agencies. And those of UK Community Interest Company includes: Social or environmental objectives, the state of independent operation, the proportion of profit distribution, asset lock, governance model of civil rights and the nature of certification agencies. In our opinion, all the above criteria are not applicable for the certification of social enterprises in China. Based on the analysis of these criteria, we propose our criteria consisting of capabilities and assurance elements from the perspective of entrepreneurship.

The definition framework of social enterprises in China includes two parts: defining criteria and categorizing criteria. The former answers the question whether an organization is a social enterprise, while the latter answers the question of what kind of social enterprise the organization is. The defining criteria include an organization's social-orientated mission, its ability to identify opportunities of transition, its abilities to solve social problems in innovative ways and the stability of its social mission. Only when an organization meets all four of these criteria can it be identified as a social enterprise. Classification criteria include organizational form criteria, revenue model criteria, and dividend policy criteria, which are used to classify different types of organizations within the category of social enterprises.

The brief definition of social enterprise in China we propose is: "an organisation that adopts socially entrepreneurial approaches to address social problems, while featuring mechanisms that prevent its social mission from drifting." The complete definition is: "Social enterprise is an organisation that has a primary organisational objective of solving a specific social problem; identifies an opportunity of making social change rooted in the government and market failures; delivers innovative problem-solving solutions; and has practices and/or systems that protect the social goal from being jeopardised by the pursuit of the business goal."

The criterion of social priority organizational mission refers to that the organization prioritizes its social mission over its financial goal when making organizational decisions. This criterion emphasizes that a social enterprise must be clear about its social mission, the social problems it aims to solve and the social impact it can make. The dominant role of social mission determines a social enterprise' decision-making logic and growing path. If an organization is driven by commercial objectives but not social mission, when the cost of solving social problems is higher than the profits it brings, the organization will tend to give up and turn to investing in activities that can generate higher profits. But if an organization is driven by its social mission, when it encounters the same situation, it will manage to transform its existing business model, and find best ways to solve social problems continuously. Fundamentally, it will take long-term tracking and observing of its decision-making process to judge whether an organization truly puts its priority on social mission over others. When the organization is in its early stages and such tracking and observation is not possible, we can make preliminary judgments by such criteria as how clear is the organization's social mission, how does it measure its social problem solving and its social impact, and how stable is its social mission, which will be discussed later.

Opportunity identification refers to a social enterprise's ability to identify social issues that haven't been effectively addressed by government or commercial enterprises. This criterion ensures that social enterprises won't waste time in solving social problems that can be solved by government and commercial organizations more effectively. For example, an organic food store that sells safe food does not meet the opportunity identification criterion of being a social enterprise because traditional commercial companies are already selling a lot of organic food. A private hospital that provides traditional medical services does not meet the criterion of opportunity identification either because in this field both public hospitals and for-profit private hospitals are providing services. Social enterprises only solve the social problems that have not been effectively solved either by the government or commercial enterprises. For example, the potential problem of food safety hazards in planting and supplier management has not been effectively addressed by the government or commercial enterprises. If an organization addresses such problems, it will meet the criterion of opportunity identification.

Solution innovativeness means a social enterprise should adopt different solutions to solve social problems other than by the traditional charity model. This criterion has two dimensions: financial sustainability and newness. Financial sustainability means that a social enterprise must either be able to obtain stable external funding or works in an effective model that can generate sustainable market operating income, for example, either one of the nine social problem solving models identified by existing research (summarized in Table 3 adpated from Alter, K. 2007. Social enterprise typology. Virtue Ventures LLC. 12: 1–124). Newness means that a social enterprise must have some characteristics that are clearly distinctive from traditional charities

Table 3 Common social problem solving models used by social enterprises

Models	Description	Cases
Entrepreneur Support Model	Provide products or training to target groups (usually vulnerable groups) to help them increase their income by selling products or services	Microloans, consulting or technical support
Market intermediation model	Buy products or services from target groups (usually vulnerable groups) and sell them on the market	Supply co-operatives (e.g. fair trade), usually in the fields of agriculture and handicrafts
Employment model	Provide job opportunities or professional training to target groups (usually vulnerable groups) to help them sell their products or services	Provide job opportunities for disabled and young people (e.g. in gardening services, cafe, printing services, etc.)
Fee-for-Service Model	Provide new payable social services in the areas where government and market fail, including education, medical care, senior care, etc	Museums on ethnic minority cultures, or mutual help senior care services
Low-Income Client as Market Model	Target low-income customers and provide quality products and services at reasonable prices	Health care (prescription, glasses), use of public facilities
Co-operative model	Provide co-operative members with services such as market information, technical support, collective bargaining, bulk purchasing, access to products/services, market entry, etc	Bulk purchasing, collective bargaining, agricultural co-operatives, credit co-operatives
Market Linkage Model	Connect target groups (usually vulnerable groups) with the market by providing services such as market information and market research	Import and export, market research and intermediary services
Service Subsidization Model	Providing free services to low-income people by selling similar but paid services to higher-income people	Counseling, psychological counseling, employment training, rental, printing and other services
Organizational Support Model	Operate a for-profit enterprise and a non-profit organization at the same time (the two often provide different services). Use the former one's revenue earned from selling products or services in the market to support the latter's social goals	Similar to service subsidies—Use the profit generated by for-profit assets to subsidize non-profit activities

in terms of its products or services, processes or application scenarios. It should be noted that the criterion of innovation is essentially an "exclusion criterion" rather than a "selective criterion." An organization which can meet the criterion of innovation infers that it is financially sustainable and innovative enough that the following two models of creating social value are excluded: (1) relying on unstable donations or one-time project inputs and being financially unsustainable; and (2) able to obtain stable donations, but not innovative in products or services, processes, and application scenarios. Typical examples of the former include irregular donations, volunteer activities, charities such as bridge repairs, etc. Typical examples of the latter include traditional study grant activities through continuous funding from companies or government. The criterion of innovation is not used to judge which of the organizations is more innovative, but to identify whether the organization meets the basic financial sustainability and innovation standards above. Apart from a definition framework of social enterprise, we are also developing categorizing criteria for the development stages of social enterprises. The purpose of using the criterion of innovation in judging the development stages of social enterprises is to help find the best ones. This is different from its function in the definition framework.

The criterion of social robustness means that a social enterprise has clear behaviors or mechanisms to ensure its social mission will not drift, or that the social mission of the organization will not be damaged by the pursuit of commercial goals. It contains the sub-factors of governance structure and profit distribution models in assurance elements. The sub-factor of governance structure requires social enterprises to prevent its social mission from drifting by improving the design of corporate governance structure. For example, to establish mechanisms to ensure all the stakeholders participate in decision-making, or to monitor and restrict decisions by organization leaders that may damage the social mission. The sub-factor of the profit distribution model requires social enterprises to limit the proportion of profits distributed to shareholders, and to reinvest part or all of the profits into the mission of solving social problems continuously.

It should be noted that in the social enterprise definition framework we put forward, profit distribution is only regarded as one of the many criteria to judge the stability of the social mission. In other words, whether and to what extent an organization distributes its profits does not constitute a decisive factor for being a social enterprise. The final judgment should be made based on all the four criteria. This opinion on profit distribution is different from many other existing certification criteria. In addition to the above two guarantee sub-factors that we found by studying current literature, we also added the following criteria to judge the stability of social mission based on the analysis of Chinese and foreign cases, including the form of asset locking, the selection on investors, the selection on target market/customers, business growth model, product development direction, senior management team's interpretation of the organization, organization members' self-identity, and decision makers' interpretation of the organization's vision and future development direction. The applicability of these criteria varies according to the specific situation of each organization. These criteria are not "cumulative," which means we cannot conclude that an organization's social mission is more stable than others just because its development will not drift from social missions on more criteria. Social robustness can be measured only through in-depth analysis from multiple perspectives on a case-by-case basis.

Categorizing criteria is used to distinguish the types of organizations within the category of social enterprises by the criteria of organizational form, revenue model, and dividend policy. In terms of organizational form, Chinese social enterprises may include social organizations and corporations established based on laws. In terms of revenue model, Chinese social enterprises can achieve financial sustainability by obtaining stable external donations or subsidies, or by generating operating revenue. In terms of dividend policy, Chinese social enterprises can adopt different policies including free dividends, voluntary partial dividends, voluntary zero dividends or no dividend per applicable laws.

Social enterprises which meet the defining criteria can be divided into two categories of major social enterprises using categorizing criteria: charity-based social enterprises and market-based social enterprises. Market-based social enterprises can be divided into the following three sub-categories: revenue-making non-profit organizations (NPOs), social purpose companies, and social businesses. Revenue-Making NPO refers to institutions that are registered with civil administrations and make revenue by selling products and/or services Social purpose companies are the most common form of social enterprises in China. These institutions are registered with industrial and commercial authorities and dependent solely or mainly on the income from market operations. It should be noted that a social enterprise can run a NPO completely depending on external funding and a registered social purpose company at the same time. In this case, it is the social purpose company that determines whether this organization is a social enterprise or not. Social purpose companies also include some B Corps. A B Corp is a for-profit enterprise that meets strict social and environmental performance standards, protects the interests of a wide range of stakeholders, and does not take maximizing shareholders' interests as its only purpose. The entrepreneurship of a B Corp is usually quite outstanding. Some enterprises may not take solving social problems as their priority, or they do not solve social problems in the area where both government and common enterprises fail. Instead, they protect a wide range of stakeholders from losses while creating value for their shareholders. They may even sacrifice some of their shareholders' interests for the interests of other stakeholders. Although these enterprises are "doing good deeds," and they go further than those commercial enterprises just carrying out activities for corporate social responsibilities, and exceed the pursuit of maximizing the interests of shareholders, they still cannot be identified as social enterprises. On the other hand, there are also some B Corps that prioritize social objectives among other organizational objectives, operate in the area where government and common enterprises fail, and have clear behaviors or mechanisms to ensure their social missions. They belong to the market-based social enterprise category and social purpose company sub-category.

The term of social business was put forward by Professor Muhammad Yunus, the 2006 Nobel Peace Prize laureate and pioneer of microfinance. It refers to a non-loss, non-dividend company that is financially self-sustainable and reinvests all of its profits in the business itself to address social problems. Legally, it is an enterprise rather than a non-profit organization. Its management model, business model and market competitiveness are the same as those of ordinary commercial enterprises, but their shareholders invest all their profits into social businesses rather than share them. Professor Yunus believes that social business is a branch of bigger social enterprise and a purer social enterprise. The fundamental purpose of social business is to solve social problems, not generating profit. In our framework, it belongs to social business sub-category under market-based social enterprise. Currently there are at least 600 social businesses in more than a dozen countries in the world, but it hasn't been found in China which can meet all the standards, so it is mainly a theoretical concept in China. Table 4 summarizes the categories of social enterprises under the definition framework of this book and their relationship with other forms of organizations that also generate social value.

On the one hand, this book uses the social enterprise identification and categorizing criteria above to analyze the enterprises in the case studies; on the other hand, by these case studies, it explains how this theoretical framework helps to understand and analyze social enterprise practices. Table 5 summarizes the categories of the social enterprises in case studies. Tables 6, 7, 8 and 9 summarizes the performance of the enterprises in case studies on the four defining criteria.

Conclusion

Based on the analysis of currently literature and case studies, we believe that using the dichotomic view, which means to consider the relationship between an organization's social goals and business models (including its profit earning models, profit distribution methods, etc.), to understand and identify if an organization is a social enterprise has limitations. We propose an entrepreneurship perspective to understand and identify social enterprise. By adding the capabilities and assurance elements to the definition of social enterprise and putting entrepreneurship rather than profit model at the center of the definition, we return the definition of social enterprise to its original spirit of entrepreneurship. In this book, we believe that if people focus only on the business solutions of social enterprise, the essential attribute of social enterprise—social entrepreneurship—will be ignored. The essence of social enterprises is not so much to adopt business solutions to solve social problems, rather than to maximize entrepreneurship to solve social problems. Social entrepreneurship, or in other words, to solve social problems with prioritized social goals, continuous innovation, and result-orientation, should be a necessary characteristics of social enterprises.

Specifically, this book proposes four criteria to define Chinese social enterprises, which include an organization's prioritized social mission, its abilities to identify opportunities for social transitions in the area where both government and the market fail, its abilities to solve social problems in innovative ways and the stability of its social mission. Only when an organizations meets all these four criteria can it be identified as a social enterprise. If an organization's mission is not to solve social

Table 4 Social enterprise categorizing criteria

	Social enterprises						
	Charity-based social enterprises		Market-based social enterprises				
	Innovative public welfare (different from traditional charity activities supported by the government)	Innovative charity (different from traditional charity activities depend on private grants or donations)	Revenue-making non-profit organizations	Social purpose companies (including B Corps in social enterprises)	Social businesses	Double bottom line enterprises, such as B Corps which are not social enterprises, low profit limited liability companies, flexible purpose companies, etc	Corporate social responsibility
Four defining criteria	Comply	Comply	Comply	Comply	Comply	Not comply	Not comply
Classification criteria: Organizational form	Non-profit registration(social organizations)	Non-profit registration(social organizations)	Non-profit registration(social organizations)	Commercial registration(companies)	Commercial registration (companies)	Commercial registration(companies)	Commercial registration(companies)
Distinguishing criteria: revenue model	No market operating revenue, and mainly depend on government budget or government service purchase funds	No market operating revenue, and mainly depend on private donations or grants	Depend not only on government subsidies, government purchases, private donations or grants, but also on market operating revenue The ratio of the two sources is not fixed	Completely or mainly depend on market operating revenue, small portion of government subsidies, government purchases, and private donations or grants are allowed	Completely or mainly depend on market operating revenue	Completely or mainly depend on market operating revenue	Completely or mainly depend on market operating revenue

(continued)

Table 4 (continued)

	Social enterprises						
	Charity-based social enterprises		Market-based social enterprises				
Distinguishing criteria: dividend policies	No dividends allowed by law	No dividends allowed by law	No dividends allowed by law	Free dividend policy: dividend can be limited or unlimited	No dividend allowed by organizational policy	No limitations on dividends	No limitations on dividends

Table 5 Categories of social enterprises in case studies

	Organizational form	Source of revenue	Dividend policies	Social enterprise categories
Xihaner Carwash	Non-profit registration (social organizations)	Mainly depends on market operating revenue, and partially on government subsidies	No dividends allowed by law	Revenue-making non-profit organization
Shared Harvest	Commercial registration (companies)	Mainly depends on market operating revenue	Free dividend policy	Social purpose companies
Chengdu Langli	At the beginning, it was registered as a non-profit, and later part of its business was registered as a company	Caring and supporting services for the seniors mainly depend on market operation revenue, and social work services mainly depend on government funding	Business registered in civil affairs departments does not share dividend according to the law, and the business registered in industry and commerce departments shares dividends voluntarily	Dual category: social purpose companies + revenue-making non-profit organization (NPOs)
Baite Education	At the beginning, it was registered as a non-profit, and later part of its business was registered as a company	Partly depends on market operation revenue, and mainly depends on external private funding	Business registered in civil affairs departments does not share dividends according to the law, and the business registered in industry and commerce departments shares dividends voluntarily	Dual category: social purpose companies + revenue-making non-profit organization (NPOs)
Daddy Lab	Commercial registration (companies)	Mainly depends on market operating revenue	Free dividend policy	Social purpose company
RiceDonate	Commercial registration (companies)	Mainly depends on market operating revenue	Free dividend policy	Social purpose company

(continued)

Table 5 (continued)

	Organizational form	Source of revenue	Dividend policies	Social enterprise categories
123langlang	Commercial registration (companies)	Mainly depends on market operating revenue, and partially on government service purchases and external investment	Free dividend policy	Social purpose company
CarbonStop	Commercial registration (companies)	Completely or mainly depends on market operating revenue	Free dividend policy	Social purpose company
0Fenbei	Commercial registration (companies)	Completely or mainly depends on market operating revenue	Free dividend policy	Social purpose company
Ride for Dream	Non-profit registration (social organizations)	Partly depends on market operation revenue, and mainly on external private funding	No dividends allowed by law	Revenue-making non-profit organization

Table 6 Social mission priority standard reference information

	Is the social mission clear or not	Can the social mission be measured clearly?	Can business growth help achieve the social mission?	Are any resources invested in systematic transformation?
Xihaner Carwash	Help intellectually disabled people learn skills, participate in work, realize their values and win social respect	Initiate "Chunlei campaign" nationwide, a mass employment plan for intellectually disabled people. The goal is to set up 1000 Xihaner car washing centers, and provide 10,000 to 15,000 jobs for intellectually disabled people	Business growth directly increases the number of intellectually disabled people being employed and therefore realizes the social mission	1. Promote policy change; 2. Accelerate the realization of its social mission through free output of its model.
SharedHarvest	Find solutions for agricultural pollution and agricultural product safety problem in China; advocate a healthy lifestyle; provide service to agricultural producers and consumers; and push sustainable rural development	Formula of social transition: When 5 consumers join, 1 mu of land can be detoxified; when 10 consumers join, 1 farmer can cultivate organically; when 100 consumers join, 5 young farmers can stay working in the countryside; and when 1000 consumers join, a more sustainable village can be built. The number of its members increased from the first 10 in 2012 to nearly 1000 in 2017. It no serves nearly 2000 families	Business growth directly reduces the use of fertilizers and pesticides, increases farmers' income and minimizes customers' food safety hazards, thus realizing its social mission	1. Carry out many social education activities; 2. Realize its social mission by outputting its model free of charge; 3. Establish "community-supported agriculture" alliance, share experience free of charge, and push industry development; 4. Extending industry standards beyond current laws and regulations.

(continued)

Table 6 (continued)

	Is the social mission clear or not	Can the social mission be measured clearly?	Can business growth help achieve the social mission?	Are any resources invested in systematic transformation?
Chengdu Langli	Recreate a senior-friendly society	By 2017, it established 36 low-cost community service centers for the senior citizens in 106 communities. Provided cheap or free senior care and social work services for more than 30,000 person hours	Business growth directly increases the number of low-income families served, thus realizing its social mission	1. Promoted policy change; 2. Developed the first assessment system and the first industry standard on senior-friendly community services in China; 3. Established a network of franchisees and suppliers of senior-friendly community service, and promoted the development of the whole industry.
Bebetter Education	Become the platform to build the capacity-building of domestic economic citizen education (financial intelligence education). Promote policy reform so that personal economic education can be gradually added to public school curriculums	Its economic citizen education service covers more than 40 cities in China. In 2017, the number of people who received its service reached 1.23 million, 105% higher than 2016. By 2020, Bebetter aims to serve 10 million children and adolescents	Business growth directly increases the number of children who received their services, realizing its social mission	1. Promoted policy change; 2. Export lessons and ability, and work with other social organizations and local governments to realize its social mission.
	Is social mission clear or not?	Can the social mission be measured clearly?	Can business at scale help achieve the social mission?	Any resources invested in systematic transition?

(continued)

Table 6 (continued)

	Is the social mission clear or not	Can the social mission be measured clearly?	Can business growth help achieve the social mission?	Are any resources invested in systematic transformation?
DaddyLab	Reduce the amount of unqualified products in China. Keep toxic and harmful products away from children	WeChat public account reached 70,000 active followers, among which 23,000 have bought their products. In 2017, the number of followers exceeded 500,000	Business growth directly increases the number of products tested and their social impact, reduces hazards incurred by toxic and harmful products, and thus realize its social mission	1. Help improve national standards; 2. Promote industry transformation.
RiceDonate	Help people become their better selves, enjoy the happiness of growing up, doing good deeds and helping others	Has more than 3 million registered users; Worked together with more than 150 enterprises who donated more than 30 million RMB; Cooperated with more than 700 public charity organizations. More than 1,500 public welfare projects have been approved, among which 1,000 have started and received feedback	Business growth directly increases enterprise donation to public welfare organizations, realizing its social mission	Promote enterprise public welfare involvement by means of activity planning and consultation
123langlang	Calling on all society to learn about children's dyslexia, improve their situation, provide specialized education, realize education equity, and help these children grow up healthily and fall in love with reading	By September 2017, there are 2 direct locations in Beijing and 42 franchise locations in other cities. The percentage of students with dyslexia in direct locations is 50%, and that in franchise locations is 5%	Business growth directly increases the number of children with dyslexia it serves, realizing its social mission	1. Carry out social education; 2. Cooperate with academic institutions and develop educational tools and standards; 3. Export its business model through franchising

(continued)

Table 6 (continued)

	Is the social mission clear or not	Can the social mission be measured clearly?	Can business growth help achieve the social mission?	Are any resources invested in systematic transformation?
CarbonStop	Reduce carbon emissions and carbon footprints	Its enterprise Carbon Accounting and Management Platform (CAMP) has more than 100 domestic and overseas customers. By applying carbon management software, it aims to help enterprises reduce 18 million tons of carbon emission by 2020; and by means of Green Conferencing, it aims to reduce 3 million tons of carbon emissions by 2020	Business growth directly reduces or increases enterprise carbon emission cost, and thus realize its social mission	1. Carried out social education at scale; 2. Promoted policy change.
	Is the social mission clear?	Can the social mission be measured clearly?	Can business at scale help achieve the social mission?	Are any resources invested in systematic transformation?
0Fenbei	Help and serve for the poorest people in China, and finally eliminate poverty	Within 1 year after its establishment, they have helped more than 7,000 poor households (about 25,000 people) find the medical, educational or other aids they need	Business growth directly increases the number of poor people served, thus realizing its social mission	Not clear

(continued)

Table 6 (continued)

	Is the social mission clear or not	Can the social mission be measured clearly?	Can business growth help achieve the social mission?	Are any resources invested in systematic transformation?
Ridefor Dream	Protect the "Road to Heaven" and ensure the safety of riders	Served 15,000 person hours in 2016, about 5% of all the travelers riding to Tibet by bicycle; 67,000 person hours in 2017, 22% of the total. In 2017, it cooperated with Tourism Development Committees along the Xinjiang-Tibet Road, and began to serve riders on Xinjiang-Tibet Road, instead of Xichuan-Tibet Road only in the past	Business growth directly increases the number of people being served, expands the scope of its service, improves its quality, and thus realizes its social mission	Encourage enterprises and a large numbers of volunteers to participate in environmental protection activities while operating its main business

Notes 1. The provided information is for basic reference. More tracking and investigation are required for judging whether the organization strictly complies with the defining criteria; 2. Systematic transformation means to solve social problems by means of transforming the external systematic elements including policies, social perception, investment, and industry ecology, instead of by conducting specific businesses themselves

Table 7 Opportunity identification standard reference information

Xihaner Carwash	Government subsidies cannot fulfill all the needs of intellectually disabled people. They can hardly adapt to the jobs in regular enterprises, so their employment rates are low
SharedHarvest	Intense commercial competition, consumer preferences for low-priced products, and increasing rural labor costs leave little room for the producers of organic agriculture to profit, resulting in market failure where profit-driven investment drives out ethical investment. On the other hand, the cost is too high for the government to transact with and supervise hundreds of millions of agricultural households. Government mechanisms and systematic solutions to agricultural pollution and agricultural product safety problems are missing, and government failure is formed
Chengdu Langli	It is difficult for the government to provide complete welfare service and products for the senior citizens. Existing welfare and support for senior citizens are not accurate and effective enough. Furthermore, due to market information asymmetry and social prejudice, companies providing services for medium-income and vulnerable senior groups find it hard for the market to accept a reasonable price that can cover their input
Bebetter Education	Government and commercial enterprises have paid little attention and invested little resources to economic citizenship education, and even less for poor children
Daddy Lab	National testing standards are not comprehensive. Even if a new standard is issued, manufacturers may replace harmful material banned by standards with some other harmful material. Government and commercial forces haven't solved the problems of information asymmetry in the area of consumer products
Rice Donate	Neither government or commercial enterprises have found effective solutions to the issues such as public's attitude to donation is inactive, and the processes and outcomes of using donations are not clear, etc
123langlang	Government intervention and response mechanisms to dyslexia are not available yet. Commercial enterprises haven't been involved in the field of dyslexia correction and training. Relevant teaching materials and teaching methods are not available
Carbon Stop	Neither government nor commercial enterprises have provided carbon emission management software and consulting services
0fenbei	Governmental poverty alleviation policy implementation is not very effective. Commercial enterprises are not enthusiastic to serve poor households registered in government systems. Public welfare institutions have to pay high cost to obtain accurate information of rural poor households

(continued)

Table 7 (continued)

Dream Cycling	The Sichuan-Tibet highway is 2,154 km long and runs through many administrative areas, but the range of each administration's responsibility and authority are vague. Therefore, it is difficult for the government to organize relevant resources to carry out road rescues and environmental protection effectively. Establishing a commercial safety rescue system for the Sichuan-Tibet line is quite difficult, and to operate and make a profit is even more difficult, so commercial enterprises are not willing to invest

Notes 1. The provided information is for basic reference. Further tracking and investigation are required to judge whether the organization strictly complies with the defining criteria; 2. Opportunity identification is to investigate whether the social problems an organization aims to solve are in the field where both government and market fails

Table 8 Creativity standards reference information

	Is the social value creation model different from traditional charity or not?	Is it financially sustainable to solve social problems or not?
Xihaner Carwash	The first car wash in China hiring mostly intellectually disabled people. Through the comprehensive system including project selection, operation procedure, ability evaluation and training, and Xihaner social adaptability improvement system, intellectually disabled children can also support themselves and participate in society	Hasn't reached a stable financial balance yet. Revenue mainly comes from service charges, and largely depends on government funding
SharedHarvest	Establish a sustainable commercial model to solve the problem of agriculture and food contamination, promote the concept of ecological agriculture, and search for the road of Rural Revitalization. It is the leading practitioner and promoter of the international "Community Supported Agriculture" model in China	Achieved financial balance within one year after establishment
Chengdu Langli	It's one of the earliest organizations in China that established a community senior service center model which operates in chain, and that realized the business model serving for both seniors and social workers. It developed 6 evaluation systems for senior adaptability services and is constructing data platforms for senior adaptability reform online service	Realized financial balance by 2012. Senior service and adaptability business mainly depend on market operation. Social work service mainly depends on government funding
Bebetter Education	It is the first economic citizenship education project and course independently developed for financially disadvantaged children in China. Adopts a model of generating social value with cross subsidy, which means to subsidize children in need by provide free services using revenue earned from selling products and services to high-income families	Hasn't reached a stable financial balance yet. Revenue mainly comes from civil donations such as foundations, enterprises and individuals. There are also a few government purchases

(continued)

Table 8 (continued)

	Is the social value creation model different from traditional charity or not?	Is it financially sustainable to solve social problems or not?
DaddyLab	It is the first to operate free product testing depending on its revenue from e-commerce business, and the first to adopt a profit model of Internet celebrity + e-commerce	Will realize financial balance by 2016
RiceDonate	The first mobile Internet public welfare platform in China, which uses its individual users as good models to motivate enterprises to participate in public welfare donation	More data needed
123langlang	It's the first to design standardized products and services to improve the reading and writing ability of both dyslexic children and general children. Adopt the social value generating model of cross subsidy, which means to subsidize dyslexic children from low-income families with the revenue earned from selling products and services to dyslexic children from high-income families	Has realized financial balance
CarbonStop	China's first carbon emission solution consisting of independent software products and consulting services. Using Internet as the medium, it helps a large number of people learn about carbon emission reduction and motivates them to make changes in daily lives	Will realize financial balance by 2014
0Fenbei	Using an Internet based business model, it provides information services for a "targeted poverty alleviation" campaign	Will realize financial balance by 2017
DreamCycling	It is the only civil rescue and monitor system in China using Beidou navigation system, forming a protective ecosystem for riders	Has realized financial balance. The revenue comes mainly from service charges, and partly from stable non-cash external donations

Note The provided information is for basic reference. Further tracking and investigation are required to judge whether each organization strictly complies with the defining criteria

Table 9 Social robustness standard reference information

Xihaner Carwash	1. Legally it is a non-profit organization; 2. Its products and services target mainly at intellectually disabled people; 3. It focuses mainly on the areas that can influence the society, such as the development of assessment modules of intellectually disabled people's performance in car washing situations.
SharedHarvest	1. Multiple stakeholders are all involved in organizational management; 2. By taking measures across the whole production chain, including giving farmers the right of pricing, fair trade, quality test, and consumers' participation in the production chain, etc., it guarantees its social mission will not be compromised by the pursuit of commercial profit.
Chengdu Langli	1. Legally it is a non-profit organization; 2. Provide free social work services and low-charge community nursing home services; 3. Make careful choices on external investors who can support its social mission.
Bebetter Education	1. Limited profit distribution; 2. Bebetter Education (non-profit organization) is the shareholder of Bebetter Technology (company); 3. Candidates' willingness to serve public welfare is an important standard of recruitment; 4. Provide services for children in need and urban community education.
DaddyLab	1. External investment will not be introduced or is introduced only when the right to control the company is ensured, to guarantee the organization's social mission and the fairness of testing results; 2. Personnel and time is invested mainly in free testing of products.
RiceDonate	1. The organization's core business and capability is to mobilize the public to support public welfare and charitable organizations; 2. Make careful choices on external investors who can support social mission.
123langlang	1. A fixed proportion of revenue is used to support dyslexic children from low-income families; 2. Make careful choices on external investors who can support the social mission.
CarbonStop	1. The organization's core business and capability is to reduce carbon emissions; 2. Make careful choices on external investors who can support social mission.
0Fenbei	1. The target customers of its products and services are low-income people registered by the government; 2. 30% of the core team members have work experience in non-profit organizations.

(continued)

Table 9 (continued)

DreamCycling	1. Legally it is a Non-profit; 2. Personnel and time are invested mostly in activities that can generate social value, such as road aids and local environmental protection and education.

Notes 1. The provided information is for basic reference. Further tracking and investigation are required to judge whether the organization strictly complies with the defining criteria; 2. The stability of an organization's social mission can be judged by checking if an organization has any mechanisms or arrangements that can prevent its social mission from drifting

problems; or the social problems that it targets to solve is not in the area where both government and market fail; or it's not financially sustainable or its operation model is not remarkably different from traditional charity organizations; or it does not have clear actions or mechanisms to prevent its pursuit of business goals from damaging its social mission—then this organization is not solving social problems in a way that uses social entrepreneurship to ensure the stability of its social mission, and therefore it is not a social enterprise.

Apart from these defining criteria, we further introduce three categorizing criteria to classify different types of social enterprises; organizational form, revenue model and dividend policy. Based on these three standards, social enterprises can be divided into charity-based social enterprises and market-based social enterprises. Public welfare social enterprise refers to social organizations that rely on stable external funding to achieve financial sustainability. The standard to identify a charity-based social enterprise is not whether it can earn profit from market operation, but its innovation and social impact. Market-based social enterprises are social organizations or companies that realize financial sustainability through market operating revenue or market operating revenue combined with external funding. These can include revenue-making NPOs, social purpose companies, and social businesses.

The definition framework of social enterprise in this book provides both a complete answer and a brief answer to the question of "what is a social enterprise." The complete answer is: " Social enterprise is an organisation that has a primary organisational objective of solving a specific social problem; identifies an opportunity of making social change rooted in the government and market failures; delivers innovative problem-solving solutions; and has practices and/or systems that protect the social goal from being jeopardised by the pursuit of the business goal." The brief answer is: "an organisation that adopts socially entrepreneurial approaches to address social problems, while featuring mechanisms that prevent its social mission from drifting." This framework has consistent connotation (defining criteria) and differentiated extension (categorizing criteria). We hope that this framework can help other forms of organizations to see their differences with social enterprises; help those who are willing to join in the social enterprise movement to find the right direction; help institutions who support or invest in social enterprises to make more accurate assessment on the social and economic value of social enterprises; and help policy makers understand the role of social enterprises in social and economic development to provide effective policies and resources to support them.

SharedHarvest: From CSA to Rural Revival

Yan Fu, Jingyue Xu, and Jianying Wang

> Organic agriculture is our belief. We only produce organic products. It's not only for our own health, but for the environment – protect the land and other natural resources, improve the living conditions of farmers, and revive the countryside.
>
> —Yan Shi, Founder of SharedHarvest

Food is humanity's primary necessity. However, in the rapid development of urbanization and industrialization, a crisis in food safety has become one of the largest social problems. The traditional farming model which has existed for thousands of years has been gradually replaced by the industrialized model using many chemicals. It's getting harder and harder for us to acquire pollution-free natural resources like air, water and land. At the same time, farmers can benefit less and less from this modernization process or are unable to earn sufficient incomes without overusing pesticides and fertilizers. These practices, together with pollution generated by animal husbandry, harm our food safety, as well as the health of farmers. Agriculture has become the biggest surface pollution source in China (Fig. 1).

Increasingly serious food safety crises are forcing us to find the solution to healthy agricultural production: can we use fewer chemicals in agriculture, and produce healthy, harmless and safe agricultural and livestock products? Can we make the best use of the achievements of modern science and technology instead of abandoning them? Can we improve the income of farmers without harming food safety and the environment? How should we rebuild the mutual trust between the producers and consumers of agricultural products? To answer these questions, a group of young people led by Dr. Yan Shi from the School of Agricultural Economics and Rural

---

Y. Fu (✉) · J. Xu · J. Wang
Business School, Renmin University of China, Beijing, China
e-mail: fuyan@rmbs.ruc.edu.cn

M. Zhao and J. Mao (eds.), *Social Entrepreneurship*,
https://doi.org/10.1007/978-981-15-9881-4_2

Fig. 1 Yan Shi and her farm

Development at Renmin University of China attempted to find the answer with their own action: "Community Supported Agriculture (CSA)[1] may be a feasible solution."

Three Rural Issues

Frankly speaking, China's agriculture is facing severe challenges, including agricultural product safety crisis, environmental pollution and a lack of mutual trust between producers and consumers. There are three major problems.

[1]The concept of CSA originated in Switzerland in the 1970s and developed initially in Japan. During this time, a niche of consumers sought safe food and farmers wanted stable customers. The two groups connected and established an economic cooperation. CSA is an agricultural model which involves direct selling and friendly cooperation between producers and consumers. The concept has since gained acceptance worldwide, developing past initial connotations of co-purchase and cooperative economies. Literally, CSA means that the entire community makes a commitment to the operation of the farm. This means making the farm become the farm of the community legally and spiritually, so that farmers and consumers can support each other and accept the risks and benefits of food production together. There are three essential objectives of CSA: to strengthen the relationship between consumers and farmers; to improve the income of the farmers engaged in ecological agriculture; and to ensure food safety. On the one hand, it requires the citizens (consumers) to pay in advance and share the natural risks with farmers (producers). And on the other hand, it requires farmers to produce various organic agricultural products in an environmentally friendly way to improve community food safety. CSA is also called Community Mutual-aid Agriculture.

The first is that overuse of pesticides and chemical fertilizers leads to agricultural soil pollution and other environmental pollution problems. Because most of the farmers use chemical fertilizer instead of organic fertilizer, and have little knowledge of scientific fertilization techniques, the basic fertility[2] of arable land is declining continuously, the supply of soil nutrients is unbalanced, and crop diseases and pests are worsening. Furthermore, the overuse of pesticides has led to serious pesticide residue and soil pollution. Data shows that the area of farmland polluted by pesticides in our country is up to 100 million *mu*, and the agricultural surface pollution will diffuse into the water body through the surface runoff generated by precipitation or farmland irrigation or soil infiltration, and cause serious water pollution and other environmental pollution. According to *2010 Bulletin of the First National Survey of Pollution Sources*, agricultural pollution sources have become the largest surface pollution sources, exceeding industrial and domestic pollution sources.

The second problem is the lack of mutual trust between producers and consumers due to agricultural products and food safety crises. Consumers are worried about agricultural products and food safety and therefore do not trust producers. From the producers' point of view, intensive market competition and consumers' preference for low-priced products have made it difficult for them to make a living by growing organic agricultural products. This resulted in market failure status where profit-based investment drove out ethical investment. Meanwhile, the cost is too high for the government to transact directly with hundreds of millions of farmers or supervise them, which resulted in government failure. With the development of market economy, non-agricultural industry in urban areas attracts a large labor force from the areas, which leads to significant rise in the cost of the agricultural labor force, this in turn makes organic agriculture disadvantaged in market competition—when its price is high enough to cover the cost, it cannot be accepted by the market; if its price is low, the income is not enough to support the farmers or motivate them to continue with organic farming. As a result, they will have to turn to chemical use to make up for shortages in labor.

The third problem is that there is no mechanism or systematic solution to agricultural pollution and agricultural product safety crisis. As early as 2007, Document No. 1 of the Central Committee has emphasized the importance of modern agriculture and called for circular agriculture and ecological agriculture. The report of the 19th National Congress of the Communist Party of China in 2017 pointed out that the issues of agriculture, rural areas and farmers are the fundamental issues bearing on national economy and people's livelihood, and put forward the strategy of rural revitalization, which raised the importance of "three rural issues" to an unprecedented level. However, in the past few decades, a complex interest pattern has been made between the industrial capital in the processing, trade, technology, and advertising of inputs and products related or leading to agricultural pollution and food safety issues. Therefore, how to adjust the existing interest pattern at a low cost and establish a new pattern which favors the development of ecological

---

[2]Basic soil fertility refers to the yield of farmland which can be produced by its own fertility without manual fertilization.

agriculture is one of the challenges facing us. In addition, governments, enterprises and consumers need to work together to makes changes, in order to build a new fair trade framework between urban and rural areas, encourage consumers to make environmentally-friendly purchase decisions, and form a positive feedback circle between producers, consumers and the environment.

Practice of CSA Model in China

In 2008, Dr. Yan Shi from the School of Agricultural Economics and Rural Development at Renmin University of China and her team introduced the "Community Supported Agriculture" (CSA) model, which was already a mature model internationally, to China for the first time. In 2012, they founded SharedHarvest (Beijing) Agricultural Development Co., Ltd. (hereinafter referred to as "SharedHarvest") and began the practice of CSA model in China.

"I hope to find a practical solution to China's food safety and agricultural pollution problems by means of business operation," said Yan Shi. "Once this business model is established, many people can refer to it for their investment or operation decisions. By promoting this business model, more people can be encouraged to get involved, and the problems of food safety and agricultural pollution can be solved more quickly."

As a new type of organic farm adopting the CSA model, SharedHarvest has been engaged in the promotion and practice of CSA notion since its establishment. It has been working to establish mutual commitment and risk-sharing relationship between producers (farmers) and consumers (citizens). They encourage producers to provide organic agricultural products without using pesticides and fertilizers or harming land health. They then require consumers to prepay for products and share risks with producers, ultimately buying agricultural products at a reasonable price based on fair trade. By doing so, they hope to realize community food safety and the sustainable development of agriculture. After six years of exploration and practice of CSA model, SharedHarvest realized the mission of promoting the concept of CSA nationwide by using alliances and platforms. Yan Shi and her team have built a successful CSA farm that produces and distributes agricultural products in organic ways. Meanwhile, they have a wide array of experiences, including food and agricultural education, CSA alliance, cooperation with new farmers and training for them, attracting talent to rural communities, and rural community environmental reconstruction. These might provide possible solutions to the "three rural issues." Looking back on how Yan Shi and her team built this farm, it's quite legendary.

Overseas Farming Experience in America

At the end of 2007, Yan Shi, who was studying for her Ph.D., learned by chance that the American Institute of Agricultural Policy and Trade was offering an opportunity to visit a local farm in the US to study CSA for six months. She leapt at the opportunity. However, the first farm she applied for turned her down since she had no outdoor work experience grew up in a big city. Later, the Institute helped her find another farm which was more focused on education. It was smaller and in a more remote area. After a lengthy application process, Yan Shi was approved.

In April 2008, Yan Shi went to Earthrise Farm in Minnesota US to study. Her tutor, Professor Tiejun Wen humorously refers to this experience of her as "overseas farming experience." This farm was certified to be an NPO in 2004 and was operating via the CSA model. For half a year, Yan Shi worked together with farmers almost every day, being a real part of their team, and receiving first-hand experience in this new agricultural operating model of CSA. Yan Shi later turned this experience into a book named *I was a farmer in America.*

Most of the work on Earthrise Farm, such as sowing and weeding could only be done manually. The farmers worked hard from early morning to late night. One time, when they were about to deliver vegetables, they found that some packed in the boxes were frozen or had even changed colors. This was because the temperature in the refrigerator was lower than it should be. The manager of the farm took out the customer contact book immediately, and made phone calls to the customers one by one to apologize. Meanwhile, he quickly arranged people to replace the frozen vegetables with fresh ones. For this experience, Yan Shi learned one thing, which is "on CSA farms, honesty is rule No.1, and it's also the bottom line. Only when members trust the farm, can the farm continue its operation." This carries on as the principle of her future work (Fig. 2).

Recalling this "overseas farming experience", Yan Shi said,

> Actually, I didn't learn much about agricultural technology in the short 'overseas farming experience.' When I ran my own farm back in China later, I learned that Chinese farmers knew more about how to produce more on small plots of land. I also didn't learn much about farm management, because there were only 33 members of the farm. Only a small amount of vegetables needed to be delivered each week, and the vegetables for each member were the same. The vegetables only needed to be delivered to the pickup spots in a few towns nearby, and the members would pick them up by themselves. Now the members of my farm exceed Earthrise Farm's by ten-fold. But that half years' experience at Earthrise Farm was just like a seed that has rooted and sprouted in me.

First Attempt: Little Donkey Community Farm

In October 2008, Yan Shi returned to China to continue her study when her internship in the US was over. She was required to report the achievements of this internship. She didn't adopt the common method of reporting by submitting papers. Instead, she chose to do it in the most difficult way—to introduce the CSA model to China. This

Fig. 2 Yan Shi used chopsticks to pick out insects in broccoli before delivery, gaining her hero status on Earthrise Farm

project was very difficult to implement, because in an environment where consumers did not trust farmers, where should they find consumers? And where should they build the farms? There were so many problems to solve, this challenge seemed insurmountable. However, young Yan Shi held firm to her convictions: "When you really want to do something positive and altruistic, the whole universe will help you." Luckily, at that time, Professor Tiejun Wen, Yan Shi's mentor, was working with the Rural Construction Center of Renmin University of China and the Haidian District Government of Beijing Municipality to establish a base of 200 mu for production, learning and research. Professor Wen allocated an area of 20 mu in this base to support her CSA practice. At the beginning of 2009, Yan Shi and her team gave this project a pleasant name, "Little Donkey Community Farm."

Tiejun Wen was known as the "research leader of China's three rural issues" and Yan Shi, the "first person sent by public university to learn farming in the United States." Their reputation won consumer trust. The first customer came to Little Donkey Community Farm after reading a report on them. With the help of such customers, Yan Shi and her team went into the community to promote their farm and recruit new members. The member count expanded from more than 50 in 2009 when it was established to nearly 1000 in 2012, and retention quite high. Every year, there were many "candidate members" waiting to join them; all attracted by the reputation of Yan Shi's project.

Join us, and enjoy healthy food and esprit de vivre!

Fig. 3 The original logo of Little Donkey Community Farm

Meanwhile, Yan Shi continued her studies and research. In 2011, she completed her doctoral dissertation, *Research on the Trust Mechanism of Alternative Food Systems*, which is the first doctoral dissertation on the CSA model in China. She received doctoral degree from Professor Tiejun Wen. Later, she went to the School of Humanities and Social Sciences at Tsinghua University to continue postdoctoral research in the direction of "social movement of food safety"[3] under the guidance of Professor Yuan Shen, director of the Sociology Department (Fig. 3).

In her research, Yan Shi found that: "history of the world and experiences of all times show that in the battle against food safety problems, consumers' self-help efforts can only solve problems temporarily at most. In the long run, a stable supply of healthy and safe agricultural products can only depend on farmers and on the sustainable development of agriculture. If farmers cannot profit from agriculture, agricultural production will be affected, and ultimately consumers will be affected."

After more than three years of development, Little Donkey Community Farm was well-known. But in Yan Shi's heart, the original commitment and dream still seems far. In her opinion, running CSA by renting land is fundamentally still a consumer self-help action. Farmers are not the main body in the business. They are just employees earning not very high wages. Therefore, she made up her mind to start over by establishing a new CSA platform. As a social enterprise, this platform would serve for agriculture by connecting farmers and consumers and letting farmers grow organic food on their own land.

[3]In September 2014, Yan Shi completed her postdoctoral research and graduated from the station. The title of his postdoctoral dissertation is "*Urban Food Safety Movement: The Four models.*"

The Young People from Mafang Village

In May 2012, Yan Shi and her partners chose to start a new business. They decided to establish a platform that could truly connect ecological farmers and consumers, and named it "SharedHarvest", attempting to expand the scale of consumers around villages. The operation model of SharedHarvest was similar to Japan's social enterprise DAICHI WO MAMORU KAI 30 years ago. This Japanese enterprise was a commercial company adopting the CSA model. It produced and delivered organic agricultural products, helped and supported small farmers to sell their products to consumers at fair prices, and helped consumers get healthy food. By doing so, it contributed to the formation of a virtuous cycle and sustainable development of agricultural production and consumption.

In the classical CSA model, farmers who produce and citizens who consume should connect directly with each other during the process of production and sales whilst reaching consensus on the concept of the CSA model. Therefore, when SharedHarvest was established, they also tried to promote the traditional CSA model and help farmers and consumers connect directly. Their plan was to look for farmers who were willing to participate, give them technical training, and require them to commit to producing on their own lands according to the organic production standards of "no chemical synthetic pesticides and fertilizers." SharedHarvest would be responsible for finding the consumers, and carrying out 191 agricultural residue tests on the products according to the European Union standards. Thus, they could bring green and healthy agricultural products to consumers' dining tables based on fair trade practices.

First of all, this model requires them to find farmers who were willing to join and promise to plant according to organic standards. However, their ambitions seemed naïve when facing reality. SharedHarvest encountered great difficulties when it tried to find its first participating farmer in Beijing's Tongzhou District. Fortunately, after many setbacks, SharedHarvest finally won the support of Guangshan Lang and his family in Tongzhou's Mafang Village. Guangshan Lang has 60 mu of land. Persuaded by his son, he agreed to join and use all of his land to plant organic vegetables for the first batch of Shared Harvest consumers. In order to work together with Lang and his family, Yan Shi and her team rented a house from Guangshan Lang as their office and accommodation. Thus, in May 2012, SharedHarvest was born with this small team of only ten members and one farmer in Mafang Village, Tongzhou District, Beijing. This group of young people with great ambition took root on this land. Soon, SharedHarvest recruited its first 120 members and obtained the first advance payment from them to pay for Lang and support their business operations. SharedHarvest established its first organic crop base. Members began to receive vegetables that meet safety standards, and the Lang family received an income higher than they would selling vegetables grown conventionally. SharedHarvest also provided interest free loans to Lang's family to build four greenhouses, while guaranteeing the vegetable purchases made by members per month.

However, they encountered problems in the very first year of their cooperation. Yan Shi said, "One morning, we found something unusual on the leaves of the eggplants that had begun to bear fruits. When we asked Uncle Lang, he replied honestly that he had used pesticides. Maybe Uncle Lang wanted to test the resolve of our mettle. Or maybe he was too worried that the red spiders would affect output. No matter the reason, we had only two choices: first, pick all the eggplants that were already bearing, and wait for the new fruits to grow; second, pull out all the eggplant seedlings, and notify the members that we could not provide eggplants this year. The team held a meeting together and decided to make the second choice, pulling out all the eggplant seedlings on nearly half a mu of land. It was a painful decision at that time, but we made it clear to Uncle Lang that the principles of our cooperation were non-negotiable. After that, such problems never happened again."

Although the problem of pesticide use was solved, things were still not easy for SharedHarvest. First of all, a lot of labor was needed for organic production, so Lang's family worked very hard. Lang's wife had frequently complained, and other farmers in the village were unwilling to join in. Therefore, it was quite difficult to carry out the plan of recruiting more farmers. Secondly, because the production base only had four greenhouses and a small amount of land facing south which store vegetables for the winter, they could only provide a limited variety of vegetables for the members to choose. In addition, the first winter after its establishment was a once-in-30-year cold winter, so the output was quite low and they could only deliver the vegetables every other week. Therefore, there had been conflicts between SharedHarvest and members from time to time. As a result, members of the founding team could only earn a low salary of only two or three thousand Yuan per month, which threatened the stability of the team. All these problems made Yan Shi realize that the original vision of SharedHarvest—to adopt the classic CSA model in China and to connect farmers directly with consumers—was not applicable (Fig. 4).

Fig. 4 The team of SharedHarvest

Localization of the CSA Model

In the winter of 2012, Director of Shunyi District Rural Economic Management Committee of Beijing, Mr. Jiao, chanced upon a recorded interview SharedHarvest. He was curious to see if there really was such a group of young people willing to devote themselves to agriculture. He took a trip to SharedHarvest's headquarters to see this phenomenon with his own eyes without informing the team in advance. As he arrived, several young men of the team were rooting around the cabbage cellar. This scene moved him deeply. Later, he found a small farm with facilities for the team in Shunyi District with more than 20 greenhouses, where the team could start their production directly. In September 2013, SharedHarvest officially rented a farm with facilities located in Liuzhuanghu Village, Longwan Town, Shunyi District, and transferred most of its personnel to this base with superior facilities. Since then, SharedHarvest has begun localized transformation of the CSA model.

Cultivate New Farmers

From this early experience, Yan Shi found that to change farmers' old farming habits was a bold and risky endeavor. Time would be needed for farmers to take the initiative in adapting to the CSA model. In addition, farmers had very little knowledge in both organic farming technology and standards, which greatly increased the cost of communication and trust building. To be sure, it was not easy to find farmers willing to produce according to Shared Harvest's organic standards. Moreover, even if Yan Shi's team could find farmers willing to join, they needed to provide continuous training and maintain close contact to ensure standards were followed. They also needed to solve various practical problems throughout production. All were grand challenges for the young team members of SharedHarvest. Lastly, in today's China, skilled farmers average about 60 years of age. From a sustainable point of view, in another 5–10 years, who will be the producer of the next generation?

After moving to Shunyi production base, Yan Shi found that although the farmers have their own land individually or collectively, they preferred to work for SharedHarvest, because they could receive a stable income without bearing the risk of product sales. Therefore, Yan Shi decided to change the original operation model of cooperating with farmers only to two paralleled models: cooperating with farmers and renting land for farmers to plant. Therefore, at Tongzhou base, they continued to cooperate with the Lang family. At Shunyi base, they rented land and hired experienced farmers as well as young people. They gave these young people training, let them participate in the whole process of production and sales and develop their full abilities in organic vegetable production, sales and distribution. Compared with the old generation of farmers (old farmers), SharedHarvest called these young people new farmers. The old farmers gave the new farmers a nickname: "college student farmers." In Yan Shi's eyes, the new farmers had a lot to learn from the old farmers.

"As a complete human being, academic achievement is not all. Living ability is also very important and it is the weak point of some young people." said Yan Shi. "The living conditions of the farms in China are mostly a struggle. If a farm needs external assistance whenever something goes wrong with water supply, power, or facilities, etc., it will be impossible for it to profit. Therefore, many problems need to be solved by us. We hope that the new farmers can improve their living ability and self-management ability even when the living conditions are limited. A good farmer should be excellent in both farming techniques and daily life."

Therefore, the most effective training method adopted by SharedHarvest was to let the new farmers learn from the old farmers and be their apprentices. The first thing they needed to learn as apprentices was the basic living skills, and then they could learn farming skills. For example, after joining the team, new farmers must follow skilled and experienced farmers to farm, attend to chores, learn basic farming techniques and gain living skills from the old farmers. One year later, they would continue to work the field and learn more advanced farming techniques. Only after that, they might have the chance to be promoted to production team leader, to manage vegetable or fruit production. New farmers who joined the team earlier are now taking management roles on the farm. By this apprentice and learning-in-working model, SharedHarvest cultivated its loyal backbone.

Besides training new farmers, SharedHarvest also worked hard on other aspects. They expanded the variety of vegetables to satisfy different consumers' needs. They searched nationwide for local vegetable types with high resistance. They learned to use refined management techniques for methods such as multi variety production, multi batch and small-scaling; techniques suitable for organic production. They searched for production machinery and production models suitable for small and medium-sized farms covering the entire production process, from stable sources of organic fertilizer, logistics insurance and distribution techniques, to temporary sale channels for excessive produce during the harvest season.

Recruit "Harvest Shareholders" and Members

Unlike the common CSA model in foreign countries, where farm owners directly contact the customers and charge only on produce, SharedHarvest needs operational funds to support its two production models. For a production model of cooperating with farmers, SharedHarvest needs to prepay a certain amount of vegetable capital to the farmers to agree on pricing and output. In the other model, the renting land model, SharedHarvest needs to pay rent for the farmland every year. Therefore, SharedHarvest was registered as an enterprise since its foundation and has been operating in a commercial way. Unlike other companies however, SharedHarvest does not accept the investment of for-profit capital.

According to Yan Shi, "All the values generated by the CSA model should be distributed within the chain from producer to consumer. The intervention of for-profit capital will bring extra pressure to the enterprise, which is already a highly risky venture that grows slowly. Such may even affect the original mission of the enterprise."

To obtain operational funds, before the first vegetable batch was planted in May 2012, Shared Harvest's founding team contacted some of its most loyal consumers, told them that they needed startup funds of 300,000 Yuan, and explained their financing plan. The basic idea of the financing plan is that each member pays 30,000 Yuan, and in return SharedHarvest promises to provide 5 years of free vegetables and 1% equity to them. It took about a month for SharedHarvest to get 10 core members to join the plan, thus they got enough startup funds, and also their first members. These members were later called "Harvest Shareholders," which is fundamentally different from common "shareholders." On this matter Yan Shi explained: "These 'Shareholders' wanted to support SharedHarvest, rather than getting any return on their investment, and actually there was no return until now. They are not involved in the daily operation of the farm, but they will be invited to our annual meeting to learn about our operation and development and make some suggestions. They are the earliest and most loyal supporters of SharedHarvest, serving to make more people believe in the CSA concept a join in."

In addition to these "Shareholders," SharedHarvest needed more ordinary members. They provide two membership options: organic vegetable home delivery service and "plant your own" service. By organic vegetable delivery service, consumers prepay for the vegetables and the farm delivers the vegetables to the customers' homes every week. By "plant your own," SharedHarvest divides the farmland into small plots of about 30 square meters and rents it to these members. The farm provides seeds, organic fertilizer, tools and technical guidance. The members plant, maintain and harvest their vegetables all by themselves. Currently, delivery service members greatly outnumber "grow your own" members. By the end of 2012, SharedHarvest had about 120 members, which provided enough funding to survive. Thanks to the word-of-mouth of their members, and media coverage, more members have joined, providing more operating funds. By the end of 2017, SharedHarvest had nearly 1,000 members, and began to make profits. Yan Shi saw not merely financial profit, but hope for rural reconstruction. In her words "The experience of SharedHarvest shows that: When every 5 consumers join in CSA, 1 mu of land can be detoxified; when every 10 consumers join, 1 farmer can plant organically; when every 100 consumers join, 5 young farmers can stay working in the countryside; and when every 1,000 consumers join, a sustainably developing village can be built."

Using the New Channel of Internet

Among the first members who joined SharedHarvest five years ago, up to 70% of them are still members. They are all solid supporters for SharedHarvest and the concept of CSA. They can understand the difficulties the farm met during its development and are willing to give their suggestions. They seldom complain about wormholes in the vegetables and imperfect appearances. They can accept plain packages and are willing to keep delivery boxes and packages for the farm to reuse. However, their number was not enough to support the operation of the farm with hundreds of mu of land.

SharedHarvest tried many sales methods such as community promotion, street vegetable stands, Taobao online stores and so on, but these channels can only attract consumers pursuing healthy living. If they cannot understand the environmental and social significance of CSA production and consumption, they would use the standard of industrial products to evaluate CSA products, and may also have doubts if the farm is really organic. For example, SharedHarvest customer service center often received consumers' inquiries about the products, they accused forchlorfenuron use since the green peppers were so big; maybe they'd failed to tend enough to the cucumbers that they were bent and ugly; were the tomatoes with stripes on their skin genetically modified? This was all because these customers couldn't fully understand the concept of CSA. They tended to apply their traditional standards of product appearance and packaging to CAS products.

To change this situation, SharedHarvest started a WeChat group and a WeChat public account to educate customers. In group talking, they encouraged consumers to share their thoughts and even debate the quality of the produce; they released weekly production reports, production issues, and product testing results; and members shared their experience on food matching and cooking. They addressed common concerns on the appearance and taste of organic products, and even taught basics in biology, and agricultural production. Thus, they gradually transformed the minds of their customers, who had been living in cities and knew little of farming and the countryside. They began to abandon their original industrial standards. They began to understand where the food comes from, what healthy agricultural processes truly entail, and that the living and working conditions of farmers differ greatly from many preconceived notions. Interestingly, there were many members who constantly questioned the produce, but they never stopped buying. Yan Shi humorously compares this to "tough love."

With the expansion of their business and the increase in product varieties, challenges were raised to their production management and vegetable combinations. They learned that when the number of a CSA farm's members exceeds 50 households, it is necessary to manage the production and marketing data systematically. The number of SharedHarvest's members was 600. It was providing 20–30 vegetable combinations, and processing about 20,000 orders every day. The disadvantages of manual processing stood out, such as low efficiency, high error rates, poor consumer experience and increasing consumer complaints.

To solve these problems, in November 2014, Cunwang Cheng, Yan Shi's husband and co-founder of SharedHarvest, founded Chengshi (Beijing) Agricultural Technology Co., Ltd. and developed China's first App specialized in CSA farm management, "Good Farm" (Fig. 5).

In "Good Farm" App, members can order food and learn the latest farm news at any time; the farm can also manage order data in real time to guide their production, picking control and distribution coordination. In addition, "Good Farm" App is actually an Internet management platform, which can integrate all CSA ecological

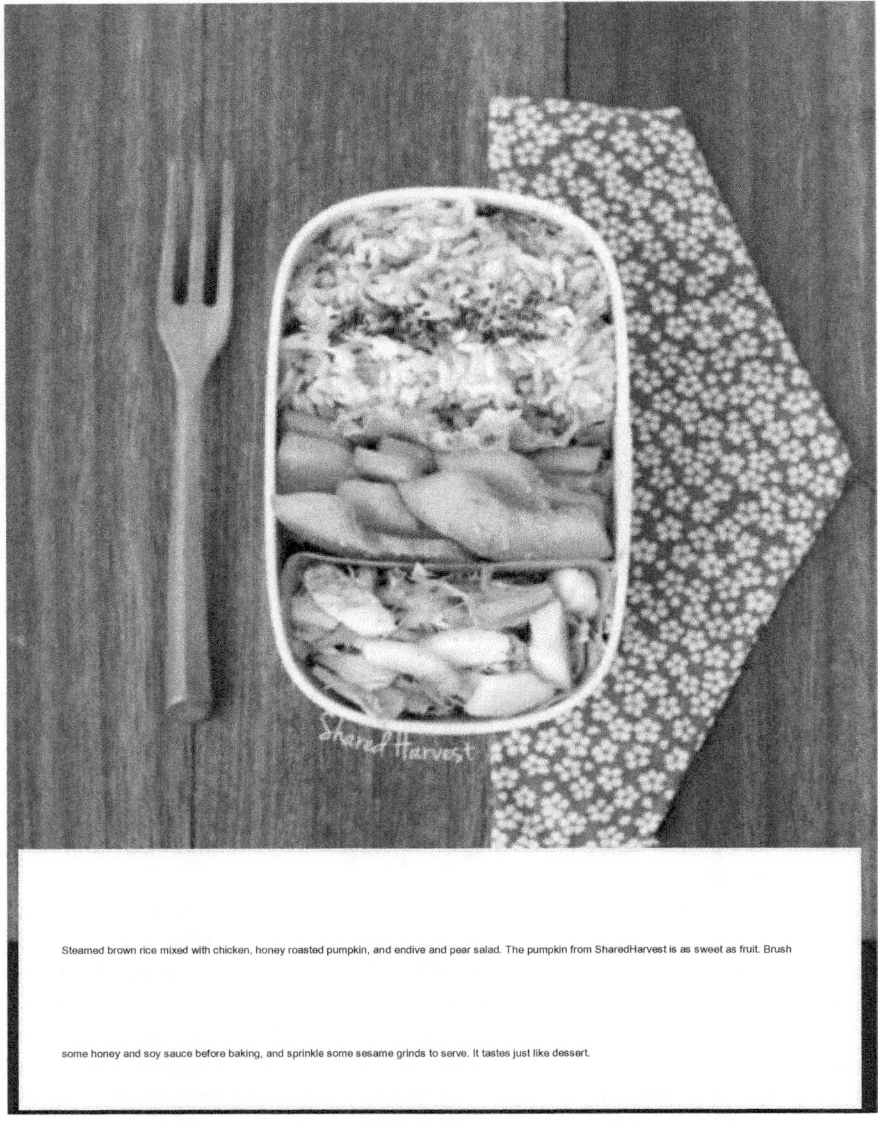

SharedHarvest
Steamed brown rice mixed with chicken, honey roasted pumpkin, and endive and pear salad. The pumpkin from SharedHarvest is as sweet as fruit. Brush
some honey and soy sauce before baking, and sprinkle some sesame grinds to serve. It tastes just like dessert.

Fig. 5 SharedHarvest Membership Team shares recipes regularly. The material is mainly from SharedHarvest food community

farms in China and provide consumers with diversified food choices. In the future, Cunwang Cheng hopes that "Good Farm" App can become the information service platform for all the CSA farms in China, providing services such as information management and member recruitment. Consumers will be able to use it to locate organic ecological farms near their homes, join the farm and purchase organic and healthy agricultural products online to meet their diversified needs. This will bring stable and increasing consumers to CSA farms, and eventually connect producers and consumers seamlessly.

Carry Out Public Food and Agricultural Education

Food and Agricultural Education first appeared in Japan, and later attracted the attention of education departments of many countries and regions around the world. In the process of bringing agricultural products from field to the table, consumers play an important role. The production of high-quality agricultural products requires not only the hard work of producers, but also the awareness of consumers. In addition to their own health, consumers should care about the health of the land too. Only in this way, we can realize the mission of sustainable agricultural development and environmental and ecological protection, while bringing healthy diets to customers at the same time. Therefore, Food and Agricultural Education focuses on the learners' personal experience in the process of food production from farmland, crop to dinner table, and let them learn about who grows crops, where food comes from, and understanding agricultural producers. The purpose of Food and Agricultural Education is to educate people and change their current lifestyles per diet. It reconstructs the human relationship with food and land, establishing an agricultural development model that is friendly both to the environment and human society. This idea is completely consistent with the concept of SharedHarvest, so SharedHarvest hopes to make some contributions in this field (Fig. 6).

In 2014, SharedHarvest launched "Children of the Land" Food and Agriculture Education Program. In Yan Shi's view, Food and Agriculture Education is a valuable part of public education. It gives power to the consumers and allows farms to find more consumers with like mindsets. The "Children of the Land" Food and Agricultural Education Program consists a series of courses, including food production, food processing, food storage, food nutrition, food culture, healthy eating, carpentry, music, art and more. At present, the Program is available for purchase in 2 forms: one is to organize families and schools to visit farms, participate in farmland activities, and join themed summer camps held in SharedHarvest base or their cooperative farm. The other is that the teachers of SharedHarvest's Food and Agriculture Education program go to the schools to teach lessons or help them build campus vegetable gardens. Currently, SharedHarvest cooperates with Hujialou Central Primary School, Shunyi Dongfeng Primary School, and Shunyi International School, to provide "Children of the Land" lesson to their students every week.

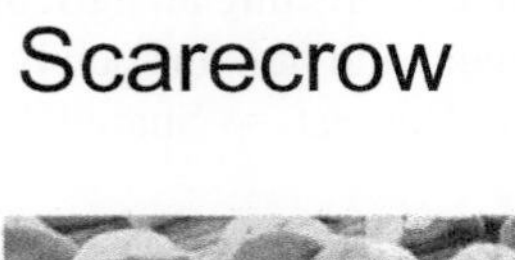

Fig. 6 2017 SharedHarvest Children of the Land summer camp

Taking Hujialou Central Primary School as an example, a teacher from SharedHarvest is assigned to give 20 forty-minute lessons per year, and a technician also goes there to help students manage the "one meter" vegetable garden on the roof. The forms of these lessons include classroom lecturing, such as teaching children to learn about the seeds and soil, and understand the conditions of germination; and also outdoor practice, such as helping students build and plant the "one meter" vegetable garden on the roof of the school building in groups and learn skills like how to preserve and cook food. SharedHarvest worked with Hujialou Central Primary School, consolidated their courses and teaching procedures into "Children of the Land Food and Agriculture Education Manual," which can work as reference material for schools and families to learn about Food and Agricultural Education.

From a Tree to a Forest

From the very beginning when Little Donkey Community Farm was founded, Yan Shi clearly knew that China's "three rural issues" could not be solved by the efforts of individuals, but by society as a whole. As the vanguard for China's CSA model, SharedHarvest should work more actively to promote concepts of CSA, teach organic production technology and cultivate future farmers.

Building Food Community

After all these years of practice and promotion of the CSA concept, SharedHarvest wins the support from more and more farmers and members. On the one hand, many new farmers trained by SharedHarvest returned to the countryside to start their own businesses. They understand and support the CSA concept, but they usually would encounter obstacles during their market development. They hope SharedHarvest can help them in sales and other areas to support their development. On the other hand, the members of SharedHarvest have demands for other products besides vegetables. Since Yan Shi and her husband have worked for more than ten years in this industry, their members trust them and hope they can also recommend good products from other suppliers. Due to the demands of these two sides, SharedHarvest is starting to build a Food Community, which sells not only the products from their cooperative farmers and their own teams, but also products they select from other reliable sources. To make sure the products they select meet standards, SharedHarvest uses two methods to guarantee product quality.

One method is to choose the products produced from the base of SharedHarvest, but by other producers who rent farmland directly from them. For example, an entrepreneur named "Mr. Mushroom" rents two greenhouses from SharedHarvest's Shunyi base. He also participates in activities and training on the farm, just like a member of SharedHarvest. The whole production process of his mushrooms is under the supervision of SharedHarvest, and it is naturally accepted by the SharedHarvest Food Community as an independent product from third-party supplier.

The other method is that SharedHarvest does on-site inspections on the supplier's farm and tests for pesticide residue in products. Only when the production procedures follow SharedHarvest's organic production standards and when the products pass their 191 items of agricultural residue tests at the same time, can the products be sold to the SharedHarvest Food Community. On-site inspections and residue tests are both necessary and equally important. This is because the final test on the product can only ensure the safety of food, but not the environmental friendliness of its production process. Both the process and the result should meet the CSA standards. By now, SharedHarvest has formulated standard organic production procedures for easier reference for farmers intending to adopt the CSA model. In addition, when doing on-site inspections on farms, SharedHarvest also inspect the weeds, leaves, planting quantity, and other details, using their rich farming experience to evaluate whether products meet CSA production standards. The final judgment will be made based on the test results from third-party testing agencies. Many times have on-site inspections been very satisfying yet final round uncovers one or two residues in the products. Even though such products can meet ordinary organic food standards, SharedHarvest still struck a veto on grounds that misconduct was highly likely during production.

The methods SharedHarvest uses to evaluate the products of Food Community are the 191-item agricultural residue testing standards created by it based on its expertise. It has won the trust of its customers. To date, the SharedHarvest Food Community have dozens of cooperative farmers supplying fruits, mushrooms, soy sauce, vinegar, snacks, meat, eggs, and more, gradually covering all consumers' daily food demands (Fig. 7).

Initiating CSA Alliance

CSA Alliance was born at the first National CSA Conference in 2009.[4] At the conference, nine community farms including Little Donkey Community Farm initiated the Citizens Agriculture CSA Alliance. At the fourth National CAS Conference in 2012, several organizations including SharedHarvest jointly initiated and joined in Ecological Agriculture Mutual Aid Network. In November 2015, SharedHarvest hosted the sixth International CSA Conference, also the Seventh China CSA Conference, which was attended by more than 800 people. At this conference, the Ecological Agriculture Mutual Aid Network officially transformed into Social Ecological Agriculture CSA Alliance. Pushed by Yan Shi and other alliance members, in 2017, the Social Ecological Agriculture CSA Alliance was registered successfully as an independent organization with the name "Beijing Shunyi District Ecological Agriculture Development Association," referred to as "CSA alliance." SharedHarvest, Little Donkey

[4]The conference was also referred to as "China Social Agriculture (CSA) Conference" and "China Social Ecological Agriculture (CSA) Conference." The short name is always "CSA conference".

春播
chunbo.com
安心健康食品的购买平台

检测结果

(Test Results)

序号 (No)	检测项目 (Test Items)		单位 (Unit)	检测方法 (Test Method)	标准要求 (Requirements)	检测结果 (Test Result)	单项判定 (Conclusion)
231	农残检测	苯氟磺胺	mg/kg	SN/T 2320	不得检出	未检出（<0.18）	符合标准
232	农残检测	异丙草胺	mg/kg	GB 23200.9	不得检出	未检出（<0.0075）	符合标准
233	农残检测	灭草环	mg/kg	GB 23200.8	不得检出	未检出（<0.0015）	符合标准
234	农残检测	氟啶草酮	mg/kg	GB 23200.8	不得检出	未检出（<0.03）	符合标准
235	农残检测	苯酮唑	mg/kg	GB 23200.8	不得检出	未检出（<0.045）	符合标准
236	农残检测	氟丙嘧草酯	mg/kg	GB 23200.8	不得检出	未检出（<0.0038）	符合标准
237	农残检测	啶虫脒	mg/kg	GB 23200.8	不得检出	未检出（<0.12）	符合标准
238	农残检测	嘧螨醚	mg/kg	GB 23200.8	不得检出	未检出（<0.015）	符合标准
239	农残检测	氟硅菊酯	mg/kg	GB 23200.8	不得检出	未检出（<0.0038）	符合标准
240	农残检测	环酯草醚	mg/kg	GB 23200.8	不得检出	未检出（<0.0038）	符合标准
241	农残检测	呋草酮	mg/kg	GB 23200.8	不得检出	未检出（<0.015）	符合标准
242	农残检测	苄螨醚	mg/kg	GB 23200.8	不得检出	未检出（<0.015）	符合标准
243	农残检测	氯亚胺硫磷	mg/kg	GB 23200.8	不得检出	未检出（<0.03）	符合标准
244	农残检测	吡唑硫磷	mg/kg	GB 23200.8	不得检出	未检出（<0.03）	符合标准
245	农残检测	三甲苯草酮	mg/kg	GB 23200.8	不得检出	未检出（<0.03）	符合标准
246	农残检测	乳氟禾草灵	mg/kg	GB 23200.8	不得检出	未检出（<0.03）	符合标准
247	农残检测	吡唑醚菊酯	mg/kg	GB 23200.8	不得检出	未检出（<0.09）	符合标准
248	农残检测	萘丙胺	mg/kg	GB 23200.8	不得检出	未检出（<0.0038）	符合标准
249	农残检测	咪唑菌酮	mg/kg	GB 23200.8	不得检出	未检出（<0.0038）	符合标准
250	农残检测	氯甲酰草胺	mg/kg	GB 23200.8	不得检出	未检出（<0.0038）	符合标准
251	农残检测	抑草磷	mg/kg	GB 23200.8	不得检出	未检出（<0.0038）	符合标准
252	农残检测	解草嗪	mg/kg	GB 23200.8	不得检出	未检出（<0.0075）	符合标准

春播品质控制实验室（北京）

Fig. 7 Testing results of 200 pesticide residues and 5 heavy metal contents on the chives produced by SharedHarvest issued by a third-party testing agency; all the testing results were qualified

Community Farm, Chengshi Agriculture, Tang Liang's Liangliang Family Farm, and Zhang Yang's Mr. Lemon Ecological Farm are all initiating members.

As the backbone of the CSA Alliance, SharedHarvest set up a special workforce to support it. In 2016 and 2017, it hosted the eighth and ninth CSA conferences on behalf of the Alliance, both of which had over one thousand attendees. According to incomplete statistics, there are thousands of production subjects running the CAS model, and hundreds of thousands of consumer families are participating in this food reform, serving to incubate countless ecological farms. A better future with safe and healthy food is not far off. From Little Donkey Community Farm to SharedHarvest today, Yan Shi and her husband have organized or participated in the CSA conference every year, promoting the concept of CSA and sharing all their achievements and experiences. Many practitioners in this field today have visited or been trained at Little Donkey Community Farm or SharedHarvest.

However, it is still difficult for most of CSA farms to support themselves, including SharedHarvest. Why would SharedHarvest allocate human and material resources to support the establishment of a non-profit organization? Many people think that SharedHarvest fostered many potential "competitors," which was not a wise move. Yan Shi interprets this differently. "I agree that many of the so-called 'competitors' in this field were fostered by us, but I don't think they are real competitors. To me, just because most of the CSA farms are struggling to survive including us, it is important for us to establish the Alliance. Only when there are more producers and consumers who understand the concept of CSA, can CSA farms and rural China have a bright future. Our original motivation in doing this is to continuously promote the concept of CSA."

Statistics show that since 2009, there have been more than 1,000 CSA farms in China that were fostered directly or indirectly by Yan Shi's team. These farms purified more than 100,000 mu of land and changed the food on the dinner tables of hundreds of thousands of Chinese families. Countless young people have been inspired by the CSA concept and returned to the countryside to engage in the development of ecological agriculture.

Incubating New Farmers

At the National CSA Conference in 2012, Yan Shi put forward the concept of the "new farmer." She pointed out that farmers should not only know about new agricultural and management techniques, but also understand the market. Yan Shi believes that to transform the producers by providing them appropriate training will be central to this rapidly-developing industry.

SharedHarvest is not a big company, but every year it receives internship applications from hundreds of college graduates. Among these young people who want to study with SharedHarvest, the majority of them have plans to run organic farms back in their hometowns, and of course there are also some people just regard this internship as a special experience after graduation.

At first, all these people were accepted to the farm as interns. The frequent turnover of interns brought a lot of management work to the farm. SharedHarvest therefore adopted two different internship models—one for learning and one for career development. For those seeking careers, SharedHarvest adopts social recruitment and provides jobs for those who can meet their standards after the internship. For those who just want the experience, SharedHarvest created a position called "new farmer intern," which allows young people an opportunity to learn new agriculture and reconsider it for their future, but makes no promises as to whether they can work in SharedHarvest after the internship.

The average age of these new farmer interns is about 25 years old, and most of them are college graduates with bachelor's degrees or above. SharedHarvest requires them to work there for at least 2–3 months. During the internship, they provide free accommodation and food. For interns who stay on longer they provide monthly subsidies. For those who work six full months, they even provide scholarships to encourage more people to join. SharedHarvest opens its door to everyone including visitors, learners and even "competitors" that will start their own businesses later on. It is the incubator of agricultural ventures. It hopes to encourage more people to join this course. We can see from the statistics that when Yan Shi and Cunwang Cheng founded Little Donkey Community Farm in 2009, there were no more than five CSA farms in China. Thanks to the practice of SharedHarvest and media reports on them, as well as the influence of the CSA Conference and great efforts from experts and scholars, CSA farms are now sprouting up around the country. There are about 1,000 CSA organic farms in China at present, of which 50–60% have studied in or visited SharedHarvest or Little Donkey Community Farm.

"After more than five years of promotion by us, there are now about 1,000 such farms across the country, serving hundreds of thousands of consumers. These farms are like pearls surrounding the cities," Yan Shi said. "Many people ask me why I would share my business model with others. What if they steal it? I just want to say that I hope more people can join in what I'm doing, so that we can improve our food safety together, because everyone should be responsible for the food on their own plates; they can even change the world in pursuit of better food."

Make the Countryside Home for the Young

Beyond building a successful organic farm, Yan Shi has a bigger dream: She hopes to create a sustainable community for these young people who devote themselves to agriculture. Yan Shi once said, "Our value comes from the land, and it will eventually return to the land and the countryside. That's why we always ask our team to live and work in the countryside." To realize this dream, Yan Shi and her team are engaging in works to reconstruct the countryside.

Building Kindergartens in the Countryside

To make the young people stay in the countryside, it is important to clear difficulties in their lives. Education is one of the most important things. Four babies have been born at SharedHarvest, and they need kindergartens. According to Yan Shi, this is not a problem faced by SharedHarvest alone, but a social problem that has to be solved on the road to the new countryside in the future. There is a training base of Rural Construction Center not far from the Shunyi Shared Harvest base, which gathers many institutions including the training base of Rural Construction Center of Renmin University of China, the practice base of Sociology Department of Tsinghua University, Liang Shuming Rural Construction Center, the training school of National Farmers' Cooperative, and the Science Committee of Slow Eating in Greater China. A lot of people are working towards rural construction in these institutions. Because this area is far from the city center, the personnel from these institutions also have difficulties in finding kindergartens for their children. If this problem can't be solved, it may have an adverse effect the working status of these personnel and even their families. It may eventually threaten the stability of these teams and their recruitment.

Yan Shi began exploring this new area. In July 2017, SharedHarvest and Rural Construction Center worked together and provided the venue, capital and technical support to set up the Rural Construction Kindergarten. They hired Tan Qin, who was studying for a doctorate in education in the United States, for curriculum design, teacher training, environmental recreation, etc. Although the kindergarten is still under construction, they can already see it in their minds that it is a small and beautiful education center with systematic courses, and extremely spacious classrooms, playgrounds, and even planting area. A dozen children study and grow up together there. They believe that education can be supported and measured by faith. "Here, children will be accompanied and grow up with a personality for finding the beauty of life," Yan Shi said.

Setting Up Pear Commune

Pear Commune is in the pear base of SharedHarvest. It is the community for new farmers, and also a place for urbanites to experience rural living. The founding of Pear Commune was related to an old pear farmer, fondly called "Uncle Yang" by the young farmers. Uncle Yang used to be a rural teacher, and later he turned to pear planting for more than ten years. At first, he used no chemical fertilizer and little pesticides and later he used biological material only. He never changed his natural way of planting even when the market was unsatisfactory or facing natural disasters. He won his credit over time. SharedHarvest began to sell Uncle Yang's pears from 2011. In 2014, Uncle Yang's ailing health prevented him from planting pears any longer. Since there were orders for pears from their members, in 2015, SharedHarvest rented an orchard of 230 mu near the farm and started to grow fruit. This orchard later became the Pear Commune. Currently there are mainly pear trees at the orchard, with a small number of cherry trees, apricot trees and plum trees.

There were two rows of old houses in the orchard. Yan Shi repaired them. A designing team from Tsinghua University Architecture School turned them into the Pear Commune today with their unique and ingenious design. Pear Commune's decor is not luxurious or exquisite, but it is quite artistic (Fig. 8).

The walls and tables are decorated with fresh fruits and vegetables. The window opens right onto the grand orchard. When spring comes, there are blossoms everywhere and even the air is sweet (Fig. 9).

Among the few rooms in Pear Commune, some of them are used as dormitories for the new farmers. The rest are reserved for the visitors coming to study CSA model or urbanites coming to experience the organic lifestyle. This unique homestay service allows urbanites to slow down and take their time to get closer to the land. Here, urban people and the new farmers live under the same roof. The lifestyle of the

Fig. 8 Meeting room in Pear Commune

Fig. 9 Homestay in Pear Commune

new farmers transforms urban people's concept of the countryside and agriculture little by little. The city and the countryside are connected together.

Training Talents with Organic Beliefs

Besides organic production, SharedHarvest also encourages an organic lifestyle, because these two concepts are closely linked. To save every scrap of resources, means to create an ecological cycle between crops and feedings produced by organic agriculture in agriculture production. In daily life, it means to transform toward an ecological lifestyle little by little. For example, at SharedHarvest, people don't use detergents or other chemicals. All the employees and visitors must take the initiative to clean up after meals. Rice bran is used to wash dishes and wastewater is collected to irrigate the farm. When vegetables are delivered to members, vegetable boxes, egg boxes, plastic bags are collected for reuse. SharedHarvest also calls on its members to donate idle items at home to the farm for second use, such as furniture, cloth, books and electric equipment. Influenced by SharedHarvest, members are also beginning to adopt an environmentally friendly lifestyle. They take initiative in participating in the construction of the farm by donating materials or making other contributions.

SharedHarvest's CSA practice is not only fostering new farmers and members with ecological beliefs, but also changing the minds of the local "old farmers." Early on, old farmers didn't believe they would have a good harvest without using chemical fertilizers and pesticides. But now, a dozen farmers who plant organically for SharedHarvest are earning a lot more than their contemporaries. Besides, local villagers are also starting to understand pollution caused by chemical fertilizers and pesticides, and the threats they make to their health. In the past, old farmers working for SharedHarvest retained methods of chemical planting in their own plots at home. Now they are also turning to organic farming. We can say that SharedHarvest not only makes the farmers feel the benefits of organic production themselves, but also allows them to earn rich experience in organic planting and have confidence in it. These changes happening to them are also influencing the other farmers in their respective villages.

To Refine or to Expand?

After nearly six years of operation, SharedHarvest now owns a planting base of 60 mu and a forest breeding base of 110 mu in Mafang Village, Xiji Town, Tongzhou District, both operating an organic production model; a planting base of 50 mu and an orchard of 230 mu in Liuzhuanghu Village, Longwantun Town, Shunyi District, providing more than 25 varieties of vegetables each week and more than 80 varieties throughout the year; plus its own chicken farms and pig farms producing eggs and meat. In addition, SharedHarvest also cooperates in the form of fair trade with dozens of small farmers across the country, such as the cooperative farmers of Heilongjiang Wuchang rice, Shandong apples, and Hebei grains, to support these young people to return to the countryside and develop ecological agriculture. Currently, SharedHarvest has nearly 1,000 members in Beijing. It is also the most famous CAS farm and urban ecological agricultural promotion base in Beijing. "Eat the food from this place and this season" is a consumption concept it promotes, influencing the whole country. However, despite all these great achievements, it still has a long way to go with its vision, which is to solve the series of problems in food safety, agricultural pollution, connections between cities and villages, improving the living conditions of farmers and reviving the countryside. What is their next step toward this vision?

According to Yan Shi, based on the current situation of organic agriculture and rural development in China, when the number of consumers of organic food reaches 10,000, organic production capabilities will be in serious shortage. Therefore, the most important task of SharedHarvest is to build a good team with strong production management capabilities. When there are still not enough qualified organic food producers, expanding the sales platform will only result in supply shortages. Therefore, no matter from the perspective of the internal management or external market environment, SharedHarvest is not ready for large-scale expansion. It should keep its current developmental model of being a small and strong business which grows slowly but healthily in the agricultural industry, influencing people and the society. In Yan Shi's own words: "For agriculture, especially organic agriculture, the turning point won't arrive in one or two years, but in another decade, perhaps longer. Meanwhile, we must strengthen the capability of our team, refine our management, build our brand, and win public trust. Thus, when the turning point arrives, we can seize the opportunity and realize our mission."

On a specific business level, Yan Shi said, we must refine our main business of vegetable and fruit production, as well as our essential techniques and management. We also need to continue to promote the concept of CSA to the public. In addition, the new businesses of "Children of the Land" and CSA Alliance are also very important and require a lot of work.

In contrast to Yan Shi's view, Cunwang Cheng prefers another more aggressive path, which is to cooperate with other farms which already have good production and management capabilities in first or second tier cities and realize fast expansion. He introduced external investors, established Chengshi (Beijing) Agricultural Technology Co., Ltd., and developed the "Good Farm" App, which has been joined by many CSA farms across the country. In terms of the management model, Cunwang Cheng and his team will allocate managers or representatives directly to the farms to supervise their production and make sure each one meets CSA standard. By doing so, all CSA farms can be quickly built up and gathered together, and a national chain farm with the brand "Good Farm" will be formed. His company will be responsible for sales and member recruitment. In the future, he hopes that agricultural enterprises can go public and donate part of their stock earning to rural construction funding.

To refine or to expand? Yan Shi and Cunwang Cheng are searching for their answers.

Further Reading

Deng Y (2012) The new adventure of a female doctor. *China Weekly* 143(6):50–54

Liu F (2012) Looking for a new road for agriculture—an exclusive interview on Yan Shi and her SharedHarvest. Green Leaf 9:73–81

Shi Y (2012) About SharedHarvest. http://blog.sina.com.cn/s/bloga11f8e0102e48u.html. Accessed 2 July 2012

Shi Y (2012) I was a farmer in America. Beijing: SDX Publishing Company

Sun Y (2010) Worries about the quality of arable land in China. Outlook 38:10–12

Wen T, Dong X, Shi Y (2010) Changes in China's agricultural development direction and policy orientation: an international comparative research. Agric Econ Issues 10:88–94

Zhang H (2015) "Good Farm" App goes online. *China Today* (Chinese version) 12:58–59

Company Information

1. SharedHarvest information links

Item	Content
WeChat	分享收获农场, 分享收获大地之子
Weibo	@分享收获CSA, @农家石嫣
Sina blog	农家石嫣: http://blog.sina.com.cn/usashiyan
Taobao online store	Search for store: 分享收获

2. SharedHarvest WeChat Public Account

3. Media reports on SharedHarvest

Beijing Wenmingban (2017) Yan Shi: post-80s returnees "new farmer" Shared Harvest with thousands of people. http://bjby.bjwmb.gov.cn/pxbd/2017/09/01/t20170904_841557.html. Accessed 4 Sept 2017

Cheng W (2013) Yan Shi: a "female farmer" wearing a doctor's hat. http://epaper.gmw.cn/gmrb/html/2013-05/30/nw.D110000gmrb_20130530_1-04.htm?div=-1. Accessed 30 May 2013

Ecological Agriculture (2012) How to rebuild a safe food chain? (Part one). http://www.yogeev.com/article/10395.html. Accessed 25 June 2012

Ecological Agriculture (2012) How to rebuild a safe food chain? (Part two) http://www.yogeev.com/article/10450.html. Accessed 26 June 2012

People's Daily Online (2013) The dreams of 100 Chinese—Yan Shi: grow food with love. http://xz.people.com.cn/n/2013/0719/c138901-19110714.html. Accessed 19 July 2013

Science and Education Channel, CCTV (2013) Returning to the countryside (Part I). http://tv.cntv.cn/video/C25153/8f963dd446f14bbb845af267de9d2cdo. Accessed 25 Dec 2013

Science and Education Channel, CCTV (2013) Returning to the countryside (Part II). http://tv.cntv.cn/video/C25153/b3bafd5bd4e44d5d9824dbdb3f9a92bc. Accessed 26 Dec 2013

Xi C (2017) Dialogue with Yan Shi: farming makes me tough. http://www.yogeev.com/article/76218.html. Accessed 2 Sept 2017

Zhang H (2015) Shared Harvest, Yan Shi has her point. http://www.chinatoday.com.cn/ctchinese/society/article/2015-03/07/content_674381.htm. Accessed 7 Mar 2015

Xihaner Carwash: Dream Home for People with Intellectual Disabilities

Xiaoguang Li, Jianying Wang, Jingyue Xu, and Qiang Wang

From being pure consumers to becoming providers of social resources, this is a great change. And Xihaner did it!

—Jun Cao, Founder of Xihaner Carwash

On August 8, 2015, Xihaner[1] Carwash, a carwash employing a dozen of people with intellectual disabilities, opened at No. 11, Kaifeng Road, Futian District, Shenzhen. It washed 11,869 cars within the very first year of its foundation. On August 10, 2016, with the help of Shenzhen Xihaner Carwash, Qinghai Xihaner Carwash opened successfully. It hired 14 intellectually disabled people and four hearing-impaired people. By the end of 2017, Shenzhen Xihaner Carwash had washed up to 32,175 cars, and a total of nine more Xihaner Carwashes had opened nationwide.

In the Sixth China Public Welfare Project Contest in 2017, which is the most influential public welfare contest nationwide, 30 public welfare projects entered the final stage among 1,617 candidates after nearly three months of fierce competitions in qualification and promotion stages. Xihaner Carwash went through all these stages and won the gold medal in the final stage on September 24.

They have been practicing their slogan "master skills, participate in work, create value and win respect" with their own actions. They are telling China's own Forrest Gump[2] story!

---

[1]Xihaner is the affectionate nickname people give to persons with intellectual disabilities. Intellectual disabilities refer to all kinds of disabilities of people mentally or intellectually, including Down's syndrome, cerebral palsy, developmental delay, intellectual impairment and autism. "Xi" means affection. "Han" is the nickname for these people. And "Er" means "forever young". Xihaner refers to intellectually disabled people who are loved and acting like children forever.

X. Li · J. Wang · J. Xu (✉) · Q. Wang
Business School, Renmin University of China, Beijing, China
e-mail: xujingyue@rmbs.ruc.edu.cn

[2]Forrest Gump is the hero of an American novel *Forrest Gump written by Winston Glum's*, which tells an inspirational story of a man with intellectual disability named Forrest Gump who persevered

M. Zhao and J. Mao (eds.), *Social Entrepreneurship*,
https://doi.org/10.1007/978-981-15-9881-4_3

Jun Cao's Pain

The Story of Cao and His Family

Jun Cao is the founder of Xihaner Carwash. Back in the year of 2002, his son was born. The joy of this new baby brought to the family was soon replaced by pain: the child was diagnosed with mild mental retardation at the age of seven months. Cao Jun said, "From then on, I was afraid of waking up at three or four o'clock in the morning. In the darkness and silence of night, thinking of my son made me sweat all over and couldn't fall asleep again. What worried me most was not the issues at the moment, but those in the future. My wife and I would grow old and gone someday. What would he do then?"

In more than ten years since the baby was born, Jun Cao anesthetized himself by working, also hoping to save more money for his son's future. He comforted himself by some optimistic ideas—his son doesn't need to participate in the fierce competitions of college entrance examinations or jobs. He and his wife encouraged each other and made life happier in many ways—the family traveled in off-seasons and enjoyed the happiness of being together. But there was still no solution to the question of the child's future.

In all those years, Jun Cao, who had entrepreneurial experience and had been working in investment banking business, began to pay attention to projects related to disabled people. He visited more than ten projects in Beijing, Shanghai, Hangzhou, Guangzhou and other cities. Most of these projects were supported by Civil Affairs Department of the government by means of providing free sites and hiring disabled people, such as restaurants, cinemas for the blind, etc. Some of them were non-governmental charities. One winter, he visited a nursing home and couldn't forget the way they bathed the disabled people. Their staff lifted up the handicapped people one by one from their wheelchairs, put them in the frame seats, rinsed their whole bodies, brushed them with soft brushes, rinsed again, and then put them all back to their wheelchairs. The whole process was just like pipelining. This scene was imprinted in Jun Cao's mind. From the standing point of nursing home, the staff was doing their best. However, this kind of operation was still unacceptable and quite painful to the families of the disabled people.

---

to pursue his own dream and created a legend eventually. As a student, Forrest Gump had to run away from other kids who laughed at him and bullied him all the time, which made him become a good runner. Thanks to that, he joined rugby team, entered University, and even became a rugby star. During the Vietnam War, Forrest Gump won a medal for saving his fellow soldiers in the battle. After he left the army, Forrest Gump started his own shrimp catching business and became a successful entrepreneur. Later, he ran across many states in America, which made him a celebrity by accident. The novel *Forrest Gump* was published in 1986, and was later adapted into a film with the same name, starred by Tom Hanks as the hero. The movie was shown in July 1994 and won six Oscar awards the next year, including the best movie, the best actor and the best director. Forrest Gump is a successful representative of persons with intellectually disabilities, and a model inspiring the group.

Jun Cao said, "I can feel the pain! I know what my child need best – he need respect. If their parents bath them, they will pay more attention to details."

Later, Jun Cao went to Hong Kong, Macao and Taiwan to investigate. In Taiwan, Jun Cao saw a variety of accessible public facilities, which allow disabled people to travel in the streets like normal people. And nobody in the streets gave pity looks to disabled people. From these experiences, Jun Cao had a deeper understanding of the situation of disabled people. He prefers the name of "disabled people with special needs" rather than handicapped people—the name of handicapped people is from medical perspective, which refers to those who have disabilities in body functions; while the name of disabled people is from social perspective, which refers to those who are capable of participating in the society equally and freely, as long as the restrictions in their environment were eliminated. It is just like nearsighted people can see as clearly as normal people when they wear lens.

In 2014, Jun Cao visited a nursing home. It was a comprehensive care center for senior people. It had a farm, an orchard, and a sports ground with fitness and entertainment equipment. It was more like an elderly care park or ecological park. The site was borrowed from the villagers, and in return, the villagers could work in the center. From then on, the idea of building a dream home for Xihaner was rooted in Jun Cao's mind. However, where should he get the fund for the construction and operation of this dream home?

Jun Cao had read a book named *Why Do We Work*, written by Taihong Dashan, a Japanese writer. Dashan Taihong is the founder of a chalk manufacturer. He once hired three or four intellectually disabled people by chance. During work, Taihong Dashan noticed that these intellectually disabled workers had many advantages: they were loyal; they were rigid; and they were quite good at mechanical operations. Later, his company hired more intellectually disabled people, who accounted for about 60% of its total employees. Inspired by this book, Jun Cao gradually realized the idea of solving social problems with commercial methods.

Jun Cao said, "Our children are growing up year by year. We can't afford to wait any longer. Why are we still working for others, instead of our children? We should create value by our own work."

The Vision of Xihaner Dream Home

After more than ten years of exploring and thinking, the idea of establishing Xihaner Dream Home began to take shape in Jun Cao's mind. In the meeting room of Xihaner Carwash in Shenzhen, when he was asked where the idea of Xihaner Dream Home came from, Jun Cao couldn't help standing up behind the table and taking a marker at the white board next to him. He drew a square on the center of the white board representing Xihaner Dream Home, and began to describe it: there will be comfortable living areas, playgrounds, sports fields, and libraries. Xihaners will live and eat together there and take care of each other. They can also get help and care from their parents and nurses. One day, when some parents get old, they will pass on their responsibilities to younger parents. One generation after another, they will continue to help each other.

Then, where should they get the funds to build and maintain the Dream Home? Jun Cao has found the solution: "By establishing a social enterprise. A social enterprise can reproduce, and can provide financial support for the Dream Home."

Jun Cao believes that the profits generated by social enterprises through selling commercialized products and services, together with government funds, social donations, as well as the inheritances from the parents, can form a common trust fund, to provide the financial support for the construction and operation of Dream Home. The common trust fund must be under supervision and its operation must be transparent, to ensure the sustainable operation of the Dream Home. Figure 1 is the road map of Xihaner Dream Home vision.

The social enterprises in Jun Cao's vision consists of business 1, 2 and so on. These social enterprises are the foundation of Xihaner Dream Home, and together they constitute a social enterprise group. Each enterprise should not only generate profits to provide the common trust fund of the Dream Home, but also provide jobs for Xihaners. Jun Cao believes that if Xihaners want to be respected by the society, they must prove their value; and to prove their value, they must work for the society.

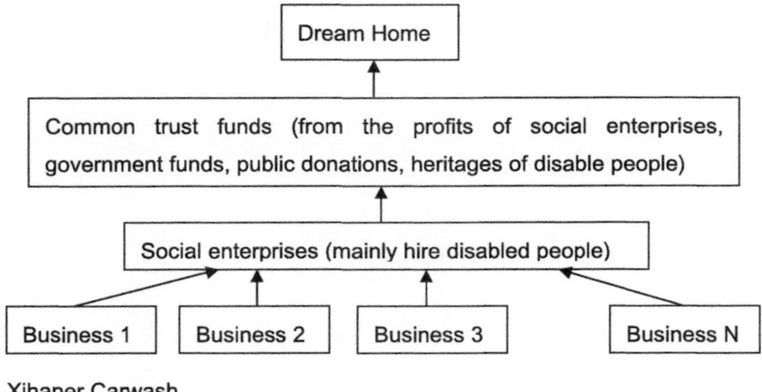

Fig. 1 Road map of Xihaner Dream Home vision

Xihaner have been growing up depending entirely on the government and their families. How could they find jobs? Are there any jobs they're capable of? How far is their Dream Home vision from reality?

The Obstacles Faced by Disabled People for Getting Accepted by the Society

The Paradox of Jungle Law

In the evolution process of the nature for hundreds of millions of years, the jungle law has been the basic biological rule, which determines and restricts the development and evolution of all the animals and plants. Natural selection, survival of the fittest, and the strong defeats the weak are expressions of this rule. The jungle law has also been dominating human society for a long time. However, human society is now developing largely by human will, instead of the jungle law. We can improve our living conditions and environment, and even modify the species of animals and plants. People begin to realize that human society is no longer dominated by the jungle law. From the aspect of earth's ecology, if human being continues to follow the jungle law and exploit natural resources without restrains, we may eventually destroy our home on the earth.

For a long time in the past when our society was following the jungle law, the disabled people have been vulnerable. Ignorance, superstition, and the fear of the public made the disabled people live in helplessness and neglect. The concept and related policies on the equal treatment of the disabled people began to develop only in the past two hundred years. On December 3, 1982, the United Nations General Assembly adopted the World Programme of Action Concerning Disabled Persons in its Resolution 37/52, which emphasizes that disabled people have the right to enjoy living conditions equal to those of other citizens, as well as to share equally the improvements in living conditions resulting from social and economic development. For the first time, the definition of disability was defined from a perspective of the relationship between disabled people and their environment.

Being "handicapped" generally refers to various functional limitations happening to some of the world's population. It includes physical, intellectual or sensory defects, or medical conditions or diseases. These defects, conditions or diseases can be long-term or transitional. The proportion of disabled people recognized by the international community is about 10% of the total global population.

Being "disabled" refers to the state of being restrained or deprived of the opportunities to participate in social life equally. It focuses on the deficiencies tangible or intangible in social environment, such as facilities, communication and education, which make disabled people unable to participate in social life equally. The term "disabled people" is used more often than "handicapped people" in today's society. It is more accurate and humane, and reflects the new social understanding of "handicapped people."

Challenges for the Development of Disable People in China

In 1982, the Constitution of the People's Republic of China first stipulated that "the state and society help make arrangements for the work, livelihood and education of the blind, deaf-mute and other handicapped citizens;" in December 1990, the 17th meeting of the Standing Committee of the National People's Congress adopted the Law of the People's Republic of China on Protection of Disabled Persons; on March 30, 2007, at the headquarter of the United Nations, Guangya Wang, permanent representative of China to the United Nations, signed the Convention on the Rights of the Persons with Disabilities on behalf of China, which marks the cause of the disabled in China has transformed to focus on the concept and policy of "equality and participation."

Table 1[3] shows the number and proportion of people of each type of disabilities in the total number of disabled people in China by the end of 2010. The total number of disabled people in China was 85.2 million, accounting for 6.34% of the total population. And the total number of families with disabled people in China was 72.25 million, accounting for 17.80% of the total number of families.

While fulfilling the Law of the People's Republic of China on Protection of Disabled Persons and the Convention on the Rights of the Persons with Disabilities, Chinese governments and organizations at all levels are also promoting the construction of social security system and service system for disabled people actively. During the 11th National Five Year Plan period, the coverage rate of social insurance for urban disabled people increased from 34.8 to 60.9%. The rate of rural disabled people

Table 1 Statistics of each type of disabled population in China (by the end of 2010)

Type	Population (ten thousand)	Proportion (%)
Visual disability	1,263	14.86
Hearing disability	2,054	24.16
Speech disability	130	1.53
Physical disability	2,472	29.07
Intellectual disability	568	6.68
Mental disability	629	7.4
Multiple disabilities	1,386	16.3
Total	8,502	100

[3]Based on the data of the sixth national census in 2006 and The Second National Sample Survey on Disabled, China Disabled Persons' Federation calculated the number and proportion of each type of disabled people by the end of 2010.

attending the New Rural Cooperative Medical System (NRCMS) reached 96%. 10 million disabled people enjoyed the minimum living security. More than 10 million disabled people received rehabilitation treatment. The level of education for disabled people continued to improve. Nearly 1.8 million urban disabled people found new jobs, and more than 6.1 million disabled farmers had food and shelter thanks to poverty alleviation measures. More and more disabled people have realized their dreams of living a happy and dignified life.

But meanwhile, the development of China's disabled people has encountered many challenges. In income, the family per capita income of disabled people is only 60% of the national average level. In education, a considerable number of children with disabilities of school age cannot receive school education. In employment, by the end of 2016, among 32.194 million certified disabled people recorded in the basic database of disabled people in China, only 8.961 million were employed, less than half of the total population. In social services, about 40% of the urban unemployed and 70% of the rural unemployed disabled people are mainly supported by their families, and nearly a quarter of the urban disabled people are not covered by any social insurance. In a word, the basic needs of disable people in income, education, employment and social services are far from being satisfied, as well as their demands to participate in social life equally. As former UN Secretary-General Kofi Annan said on the day of the adoption of the Convention on the Rights of Persons with Disabilities, "The situation of persons with disabilities reflects the darkest side of human nature. On paper, persons with disabilities have enjoyed the same rights as others; in real life, they have often been denied the opportunities that others take for granted."

The situation of the intellectually disabled people is even worse. The employment rate is only 2%, far lower than the average employment rate of the disabled. On December 10, 2017, China's Top Ten Incidents of Intellectually Disabled Persons' Right were first released in Beijing. These incidents were all selected from public reports released in 2017. The publication of this list shows that the society is paying more attention to the needs of intellectually disabled groups. But at the same time, it also reflects the bias of the public toward the disabled people, and the challenges in policies, legal protection and social services for disabled people. From adopting the new concept of disabled people's "equal rights and social participation," to transforming this concept into policies, and finally to implementing the policies to make changes, our society still has a long way to go.

How to allow the disabled people participate in the society equally, and let them create value and serve the society so as to win respect? That is the problem that takes the joint effort of the government, the society and the families to solve. Jun Cao and his Xihaner are already on their way to find the answer.

Founding of the Dream Home

Searching for the Right Project

Jun Cao had been communicating his concept and vision of Xihaner Dream Home to other Xihaner's parents once he got the chances. Finally, he convinced ten pairs of parents and together they raised one million yuan. The course of building Xihaner Dream Home could finally be launched. A journey of a thousand miles begins with one step. But things are always difficult at the beginning. What project should he choose to invest in with this one million yuan? During the process of selecting projects, Jun Cao summarizes his own project evaluation standards.

(1) Fits Xihaner's characteristics and abilities

First of all, the choice of the projects should be based on the rehabilitation theories and the comparative advantages of the disabled people. Specifically, the project should fit the characteristics and abilities of Xihaner. Xihaner's intelligence level is close to that of children. And their behavior model is similar to children too. If they find something interesting, they will focus on doing it and never feel tired. As for the comparative advantage of Xihaner, they are good at big movements, instead of delicate movements. There is a Chinese saying "quick minds and nimble fingers," which shows the relationship between the brain and body.

Jun Cao once visited a production line of boxes. More than ten workers worked together in a line to make one box. Each of them sat in their own seat. One worker folded and pasted one side of a box, then passed it on to the next worker, who continued to fold and paste the other side and then passed it on for the next step, until the box was done. Folding and pasting is refined works unsuitable for Xihaner. If they do such jobs, reject rate will be very high. So this project was eliminated.

(2) Market demand should be rigid and frequent

When selecting the project, they should also consider the market and customer demand. The market should be large enough and the demand should be frequent. Customer acceptance level should also be considered.

Jun Cao investigated gardening and planting projects. These projects are quite simple, but the market demands are neither strong nor frequent enough.

(3) Deciding on carwash project

After painstaking investigation and analysis, they finally decided on carwash project. Carwash business does not require big investment or high techniques. It's easy to operate and fits the ability and characteristics of Xihaner. Xihaner can have fun in work, which is quite lucky for them.

Jun Cao said, "first of all, playing with water and bubbles is fun for the boys. When my family washes our own cars, my son is always happy to help. Secondly, car washing requires big movements, which are within Xihaner's capabilities. Finally, car washing has rigid and frequent demand, and the market is big. Even if cleaning and rinsing would be done by machines in the future, manual work is still needed for drying. So the demand is permanent."

Will the car washing business succeed? Jun Cao said, "We need to verify three questions by trial operation: if they can get the job done; if they can get the job done well; and if the business can sustain."

The first and the last questions are to verify whether the job fits Xihaner's ability and characteristics: "if they can get the job done" aims to verify if the car washing business matches Xihaner's comparative advantages; "if the business can sustain" aims to verify whether the business matches Xihaner's interest.

The second problem will be verified mainly by customers' response and recognition. Jun Cao believes that at first people would be happy to come to show their support. But in the long run, the business cannot survive by immorally kidnapping the customers and forcing them to purchase the service. The key to attract long-term customers is to "get the job done well," which means the business should operate by commercial means and reach average industrial level.

Foundation of Xihaner Carwash

(1) Trial operation

In the beginning of July 2015, the first Xihaner Carwash in China began it trial operation in Futian District, Shenzhen. There were 12 core employees, including several graduates from Shenzhen Yuanping Special Education School, several Xihaner recruited from the Welfare Institute and the society, two managers including Jun Cao, two special education teachers and three car washing master workers. The Carwash was only open to Xihaner's families and friends during trial operation.

On the day of its trial opening, Shenzhen Business Daily released the news of its opening in its report "Graduates from Yuanping Special Education School Now Have a New Choice" in Civil Affairs Section. On July 15, the reporter from Yangcheng Evening News made an on-site interview at Xihaner Carwash, and published a report entitled "A Carwash Opened in Shenzhen Hiring 12 Xihaner," using 1/4 of a page. After that, Futian District Government's WeChat official account reprinted the report of Yangcheng Evening News. The WeChat article was forwarded more than 300 thousand times on the first day, and more than 100 thousand times every day for several days afterwards.

(2) Media effects

Media effects were accumulating. On August 6, three reporters from Xinhua News Agency came to the Carwash taking their cameras and made a thorough interview, and then published a report entitled "Pleasant Home and Workplace for Persons with Intellectual Disabilities - A Visit to Shenzhen Xihaner Carwash." Various media rushed to the Carwash when they saw the report, and Xihaner Carwash immediately

Fig. 2 Opening ceremony of Xihaner Carwash

Fig. 3 Xihaner at the Carwash received their salary earned by themselves for the first time

went viral. On August 8, Xihaner Carwash opened to the public earlier than planned (Figs. 2 and 3).

On the same day, Xihaner at the Carwash received their salary earned by themselves for the first time.

In the next few months, Xihaner Carwash was crowded with customers every day. At most, they washed 70 cars in one day. They could feel the support and care from the society. The Carwash had a successful opening. During the trial operation, they verified the first question "if they can get the job done" successfully. However, the other two questions still needed to be verified.

Adjust Jobs to People (Operation Model Exploration and Innovation)

Adjust Operation Process to Xihaner

Compared to ordinary carwashes, who have mature operation procedures and operation standards for reference from the beginning of their business, Xihaner Carwash, as the first Carwash which hires mainly intellectually disabled persons, they don't have any information for reference. Everything is new and awaits them to explore and create. First of all, Jun Cao's team set objective, principle, basic procedures and standards, and then summed up a set of operation models and practices during their business operation.

(1) Objective

The objective they set is to reach the average industrial level, so as to verify the problem of "if they can get the job done well," and find out if the customers are satisfied with their service.

Jun Cao said, "Customers came for the first time just for support. The fervor will gradually chill down in a few months. If Xihaner wants to attract and retain customers, it must do well and reach the average industry level both in cleanness of cars and waiting time."

(2) Principle

The basic principle is to verify the question of "if the business can sustain," by means of which the expected objective can be achieved. Since Industrial Revolution, the basic principle of production and business operation is to let employees adapt to machines and procedures. In order to improve labor productivity, business owners must hire first-class employees, give them trainings on standard operation, use standard tools, and standardize the working environment. These are the requirements of Taylor's Scientific Management System on employees. However, for a workplace like Xihaner Carwash, operation procedures and standards must be adjusted to people. This is the basic principle.

In addition, among all the intellectually disabled persons, only less than 5% of them are mild in the disability level, and more than 95% are moderate to severe. Therefore, to realize full employment of this special group, they cannot just hire the best of them. Instead, they must "divide the jobs into smaller tasks and let all the special workers cooperate as a team."

"For people with special needs, like Xihaner, machines and processes should be adjusted to fit them. Just like in optical shops, lenses should be chosen to fit people's sight, rather than the other way around." Cao said.

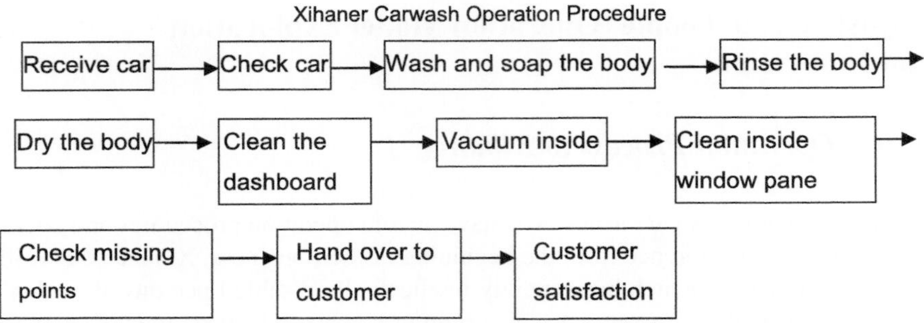

Fig. 4 Operation procedure of car washing

Fig. 5 Washing zone

(3) Basic procedures and standards

Based on the objective and basic principle above, Jun Cao's team simplified the operation procedures and standards as much as possible, and standardized and refined the washing and cleaning procedures down to each task and step. They even use towels of different colors to clean different parts. Figure 4 shows the operation procedure of car washing The car washing procedures take place in two operation areas—washing zone and drying zone—as shown in Figs. 5 and 6 respectively. Four steps are done in washing zone, including car receiving, car checking, car washing, and car rinsing. In car drying zone, there are six steps, including car body drying, dashboard cleaning, vacuuming, inside of window pane cleaning, inspection and handover.

(4) Improve procedures and standards quickly in practice

After the team set up their objective, principle, basic procedures and standards, they also need to improve the operation procedures and standards in practice. During trial operation, many problems were exposed at the Carwash. The master workers

Fig. 6 Drying zone

ran around to guide Xihaner. It was almost out of control. As a result, the cars were not clean enough and the waiting time was too long.

Based on the problems occurred during trial operation, the team improved their operation procedures and standards, and formed the best practices. Jun Cao said, "If Xihaner wants to attract and retain customers, we must reach the average industry level both in cleanness and waiting time. What should we do then? We must give ability evaluation and training to the staff."

Professional Ability Evaluation System

Jun Cao's management team planned to verify the three questions in trial operation in the first month. But the blockbuster effect of the trial operation forced them to open to the public earlier than they planned, and also accelerated their exploration and experience accumulation process. After two years of operation, the team has developed a complete set of professional ability evaluation system and training system. They summed up their principles to "scientific evaluation, make best use of advantages, divide jobs, and team work." And they also found the best practices suitable for Xihaner.

(1) Professional ability evaluation system

Professional ability evaluation is to learn the ability of the employees by giving them evaluations, to guide work assignment and training based on the results (Fig. 7).

Currently, Xihaner has upgraded its professional ability evaluation system to the fifth version.

The ability evaluation template is a white board (see Fig. 5), which is 3.6 meters long, 1.85 meters high and 0.25 meters from the ground. It simulates the body of a real car: its height equals to that of an SUV, its length equals to that of ordinary car,

Fig. 7 Professional ability evaluation templates

and the distance from its bottom line to the ground equals that of the chassis of cars. The white board simulates the scope of Xihaner's work place. Every new Xihaner must pass the evaluation using this template.

(2) Evaluation procedures

First, the evaluator sprays water on the template with a watering pot, and then taps some chalk dust on it to simulate the dust on the car.

Then, the evaluator asks a Xihaner to clean the template with a towel. The team developed a scale to rate all the details of the evaluation: Is the Xihaner willing to squat down or bend down to wipe? Does he turn over the towel to the other side when one side is dirty? How long does it take to finish cleaning? And so on. These are all rating points.

When the worker finishes his work, the evaluator turns on the light, and all 18 cells will light up. Each cell is of different difficulty levels and has different points—the cells in the middle are the easiest, and the point is lower; the cells on the edges are the most difficult, so the point is higher. Each clean cell adds points. And each cell that is not clean does not add points.

The final points of all the cells show the ability of the worker. Those who get 80 or 90 points will be appointed to important positions in their future teams. It has been proved that this ability evaluation system is effective in evaluating the worker's actual working ability.

(3) Assigning jobs based on evaluation results

Based on the results of professional ability evaluation, managers can divide the Xihaner into teams and assign different jobs to them. Specifically speaking, they will divide the workers into several teams and make sure the average disability level of each team is basically the same. For example, each team has one worker of mild disability level, three medium and one heavy; or one mild, two medium and two heavy. Members in each team cooperate with each other and work together.

Jun Cao said, "no matter how mild a child's disability level is, he can't clean the whole car by himself. They are not capable of it. Therefore, jobs have to be divided into smaller tasks and done by teamwork. Workers with disability of mild level do more, those of medium level do less, and those of heavy level can just do one task. Thus, five or six workers can clean the whole car by teamwork."

Then how to ensure cleanness and waiting time? The answer is by professional training.

Professional Ability Training System

Workers who passed professional ability evaluation will be divided into teams of five or six members. Each team can finish cleaning a car in 20–30 min, about the average industry level in waiting time. Jun Cao's team also invented the concept of "starting point" and the method of "avoiding major and minor negligence," to make sure they can achieve the average industry level in the aspect of cleanness.

(1) Avoiding major negligence using the concept of starting pointing

Before receiving professional training, when Xihaner were giving the task of cleaning the doors or the windows of a car, the following situation may happen: when they finished cleaning one side of the car and went to the other side of the car, they would find the other side looks the same and think it has been cleaned already. This kind of negligence is called major negligence.

Jun Cao's team found a solution to it, which is to always start cleaning a car from the starting point—the reversing mirror on the left side of the car—and then continue with the windows, tires, doors, etc. on both sides in order, and finally go back to the starting point. Thus, major negligence can be avoided.

Jun Cao said, "first of all, we will train the kids about the concept of starting point. After training, when they are asked to clean the template, they should ask their trainer where is the starting point, which means the training is successful. Then the trainer will tell them to start from the reversing mirror on the left side of the car."

(2) Avoiding minor negligence using the concept of starting pointing

Similarly, before receiving professional training, Xihaner usually clean randomly when they clean the car. As a result, the stains and dusts cannot be cleaned thoroughly, and will show up again once the car dries up. This kind of negligence is minor negligence.

Jun Cao and this team found their solution to this kind of minor negligence, that is, to divide the car into smaller parts, including window panes, door panels, head cover, trunk cover and roof. Xihaner are trained to clean each part one by one.

Fig. 8 Xihaners in professional trainings

When cleaning each part, they should always start from the top left corner and wipe horizontally with a small angle until the bottom of that part, so as to ensure that each part can be cleaned thoroughly. Thus, minor negligence can be avoided (Fig. 8).

Jun Cao said, "In real work, each worker will be responsible for a few parts and cooperate with other team members, just like in training. When they finish cleaning one part, they will have a sense of achievement. It's just like winning a little red flower. Thus, they win self-confidence from working."

By applying the concept of "starting point" and the method of "avoiding major and minor negligence," they can reach the average industry level in the aspect of cleanness. By now, Jun Cao's team has given this training to two or three hundred Xihaner, and 90% of them achieved the working ability as they expected, which proved the effectiveness of their training system and methods.

(3) Reaching the average industry level

Xihaner who received professional ability evaluation and training demonstrated good cooperation spirit and professional ability in actual work. They verified the three questions successfully, and reached the average industry level both in cleanness and waiting time. It's safe to say that their car wash project is a success.

Jun Cao once said excitedly, "Every time we clean a car for a customer, the customer will pay us 35 yuan as remuneration for our service. This is fair trade. When customers come for the second time or make special requirements on our services, it means that customers are taking us as a standard carwash, and that we have reached the average industry level."

Testing Ground for Social Adaptability

Xihaner Carwash is not only a place for Xihaner to work, but also a testing ground for their social adaptability.

When Xihaner are under the age of 14, their families do their best to provide Xihaner with basic education and rehabilitation. The government and the society also invest money and resources to help them. When they are older than 14, the target naturally transfers to developing Xihaner's social adaptability. The reality faced by most Xihaner in today's China is that when they grow up, there are hardly any jobs suitable for them. So they are forced to stay at home, and don't have any opportunity to adapt to the society, and eventually become burdens to their family and the society. In this sense, Xihaner Carwash provides opportunities for Xihaner to adapt to and integrate into the society, and therefore solved the problems of both their families and the society.

Developing Social Adaptability

The goal of social adaptability development is to let Xihaner enter the society, participate in work, create value, develop social adaptability and finally win the recognition of the society. Now, every Xihaner has to go through one month's evaluation and training after they join the Carwash. Professional training usually takes only a week, and the rest of the time is spent on social adaptability development.

Yan Huang is one of the managers of Xihaner Carwash. She used to work in Shenzhen Disabled Persons' Federation. When she met Jun Cao and exchanged ideas with him, she totally agrees with his concept. Therefore, Yan Huang resigned in May 2015 and worked together with Jun Cao to found Xihaner Carwash. "In order to develop Xihaner's social adaptability, we need to develop their cognition and ability in four aspects, including basic cognition, working ability, cooperation ability, and autonomy ability," said Yan Huang.

Basic cognition is the basic requirement for Xihaner, which is to make Xihaner understand that the workplace is different from their schools or homes, and they should follow certain rules in manners, etiquette and clothing, to show respect to the customers and to themselves too. Xihaner Administration Rules in Table 2 aims to develop and standardize their basic cognition.

Table 2 Some items of Xihaner administration rules

• Working area and rehabilitation area should be kept clean and tidy. No shouting or chasing is allowed. No snacks or chatting is allowed during working hours. Workers should follow the schedule and arrangement of their supervisors
• Keep good working spirit during working hours. Always wear uniforms and welcome the customers warmly. Respect leaders and colleges, and care for each other
• Keep the Carwash clean and tidy. No spitting or littering is allowed. Follow the rules when taking and returning working or sports tools and materials
• Follow the attendance rules of the Carwash. Do not be late or leave early. Always report to supervisors for approval in advance in case of special occasions
• Working hours: 9:00–12:00 in the morning; 14:00–18:00 in the afternoon

Fig. 9 Ability training room (for trainings both on working ability and social adaptability)

Working ability and cooperation ability are basic employment requirement for Xihaner. Although the car washing procedures and standards can be adjusted to fit Xihaner to some extent, their working ability and cooperation ability still needs to be improved by applying the principles of "scientific evaluation, make best use of advantages, divide jobs, and team work," so as to serve the society better and create more value by working. Autonomy is a higher requirement for Xihaner, and it is also an important factor to measure their social adaptability (Fig. 9).

Testing Results of Social Adaptability Training

As the testing ground for Xihaner's social adaptability training, how did Xihaner Carwash do after two years of experiment?

Jun Cao tells such a story about a Xihaner called Xingyou Chen. Xingyou Chen is intellectually disabled of the heaviest level. Before he worked for the Carwash, he had never left his house or taken a bus by himself. When he first joined the Carwash, he had two or three incontinence every week. Master workers or other coworkers had to wash and change clothes for him. He needed to go to work by bus. At first, his grandparents sent him to the Carwash in the morning and pick him up again after work. Gradually, they just sent him to and pick him up at the bus stop near home, and the teachers picked him up at and sent him to the bus stop near the Carwash. Later, in order to train his independent living ability, the teachers and his grandparents would just follow him to the bus stop behind him. And soon, he was able to take the bus to work all by himself. And incontinence never happened again for more than one year. In the aspect of working ability, he could only clean one tire at first. And now he can clean all the four tires, and even help his coworkers with soaping. This is a big progress.

There is also a Xihaner with cerebral palsy who can't land his heel due to muscle tension. After he joined the Carwash, he has to squat down, get up, and stretch his arms and legs repeatedly in work. Gradually, he can land his heel on the ground, and can even run a few steps. Some of the Xihaner even learned to use shared bicycles to commute.

"Over the past two years, Xihaner's social adaptability has been improved comprehensively. The achievement is even more remarkable than professional rehabilitation training," said Yan Huang. In the aspect of working ability, some Xihaner are not only capable of the jobs assigned to them, but can even shift between multiple positions. This is an amazing achievement.

Frequent customers are also surprised to see the changes of Xihaner's mental state. One of them said, "When the Carwash just opened, Xihaner were shy and would hide in the corner. But now they can take the initiative to receive the car and greet people."

The workplace has become a platform for the young people to communicate freely and happily. They have their own language. They play, joke, and fool around with each other and sometimes have good laughs. The pay-day is the happiest day. They buy Coke and Sprite to treat each other and celebrate together.

"People's Daily once wrote a report on us named 'They did it'," Jun Cao said. "I'm really proud of us! These children proved themselves. They did it, and they did it well!"

Always on Road

Since its establishment two years ago, Xihaner Carwash has been practicing its mission of allowing intellectually disabled persons to "learn skills, participate in works, realize their values and win social respect," and transforming them from pure consumers of social resources to providers of social services. On September 24, 2017, Xihaner Carwash won the gold medal in the final round of the Sixth China Philanthropy Project Competition. This shows that it has become a leading social enterprise that solves social problems by means of social innovations.

(1) Model effect

On the first anniversary of Shenzhen Xihaner Carwash, Qinghai Xihaner Carwash opened with the help and support of the former one. After two years of operation, Xihaner Carwash streamlined, standardized and modularized its car washing process, and formed a complete professional ability evaluation system and professional ability training system. Currently, with the help and support of Shenzhen Xihaner Carwash, there are a total of nine Xihaner Carwashes in China, and more than 20 under construction (Fig. 10).

Fig. 10 Qinghai Xihaner Carwash

Xihaner initiated "Chunlei Campaign" nationwide, a mass employment plan for intellectually disabled people, aiming to set up 1000 Xihaner Carwashes, and provide 10,000 to 15,000 jobs for intellectually disabled people.

(2) Spreading positive social energy

Xihaner Carwash has attracted the attention of many media around the country. Xinhua News Agency, Guangzhou Daily, Yangcheng Evening News, Ta Kung Pao, Southern Metropolis Daily, Nanfang Daily, Shenzhen Special Zone Daily and Shenzhen Daily (English version) all reported on them. CCTV-13 broadcasted a program on them in Live News. Charity Network published a report with the title of "Xihaner Carwash: the Road to Dream Home." All these media reports enhanced their social influence.

On March 8, 2016, Xingrui Ma, then Secretary of the CPC Shenzhen Municipal Committee, said to Jun Cao when visiting Xihaner Carwash, "you have done a great job. You helped them win respect and realize their value. You promoted righteousness and passed positive energy to the society."

(3) Promote the introduction of relevant policies

Xihaner Carwash has been exploring to provide a commercial solution to social problems that cannot be solved by the government or the market alone. It has taken a solid step toward Xihaner Dream Home. Social problems need the participation and support of many parties, especially the policy support of the government. Just like there are special policies of massage shops for the persons with vision disability, maybe there can be special policies of carwashes for persons with intellectual disabilities. On February 23, 2017, Kai Cheng, vice president of China Disabled Persons' Federation and Yong'an Zhang, president of Guangdong Disabled Persons' Federation visited Xihaner Carwash. Their visit shows Xihaner has won government recognition and their social influence is wide.

Jun Cao said, "Just like targeted poverty alleviation policies, persons with disabilities also need targeted support policies. It should be a complete set of solutions including accurate identification, accurate assistance and accurate management. If we can successfully promote the government to issue special support policies for intellectually disabled people, it will be the best contribution we can make for them."

(4) Demonstration role of a successful social entrepreneur

As the founder of Xihaner Carwash, Jun Cao won the nomination award of the third "CCTV Charity Celebrity of the Year" in 2016, and was invited to be the director of the Sixth Council of Shenzhen Disabled Persons' Federation in 2017. As a successful model of social entrepreneur, Jun Cao encourages young people to explore innovative commercial solutions to social problems.

Government support is indispensable for the development of Xihaner Carwash. Xihaner Carwashes provide jobs mainly for Xihaner. They aim to explore innovative solutions to Xihaner's employment and society adaptability. They need to work together with the government, society and Xihaner families to solve social problems. At present, their operation revenue can cover their employees' salary and daily operation and management expenses. But it can hardly cover other expenses, such as site leasing, expenses for teachers and assistants and so on.

People asked Jun Cao why he decided to open Xihaner Carwash before getting any government support, he replied, "Just do it and don't hesitate. Government support will be in place when you prove yourself." At about six months after its opening, the Carwash was visited by Ma Xingrui, then Secretary of the CPC Shenzhen Municipal Committee, who committed to provide them with free work site and expenses for teachers and assistants right away. Currently Shenzhen Xihaner Carwash is running on free site provided by the government. Xihaner Carwash streamlined, standardized and modularized their car washing process, and formed a relatively complete professional ability evaluation and training system. Once it gets government's support in work site and expenses for the teachers and assistants, Xihaner Carwash can hire a large number of people with intellectual disabilities, and therefore its model can be duplicated fast.

Xihaner Carwash is the first social enterprise founded by Jun Cao's team as part of their Xihaner Dream Home. They are also exploring other projects suitable for

Xihaner. Recently, a negotiation on a rice processing project is going between the team and an enterprise in Heilongjiang Province and it will come to an end soon. Jun Cao and his team are taking steady steps toward their vision of the Dream Home.

As for the future challenges, Jun Cao said, "the success of Xihaner Carwash has proved that Xihaner can integrate into the society, create their own value, and win respect and recognition of the society. But there's still a long way to go to change the public attitude toward the disabled people, as well as to formulate and implement new policies required by the new concept of disability."

The families, the society and the government should work together, to transform public perspective on disabled people from handicapped people to people with special needs, to change the focus of future work from medical treatment to society transformation, from equal participation to value creation, and to transform the new concepts into new policies and implement them.

Further Reading

Bulletin of Main Data of the Second National Sampling Survey of Disabled Persons in 2006 (No. 1). 1 December 2006

Website of China Disabled Persons' Federation. http://www.cdpf.org.cn

Company Information

Feng L, Bai Y (2015). Shenzhen Xihaner Carwash: dream home for persons with intellectual disabilities. http://www.xinhuanet.com/politics/2015-08/18/c_1116296397.htm. Accessed 18 Aug 2015

Guan Y (2016) Shenzhen Xihaner Carwash opened its first flagship store in other cities. http://sz.people.com.cn/n2/2016/0817/c202846-28846095.html. Accessed 17 Aug 2016

Gui C (2018) "Xihaner" also has a wonderful life. http://theory.people.com.cn/n1/2018/0401/c40531-29900761.html. Accessed 1 Apr 2018

He L (2018) Founder of Shenzhen "Xihaner" carwash: Morally Hijacking people with compassion is not an option. http://www.thepaper.cn/baidu.jsp?contid=2037589. Accessed 22 Mar 2018

Lv S, Xia F (2017) Working while receiving training and education at the same time, they did it. http://gd.people.com.cn/n2/2017/0728/c123932-30541212.html. Accessed 28 July 2017

News Channel, CCTV (2016) Every cloud has a silver lining: the story of Jun Cao. http://tv.cctv.com/2016/05/11/VIDEj4jaxXWWE371iwNY8Hgz160511.shtml. Accessed 11 May 2016

Shenzhen Economic Daily (2015) Xihaner Carwash is paying the salary. http://news.sina.com.cn/o/2015-08-10/doc-ifxftkpe3077813.shtml. Accessed 10 Aug 2015

Shenzhen Evening News (2016) Creating value by working, Xihaner wins respect—Xihaner Carwash won the title of "The Third Pengcheng Public Welfare Project Model." http://wb.sznews.com/html/2016-09/06/content_3613276.htm. Accessed 6 Sept 2016

Shimiaofanren (2018) Xihaner can have their spring. http://www.iqiyi.com/wrw8xfhgx.html. Accessed 17 Jan 2018

Shouxun Video (2017) Jun Cao: Xihaner employment action—creating value and win respect by working. https://v.qq.com/x/page/b0522d85z2b.html. Accessed 21 Dec 2017

Sun Y (2017) Xihaner Carwash won the public welfare award. http://www.oeeee.com/nis/201709/25/525309.html. Accessed 25 Sept 2017

Xinhua Net (2015) Shenzhen's first "Xihaner Carwash" opened yesterday. http://health.cnr.cn/jkgdxw/20150809/t20150809_519482064.shtml. Accessed 9 Aug 2015

Yang Cheng Evening News (2015) A Carwash opened in Shenzhen hiring 12 Xihaner. http://shenzhen.sina.com.cn/news/n/2015-07-15/detail-ifxewxfu4183527.shtml. Accessed 15 July 2015

Chengdu Langli: Recreate a Society Adapted for the Elderly

Jianying Wang, Jingyue Xu, Xiaoguang Li, Qiang Wang, and Yuyu Liu

> If in ten years, adaption for the elderly can be part of architecture standard, or a system, just like the floor boards or tiles in our homes, our mission will be achieved. There are so many hidden dangers for the elderly people in our homes that need to be solved as early as possible. However, this mission can't be achieved by Langli along, but the whole society.
>
> —Qinghai Zhu, founder of Chengdu Langli

According to international standards, China has entered the aging society since 2000. Moreover, the aging speed is fast, and the scale and proportion of the aging population are both growing rapidly. These have led to great challenges to the goal of "every elderly person is properly supported and cared." Before 2011, family has been the major provider of elderly care in China, supplemented by government sponsored nursing homes and other elderly care organizations. But the number of such organizations is too small to meet the social demands. Statistics show that by the end of 2010, the number of beds in elderly care organizations was less than 30% of the total population of disabled elderly people. Nearly half of the organizations made it clear that they only accept or mainly accept self-care elderly people, not disabled elderly people. In terms of elderly care nurses, only less than 30% of them graduated from nursing and related majors. In addition, the elderly care organizations are usually far away from the city centers, which means that the elderly will be separated from their

J. Wang (✉) · J. Xu · X. Li · Q. Wang · Y. Liu
Business School, Renmin University of China, Beijing, China
e-mail: wangjianying@rmbs.ruc.edu.cn

J. Xu
e-mail: xujingyue@rmbs.ruc.edu.cn

X. Li
e-mail: lixiaoguang@rmbs.ruc.edu.cn

Q. Wang
e-mail: wangqiang@rmbs.ruc.edu.cn

Y. Liu
e-mail: liuyuyu@rmbs.ruc.edu.cn

M. Zhao and J. Mao (eds.), *Social Entrepreneurship*,
https://doi.org/10.1007/978-981-15-9881-4_4

familiar environment, and it is inconvenient for their children and grandchildren to visit them frequently. This is quite different from the tradition Chinese ideal elderly life of "living with the families and surrounded by grandchildren."

In 2009, Qinghai Zhu, a Shandong native who had been doing business for more than ten years, decided to enter the home-based elderly care service industry after doing a lot of investigations together with his team. In 2011, they established Chengdu Langli Elderly Care Service Information Consulting Co., Ltd. (hereinafter referred to as "Chengdu Langli").[1] At that time, the whole society focused on the construction of high-end elderly care real estate and large-scale elderly care organizations. But Chengdu Langli made a different choice to provide community elderly care services for ordinary people. Over time, they established a chain of small multi-functional community elderly care service centers. As the company grew, Chengdu Langli expanded its business to social work services, which is closely related to home-based community elderly care services. It established formal social work centers, recruited volunteers, and undertook government projects, so as to enter families and communities to carry out various professional social work services, with elderly care as the core. By 2014, Chengdu Langli has formed a business model driven by both elderly care services and social work services, which can support each other.

Based on its rich nursing experience for the elderly, Chengdu Langli formed its service standards, and discovered the rigid demand of elderly. It finally decided to take elderly adaptive transformation as their business development direction, and proposed a new home-based elderly care model. It promoted and worked on the construction of an all-round elderly adaptive environment transformation from home to community and the society, to prolong the period when the elderly people can take care of themselves in their own homes and in the society. From promoting the basic elderly adaptive products to the consumers to building an elderly care service information platform, from working as one company to establishing an alliance of the organizations with common values across the country, Chengdu Langli has been working hard to promote the concept of all-round elderly adaptive services from families to the whole society and realize ideal elderly care models.

The Discovery: Elderly Care Market with Opportunities and Challenges

In 1997, Shandong Material Bureau cut down the number of its staff. Qinghai Zhu left the Bureau and started his own business. For more than ten years, his did business in importation, hotel, engineering projects and other fields. And finally, he began to look for new investment direction of his company. In 2009, when Qinghai Zhu and his management team visited Europe, they were deeply impressed by the local elderly care system. They admired the living conditions and the welfare enjoyed by the local ordinary elderly people very much. According to Qinghai Zhu, the market of crowd

[1]1 Now is Chengdu Langli Elderly Care Industry Development Co., Ltd.

service in China consists of three fields: women, children and the elderly. The former two have been developed for a long time and even over developed, while the elderly market is basically a blank. The situation of elderly care in foreign countries has set the goal for them. "The elderly people in China deserve the same living standard as those in Europe." Therefore, they decided to invest in Chinese elderly care business and began to investigate it.

Opportunities in Aging Society

Compared with developed countries such as Europe, America and Japan, which entered the aging society in the middle of the twentieth century, China was late for nearly 50 years. However, due to the long-term implementation of family planning policy and the increase of life expectancy in China, the aging rate is faster than developed countries, and the scale and proportion of the aging population are growing rapidly. According to the data of the sixth national census, at the end of 2010, there were 178 million people aged 60 and over, accounting for 13.26% of the total population, including 119 million people aged 65 and over, accounting for 8.9% of the total population. The total number of disabled and semi-disabled elderly people in China reached 33 million, among which disabled elderly people was 10.84 million. It is estimated that by 2020, the population of elderly people over the age of 60 nationwide will increase to about 255 million, accounting for about 17.8% of the total population; elderly people over the age of 80 will increase to about 29 million. Elderly people living alone or without children will increase to about 118 million.

In recent years, the government has been reforming its policies on elderly care services from depending mostly on the government to using market-oriented means, including purchasing social services. However, all the elderly care service providers in the market are facing challenges, whether they're elderly care real estate projects for high-end customers, or community elderly care service providers. According to the Research Report on the Development of China's Elderly Care Organizations issued by China Research Center on Aging, the vacancy rate of beds in China's elderly care organizations is up to 48%; 48.1% of these organizations achieved financial balance; 32.5% of them are in deficit; only 19.4% are in small surplus. Most of the community elderly care organizations rely on government subsidies to operate. The trend of aging and the current situation of the elderly care industry represent great business opportunities in Qinghai Zhu's eyes.

Lack of Elderly Care Services for the General Population

On the one hand, many high-end elderly care real estate projects and community elderly care service organizations are struggling to survive, and the empty bed rate is very high. One the other hand, elderly care services for the general population is in serious shortage. There are two major reasons for this situation:

First, the demand and the supply do not match. The elderly care supply in the market does not match the effective demand affordable to the general population. Research shows that a well operated elderly care service provider need to charge about 3000–4000 yuan per elderly person to cover the cost. However, by 2014, the average pension of enterprise retirees is only about 2000 yuan after "10 consecutive increases" by the government. Due to this gap, a large number of elderly people cannot afford the elderly care services they need. In addition, the average qualification of elderly care staff is not so good. And elderly care service is a special service. Therefore, elderly people and their families who can afford have doubts in the quality of the service. Some elderly people who have purchasing power don't want to purchase the service due to their traditional thrifty thinking. This kind of consumption environment makes it difficult for elderly care service providers to price their services properly to cover their input.

Second, government welfare is insufficient. Family has been the major provider of elderly care in China. It is difficult for the government to change this situation in short time and provide elderly care welfare to cover the general population. The existing welfare and support provided by the government for the elderly is ineffective because it cannot match the demand very well.

Locating the Target Market: Providing Elderly Care Service to the General Population

"Improving the living quality of the elderly and releasing the burden of their children" is the business goal of Chengdu Langli. It finally chose the ordinary elderly people as its target customers.

Chengdu Langli is very clear that in order to survive in this market, it must solve the problems lies in existing elderly care providers. First, it must help the government to solve problems in this field and prove it's trust-worthy. Second, it must find its own way to survive in the market independently and at the same time improve the environment for its future development, especially the policy environment. Therefore, it is very important to take both the middle and high income groups with purchasing power and the low-income groups relying on the government support as their target customers, and to find a business model that can serve them at the same time.

Starting the Business: A Service Model Driven by Both Elderly Care and Social Work

Investing in Chain Community Elderly Care Centers

"Since our capital is limited and can't afford to invest in big elder care centers which requires long payback period and of high risk level, then I will start with what I can do."

Chengdu Langli's team visited many countries in Europe and America and found that their cultural and social security systems are quite different from those in China, so it is not practical to learn from them. However, when they were visiting our neighboring country Japan, they found a small-scale multi-functional elderly care facility suitable for Chinese people, which can expand gradually by phased investments. This small-scale multi-functional elderly care facility provides support for the elderly in their homes and communities, which provides 24-hour personalized nursing services for the elderly without separating them from their families and neighbors. This type of elderly care facility has been actively promoted by the Japanese government in recent years.

Learning from this business model, Qinghai Zhu and his team started their preparation, and after one year they registered a non-profit organization in Civil Affairs Department, and also an enterprise named "Chengdu Langli Elderly Care Service Information Consulting Co., Ltd." in industry and commerce departments for better development in future. On October 8, 2011, Langli opened the first community nursing home with 11 beds (later referred to as "community elderly care service center") which was an NPO, in a community service building in Qingyang District, Chengdu. Being persuaded by Qinghai Zhu, the local government agreed to provide the venue. The local government paid a lot of attention to this innovative elderly care model, and "hoping to improve the overall community supporting facilities" through it. So it provided this site of 300 square meters to Langli free of charge. This was a great financial support for Langli who had just started its business.

About the first community nursing home, Langli team once said, "We hope it can represent our understanding of home. We spent a lot of efforts in software building to improve the services and the environment to make the elderly people feel like being at home. As for the hardware, we chose the colors that were seldom used by traditional elderly care organizations. We paid attention to all the details, even the color of our uniforms. (Fig 1)"

Chengdu Langli has rich marketing experience from years of commercial operation, and uses it in promoting the nursing home to the government and community. In less than two weeks, the nursing home welcomed the first resident. And in less than two months, the nursing home is fully occupied.

The price of the service center is 2000–3000 yuan /month /person, which is close to the per capita salary (34,008 yuan /year) of Chengdu in 2011. Each service center has about 15 beds, and seven or eight staff numbers, including one head, two nurses, three or three nursing workers, one chef, and one cleaner. The center provides

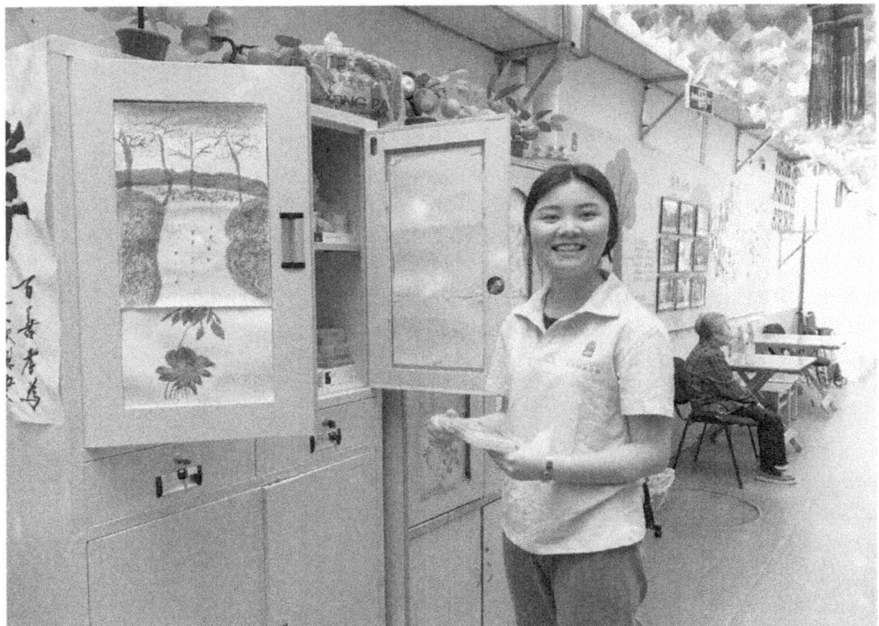

Fig. 1 Chengdu Langli Community elderly care service centers

boarding care, day care and temporary care and has stable customers, which can support their basic operation. Meanwhile, it continues to expand its business. It undertakes purchasing services for the government and citizens, and provides home-based catering, rehabilitation, sanitation and other services for the elderly people in the community.

Expanding to Social Work Services

Qinghai Zhu's believed that "community elderly care service center was a typical neighborhood business, which depends on the trust by the people in the neighborhood. The biggest investment we made is time. The first thing a successful neighborhood business needs is time." To make the neighborhood business better, Chengdu Langli chose to do more for the community.

On the one hand, based on the community elderly care service center, Chengdu Langli applied for government support or used its own fund to sponsor community organizations, such as the elderly chorus. On the other hand, Chengdu Langli's young team also attracts young volunteers including college students. Chengdu Langli provided venue in the community elderly care service center for the volunteers to chat, have parties and do other activities. They carried out various activities, such as visiting the elderly people living apart from their children, free medical services for the elderly people, etc.

At the end of 2012, the Ministry of Civil Affairs and the Ministry of Finance issued the Guidance on the Government's Purchase of Social Work Services, which provided documentary support for the government's purchase of social work services. This inspired Chengdu Langli. "We have been thinking that now we can only meet one need of the community, and the services of our volunteer workers are not professional. What kind of service is more professional? The answer is social work. And elderly care service is part of social work too." At the beginning of 2013, based on the existing volunteer workers, Chengdu Langli established its Social Work Center. As a formal organization, it can apply for government projects related to community elderly care, and provide comprehensive and professional social work services in the homes of the residents. It can also lead the original volunteer workers to carry out more professional voluntary services to the residents' families and the community. For example, Chengdu Langli Social Work Center organized a large-scale voluntary training activity "100–1000 volunteers" that went on for half a year. It helped Langli expand its volunteer's team to more than 1000 people. Langli volunteers came from Chengdu Langli, Sichuan University, Yulin Middle School, Experimental Primary School and various organizations and they provided free voluntary services including rehabilitation, sanitary, public lecture, and artistic photography for the elderly people in seven communities, and provided training for volunteer groups from various enterprises and organizations.

"We have both elderly care business and social work business. We can extend elderly care services to the communities that have our social workers."

Langli cooperated with local government and established a comprehensive community administration platform, which can support not only elderly care service, but social services for all social groups including the elderly, children, women and the disabled. With this platform, Langli can meet all kinds of social service requirements.

With its rich experience in nursing and rehabilitation gained from its community elderly care service center, Langli Social Work Center can select and apply for suitable government social work service projects related to elderly care, such as the community-resident elderly people service project of Li Ka Shing Foundation of the Ministry of Civil Affairs "The trip of great love—Sunshine to the nest," Alzheimer elderly people rehabilitation project of Welfare Lottery Foundation the "Guardian angels," and the "Rehabilitation and bath aid project for seriously ill and bedridden elderly people in Chenghua District" supported by central government finance.

Langli Social Work Center undertook a lot of government projects, which raised Langli's brand awareness in communities, and won their trusts. It helps Langli's community elderly care service centers enter more communities and even extended to paid home services. In just one year, Chengdu Langli opened another 11 community elderly care centers, and the number reached 36 by the end of 2017. Chengdu Langli has developed and runs almost all home-based services for the elderly, such as meal delivery, massage, rehabilitation, sanitation, spiritual comfort, social work services, etc.

Chengdu Langli sorted out their experience of elderly care and social work services, and draw up company workflow system and training system. The team also actively contributed valuable suggestions to the government for making relevant policies, and two documents of standards on the development of home-based elderly care organizations have been issued with their help—Chengdu Community Elderly Care Service Management Specification and Home-based Elderly Care Service Management Specification.

Where to Go Next: From Service to Products

Worries About the Company's Future Development

"In the market targeting the elderly people, one common feature of the companies who sell fake medicine or health care products is that they all provide very good services—They are willing to spend time to accompany the elderly people and win their trust, then sell the products and gain high profits; and with high profits, they can invest more people and time to please the elderly people. On the contrary, companies who sell qualified products can hardly make enough profits to afford such kind of service."

As the foundation of Langli's main business and its core competitiveness, its nursing service business for the ordinary elderly population is restricted by the regional differences in accents, culture, habits and other aspects when it was trying to expand to other regions of the country. So far, Chengdu Langli's community elderly care and social work services are only available in Chengdu.

In Chengdu, Langli is also facing challenges of serious shortage of community infrastructure. For example, old communities where most elderly people reside usually lack the venue for elderly care centers, while the new communities with enough venue are usually home to young people.

Community elderly care centers can only provide beds for limited number of people, while other home-based services such as home delivery, cleaning, rehabilitation, and social work are neither unique service of elderly service enterprises, nor required by every elderly person.

Chengdu Langli deeply realized that the solution to the operating difficulties faced by all the responsible elderly care service providers in China is to find the real rigid demands of the elderly population, and provide products affordable to most families to meet such demands. Thus, elderly care enterprises can find a balance between providing high-quality services and obtaining reasonable benefits at the same time, and survive in this field. If we can't find the answer to this question, we can't really solve the problems faced by the elderly people, and the enterprise can't really form the core competence and competitiveness in the field of elderly care.

Trying New Businesses in Small Steps

In order to develop, Chengdu Langli has been developing new products and services related to its core community elderly care service continuously. Chengdu Langli found that its rich experience in elderly care and social work services was urgently needed by many real estate developers and elderly care providers who just entered the field. Therefore, Langli began to provide relevant training for all the enterprises and organization in need. In addition, Langli has won the trust and word-of-mouth in the elderly group by years of services, and it has sufficient medical and nursing resources. Therefore, it can also organize national and overseas theme holidays and tours for elderly people. However, these consulting and tourism services are still difficult to duplicate and expand.

Chengdu Langli once again turned to Japan for inspiration. There, they found a nursing and prevention system for the elderly, which carries out a series of professional evaluation on the condition of the elderly people, then proposes a personalized exercise and health improvement plan. Based on this plan, it guides the elderly people to do exercises with professional equipment, to improve their body function and prevent disabilities from happening. Langli believed that it would be very help for the elderly to improve the quality of their lives. The system design was quite rigorous and scientific, and every elderly person could benefit from it. Would it be accepted Chinese market? They invested more than 100 thousand yuan and introduced one set of equipment. The business attracted some customers after its opening, but very soon, "it was defeated by the square dance, the favorite sports of Chinese elderly people!"

Enlightened by a Failed Attempt

When performing government procurement projects, Chengdu Langli's employees meet a lot of difficulties in providing services for the elderly. For example, when they cleaned homes of the elderly people, some elderly people would forbid them from touching the staffs that carry their memories. This made the cleaning work difficult for both the cleaners and the elderly. As for the consolation service of government procurement projects, the service period was usually too short to provide real accompany to the elderly. Some elderly people even suspect that they were just trying to get subsidies from the government and their service was a waste of money.

Once, when one of their employees was trying to carry out service of government procurement project, the customer refused him directly. It's not that they didn't do their jobs well, but that this service could not improve the living quality of the customer. Besides, the customer had to wait at home, sign, take photos, and go through a series of processes required by the government procurement project (for the sake of record and archive). However, existing government procurement orders had to be performed. Through observation, they found that many elderly people had difficulties to move around at home. So they began to think if it was possible to introduce the existing adaption facilities in the elderly care centers to the elderly people's homes. After getting government's approval, Langli replaced their original service to installing simple assistant facilities in the elderly people's homes. This new service was immediately accepted and welcomed by the elderly. They worked with the government to promote this home adaption experiment for the elderly right away, and replace the services of cleaning and accompany in original government procurement list with home adaption service at the same price. In May 2016, Langli carried out the first batch of elderly adaptive transformation service purchased by Liucheng Street government of Wenjiang District, Chengdu, and completed home elderly adaptive transformation for four elderly people in need.

After the reconstruction, an old man with hemiplegia who had been lying in bed for more than ten years stood up by himself and walked to the window for the first time without the help of his old wife, who also had difficulties to walk. Tears of excitement filled his eyes, and all the staff on site were also moved to tears. In the past, Langli staff had often been asked by the elderly people and their families to purchase some basic elderly products for them, such as special crutches, adult diapers, etc. But this time, they found the rigid demand of the elderly - home environment adaptive transformation, which can help the elderly people live a life with dignity.

Chengdu Langli's pilot project of home environment adaptive transformation was also the most suitable project for local government's accurate elderly assistance plan, and thus was recognized by the government. Each transformation project is designed, installed and adjusted according to the needs of each individual person. It substantially improves the elderly person's ability to live independently at home, and has been highly recognized by the elderly. Such use of Elderly Fund is quite effective. The elderly people are very satisfied with this government procurement project, and the government performance is improved accordingly. Meanwhile, for the government, the process and result of using the Elderly Fund is traceable and verifiable, and the products and services can be kept for a long time for the government and the higher authorities to audit in the future.

The government's acceptance and recognition of the home adaptive transformation surely helps Chengdu Langli promote the concept of elderly adaptive transformation to the public and expand this market. The implementation of the government procurement adaptive transformation project for low-income elderly people has also made the other residents in the neighborhood learn about the benefit of this service, and want to buy it for themselves. At present, Chengdu Langli has carried out home adaptive transformation for nearly 1000 families, of which more than 600 are purchased by the government, and the rest are by individual customers.

Promoting Home Adaptive Transformation Service

Chengdu Langli is very optimistic about the future of its home adaptive transformation project—compared with ordinary elderly care services, adaptive transformation products and services are easier to be carried out by intensive operation, especially when using domestic equipment, the cost and price can also be reduced significantly. This project can improve safety and comfort of the elderly at home, and improve their quality of life, so every elderly person will need it at a certain stage, and be willing to pay for it. Compared with the service of community elderly care center, adaptive transformation project can be quickly promoted to larger regions by franchising, authorization and other means, and the installation and following-up services can be standardized. In turn, the profit brought by home adaptive transformation project can be invested to elderly care business, to improve the enterprise's ability to survive and make profits.

Statistics of the World Health Organization shows that every year about 30% of the elderly over the age of 65 fall, and 15% fall twice or more. In 2016, there were 150 million elderly people over the age of 65 in China, and 40 million of them fell. Among these accidents, 40–70% of the injuries caused by falls need medical treatment. Falls may shorten the life span of the elderly by five to seven years. Home adaptive transformation, on the one hand, can prevent the elderly from falling to the biggest extent, prolong the life span of the elderly, and ease their psychological pressure; on the other hand, it can also reduce the conflicts between the family menders due to the shortage of labor and financial resources required by daily care for the elderly. Qinghai Zhu put this as reshaping of China's "family culture."

However, home adaptive transformation project still face challenges because the elderly people are unwilling to try new things and consume by nature. On the one hand, Chengdu Langli expended its cooperation with the government to carry out more home adaptive transformation project to low-income elderly families and elderly people with advanced age, which increased its fame effectively among the neighborhood and community through word-of-mouth; On the other hand, it also promoted this service to the children of the elderly and relevant knowledge to them. They developed the image of panda "Mighty" and created animation about home adaptive transformation. They also made TV interviews. By these means, the children who were actually taking care of the elderly people realized the importance of improving home safety and preventing the elderly from falling (Fig. 2).

In 2015, Chengdu Langli organized a team to studied the existing elderly products on the market, summarized their experience of elderly care service, sorted out the potential hazards in the home of the elderly, conducted special survey on more than 300 elderly people, and went to Japan many times to learn their experience and introduce appropriate home adaptive transformation products to China. Meanwhile, Langli believed that "every first-line employee is the designer of products." It developed a series of elderly care products independently with its own brand, and selected high-quality manufacturers in China as their OEM to produce its own products. In

Fig. 2 Cartoon image of Chengdu Langli home adaptive transformation project

just one year, Langli established the Internet of Things for a series of software and hardware elderly care products.

In order to meet the requirements of customers with different purchasing abilities and health conditions, Chengdu Langli developed a variety of products and services. With these differentiated products and services and their combinations, Langli can provide personalized adaptive transformation for each family. They developed a variety of product combinations with the price range from less than 100 yuan to 100 thousand yuan that solves the same problem on different levels. Customers can make choices according to their purchasing abilities and preferences, or buy the products by steps according to urgent levels.

Form Chengdu to the Whole Nation: Home Adaptive Transformation Platform Management System

Qinghai Zhu estimated that China's home adaptive transformation market worth at least 106 trillion yuan. The prospect of this market is so promising, but ordinary people still know very little about the concept. In many people's understanding, it just means selling products to the elderly. Chengdu Langli clearly knew that for better development of their enterprise, they should do much more than just choosing and designing home adaptive products. Based on the development of home adaptive transformation business, they set their next goal as building elderly service management platform.

Structured Experience—"Six Evaluation Systems"

Langli believes that home adaptive transformation should be a personalized service due to the different physical conditions and home environment of each elderly person. The promotion of this service must rely on a large-scale and reproducible operation system. At the end of 2015, Chengdu Langli officially set home elderly adaptive transformation as their most important new business in the future. They would continue to develop Langli home adaptive transformation products, and began to build a comprehensive standardized evaluation system. After reviewing and classifying various conditions and problems encountered in home adaptive transformations in the past, Langli standardized the assessment content and procedure, formed a set of scientific transformation plan, to reduce the possible influence of objective judgments in practical operations. At the beginning of 2017, Chengdu Langli finally completed the preliminary construction of home adaptive transformation management platform.

The six evaluation systems were created based on the experience of Chengdu Langli elderly care center, social work center and home adaptive transformation project. It is the essential competitiveness of Chengdu Langli home adaptive transformation business, and the foundation of the future home adaptive transformation information platform. It inquires and evaluates the conditions of the elderly people from six aspects to provide accurate data support for proposing personalized home adaptive transformation plans and follow-up services.

The six evaluation systems include contents of six aspects, including living ability evaluation, family relationship evaluation, assistant needs evaluation, home environment evaluation, personality and psychological evaluation and policy evaluation (see Fig. 3). Among them, living ability evaluation about the elderly self-care ability (such as eating, dressing, bathing and other specific life skills); family relationship evaluation is about the family members of the elderly people; home environment assessment is about the safety of hardware such as the floor, lights, accessible equipment and so on in the home environment of the elderly.

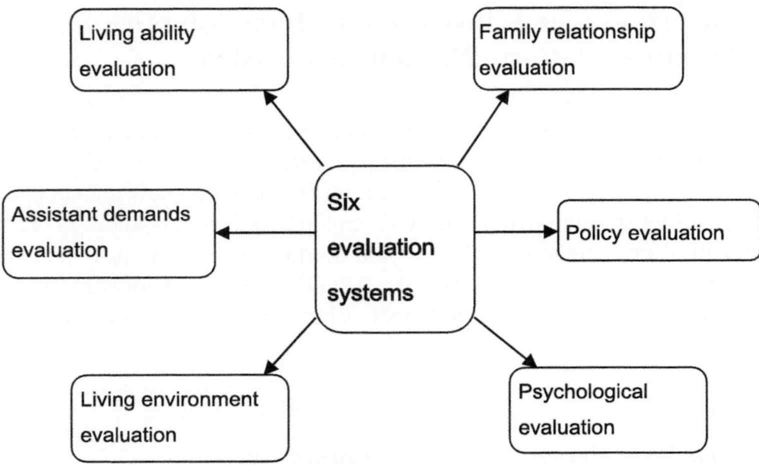

Fig. 3 Langli's six evaluation systems

Standardized Data Analysis Supporting Personalized Transformation

The evaluation personnel of the home adaptive transformation project visited the elderly people and carried out on-site questionnaires and technical tests with their evaluation toolkit designed by Langli. Then, they input and uploaded result of their evaluation to Langli's adaptive transformation platform directly through the APP installed in their hand-held iPads. And the platform would automatically generate the evaluation report and the transformation plan in real time, and send them back to the iPads of on-site personnel to show to the family members of the elderly. Finally, a personalized home adaptive transformation plan for this elderly person was generated. The elderly person and their families could make their choices and suggestions in proposed transformation plan, and decided on an affordable final plan, to guide the future transformation.

Upgrading the Data of Home Adaptive Transformation

The home adaption evaluation toolkit and training provided to franchisees made it possible for them to obtain evaluation contents of the six systems, and also extend data collection to the whole country at the same time. The diversity of franchisees also made it possible for them to add new contents to the system in order to serve the customers that they mainly focus on. For example, franchisees who focus on the service for disable people can add evaluations contents for these people. This will keep on upgrading the content of the evaluation systems and may produce subsystems for different customer groups in the future.

With the development of its Internet of things products, Langli can provide a variety of intelligent elderly appliances, such as smart watches, smart crutches, positioning shoes, etc. It hopes to collect and update the data in real time through these products, and provide further follow-up services for the elderly and their families, such as warning.

Chengdu Langli hopes to utilize the customer data collected from the adaptive transformation management platform to find and analyze customer needs in real time, maintain interaction with them and meet their potential needs accurately and in real time (see Fig. 4). Since it has two business development channels—marketing promotion and government procurement—Langli developed two sub management systems for different channels under this management platform:

Franchisee Management System and Government Procurement Quantitative Service Management Platform, which provide home adaptive transformation management services for franchisees and government clients respectively. This improvement also provide Chengdu Langli with the foundation for data update, customer maintenance and platform improvement in the future.

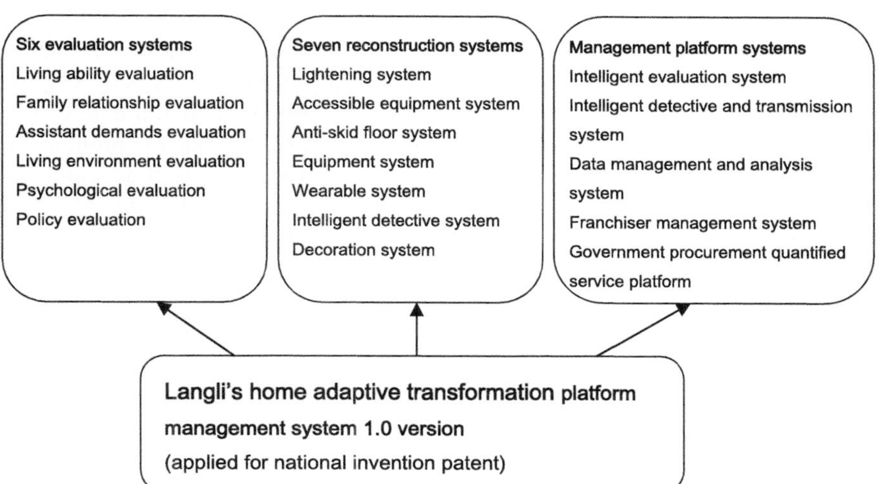

Fig. 4 Structure of Langli's home adaptive transformation platform management system

Products + Services + Data to Improve Customer Stickiness

In recent years, there are more and more enterprises participating in the sales and installation of elderly adaption products in the market. Chengdu Langli has been thinking about how to improve customer stickiness with the help of its elderly adaptive transformation service.

In addition to elderly adaption evaluation and construction personnel, in Chengdu Langli's elderly adaptive transformation team, there are also elderly care personnel. As members of the team, they can make suggestions and answer consultations during the whole process of evaluation and construction, and provide follow-up services. For example, when making evaluations for elderly adaptive transformation projects, elderly care personnel can make proper rehabilitation suggestions for the elderly people who suffer from movement disorders caused by stroke, and work with the rehabilitation professions to carry out rehabilitation services; or recommend them to participate in free activities or enjoy other social work services provided by Langli social work center according to their different interests. At present, the home-based services associated with home adaptive transformation are all provided free of charge. By doing so, the company hopes to distinguish it from other enterprises that simple sell products or services, and build its brand and reputation in the field of home adaptive transformation.

The Promotion of Elderly Adaptive Transformation Model: Franchisee System and Concept Popularization

Chengdu Langli's successful experience in elderly care and management, and its standardized evaluation system and evaluation techniques it created attracted many other enterprises and organizations to join in the elderly adaptive transformation business. Qinghai Zhu believes that to form and develop the market of elderly adaptive transformation, more people need to join in. Chengdu Langli cannot fulfill the elderly adaptive transformation demands nationwide by itself, so it decided to promote the service through franchising. At the end of 2016, at several rounds of amendments, the package of elderly care service franchisee system was officially launched, which include the principles of franchisee selection, franchising model and public welfare terms of franchising.

Selection of Franchisee

1. The selection of franchisees is an important strategic issue for Chengdu Langli which had been discussed and adjusted many times. Langli is very clear that its core competitiveness was formed by its long time of practice of always serving for customer interests by all its employees. Patience and sincerity are the key factors for its survival in the elderly care industry. Even for the elderly adaptive transformation business which is more commercial, "we also require the team to serve for more than three times during installation stage. Because the elderly people usually would contact them and ask questions like if the equipment is fine, or is it stable, and so on, so our service can't be measured or settled by efficiency. At present, the biggest service capacity estimated is installing for four families each day by four teams of two workers."

At first, Langli would interview the applicants and make judgment on whether they can perform the adaptation reconstruction and follow-up services according to its quality standards based on its experience and intuition. In addition to ensure that the applicants' resources and capabilities (such as its local social resources, influence in the customers, etc.) in the local area should be complementary to that of itself, Langli should also examine if the applicant is patient enough. Langli believes that only those applicants who can accept the fact that the return cycle of elderly care industry is slow can provide high-quality services and maintain long-term cooperation. "It's very important to judge whose fund we should accept. We are not looking for fund, but the correct people who provide the fund. The right people are much more important than the fund itself." Through careful screening, Langli finally selected 14 franchisees and began with detailed cooperation procedures.

However, during their cooperation, Langli found that this objective selection method was not very effective in identified cooperators with common values. Some franchisees made serious problems due to different values and beliefs. Langli resolutely refunded them their franchise fee and cancels the cooperation.

From then on, Langli changed its idea. With the deepening of Langli's communication and participation in the field of social enterprises at home and abroad, it began to change its attention to social enterprises and organizations. Different from ordinary commercial enterprises, these organizations and enterprises often take serving the vulnerable social groups as their organizational goals. They pay equal attention to the achievement of commercial goals and social goals in their operations, and have much in common with Chengdu Langli in values and innovation. For example, Wuhan Aite Children' Special Education and Training Center, is such a social organization who provides special education for disabled children. Ms. Hu Hong, the founder, visited Chengdu Langli during a social enterprise exchange activity. After learning about Langli's elderly adaption product system, she decided to start their cooperation right away. Her enterprise served for special children and their families. It provided nursing services similar to elderly care, and needed the same targeted products and services. "Elderly adaption" means "ability adaption" in her eyes. After becoming a franchisee of Langli, Hu Hong's team has obtained various resources and strong support from Langli. It reached financial balance in only half a year. It also added contents for the evaluation of disabled persons to Langli's original evaluation system, which may help to upgrade the system in the future. Therefore, Langli made it clear to select franchisees only among social enterprises and similar social organizations.

Franchise Models

Chengdu Langli has four franchise models:

First, the franchisee pays a certain amount of franchise fee in one time. The amount of this fee was reduced after Langli changed its way of franchisee selection. Chengdu Langli entrusts franchisees with the right to operate in a certain region. It not only provides franchisees with a set of special toolkit for elderly adaption evaluation, but also gives them a series of guidance, including providing all-round elderly adaption trainings and reconstruction, communicating with government for cooperation, giving them trainings on elderly care service, and inviting them to participate in trainings and visits given by Langli's elderly care experts from Japan. It also gives them real-time guidance and suggestions during the whole process of the operation, including helping them select the right address of and build the exhibition hall, and giving them suggestions for participating in government procurement, hosting public welfare activities, and so on.

Second, franchisees can use the franchisee management system in Langli's elderly adaption platform management system and Langli evaluation system and methods, purchase products produced or recommended by Langli to carry out adaptive transformation, and receive Langli's systematic training. Franchisees can develop other elderly care service businesses according to their own resources, and Langli will not charge any commission for their income of product and service sales.

Third, when carrying out home adaptive transformation projects, the franchisee needs to use Langli's standardized evaluation system and the toolkit to do the evaluation as required by the standard procedures, collect evaluation data, and use the data analysis results to help the elderly people choose suitable products and services. During and after the reconstruction, the remote data collection system carried by relevant intelligent products will collect and upload the use data and physical sign data of all users. Franchisees can add systematic evaluation items according to their own needs. All data will enter Langli's elderly adaption platform management system, and turn the system into a large database of elderly care services, elderly adaptive transformation, and information of elderly users and other user groups, providing data support for further product and service development.

Langli hopes to use these data in cooperation with more partners in the future, to make it become a cooperation platform for the elderly care field, on which partners can achieve mutually beneficial cooperation.

Fourth, in their own authorized regions, franchisees can not only carry our elderly adaptive transformation projects, but also copy Chengdu Langli's community elderly care service center model, learn from Chengdu Langli's community mobilization and government cooperation models and the nursing home management model in the future.

Public Welfare Term in the Franchise Agreement

Chengdu Langli added a special term in its contract with the franchisees: "The franchisee must perform one of the following public welfare obligations as suitable to the specific conditions of each franchisee and its region, including donating a certain amount of money or a certain ratio of the franchise fee to the local charity association or a certified public offering foundation; or establishing a special public welfare funds for elderly adaptive transformation; or carrying out free adaptive transformation for families with financial difficulties or special needs in the region; or raising funds using its own resources. Langli requires its franchisees to make a certain amount of donations every year. Qinghai Zhu said, "We want to take the initiative to establish a nationwide foundation. It would be the best if it could attract other social resources." By doing this, Chengdu Langli hopes to encourage its franchisees to increase local society's awareness of elderly adaptive transformation."

Popularization of the Concept of Elderly Adaptive Society

In addition to providing elderly care home services through franchising, Chengdu Langli also thinks it is necessary promote the concept of community and social elderly adaptive transformation. The elderly not only need assistance in their homes, but also need to go to the communities and even participate in social activities. Therefore, it is imperative to promote elderly adaptive transformation in the communities and the society.

In the process of providing elderly care service and home adaptive transformation service, Chengdu Langli realized that the elderly people also meet obstacles outside their homes. Even for the community elderly care service, it is still a burden for the families to send and pick up the elderly persons who are unwilling to spend the night in the center but still need day care because their home environment is not suitable. Home and community elderly adaptive transformation and door-to-door elderly care services allow the elderly people to live freely at home without depending on other family members and ease their burdens, so that family members can enjoy traditional close relationship between them without unnecessary trammels.

With the help of elderly adaption equipment and information system, the empty nest elderly and their families can rebuild their close relationship. The family members can monitor the safety and living conditions of the elderly remotely, and remind them to take medicine, rest, and exercise.

In Langli's concept about the mission of the enterprise, elderly adaptive transformation does not only mean to physically protect and monitor the elderly at home, but also an ideal to reshape the healthy ecology of the family, and a practical way to reshape the traditional Chinese "family culture."

When Chengdu Langli has a clearer understanding of the relationship between elderly adaptive transformation, elderly care services, and home-based elderly care, the social goal of this enterprise is clearer too.

In Langli's vision, in the future, more elderly people will able to live at their own homes with the help of elderly adaptive transformation and enjoy community elderly care services. Community elderly care service centers will slow down their development due to limited demands. And large and medium-sized nursing homes will be built in places far away from the community where land can be acquired more easily, to accept the elderly people who have no independent living ability for nursing services.

If the elderly adaptive transformation of the whole community and the whole society is completed, the proportion of home-based elderly care may be further increased. The ultimate goal of China's elderly care pattern is "9802," that is, 98% of elderly care is home-based care, and the rest 2% is nursing and palliative care in large and medium-sized nursing homes.

Langli needs to promote the elderly adaption process from home to community and to society, and the ideal elderly care pattern of "9802" consisting of home-based elderly care and nursing home professional elderly care. Therefore, Chengdu Langli began to accept more media interviews and made "Mighty" family safety cartoons. The founder was invited to be a member of the expert group of the Elderly Care Standard Committee of Chengdu Civil Affairs Bureau to make suggestions for government policy making, and participate in the formulation of local standards in related industries. On December 18, 2016, Chengdu Langli Elderly Adaption Service Project Press Conference and the launching ceremony of Elderly Adaption Service Research Center were held in Chengdu. Langli, together with all sectors of society, established the first elderly adaption service research center in China. Scholars from China Institute of Elderly Industry Development, Sichuan Academy of Social Sciences, some colleges and universities in Chengdu, other domestic researchers on aging issues, experts of elderly adaption from Japan, etc. attended the conference and gathered together study and promote elderly adaptive transformation services in China.

"We can't do it by ourselves. We need to increase the awareness of the whole social on this issue. We want to share Langli's community service experience, and our ideas and solutions about the elderly industry through these activities, to influence the society."

System Guarantee: Risk Control and Team Building

Risk Control of Elderly Care Services

There are two major risks of enterprises in the elderly care service industry: first is the emergencies happen to the elderly; second is the objection of the community residents during business expansion. Chengdu Langli met many challenges in years of community and home-based door-to-door elderly care services, accumulated rich experience, formulated a systematic response procedure, and carried out related trainings and drills.

1. Prevention in advance

Before accepting each resident or providing home-based service, Chengdu Langli community elderly care service center will do the initial evaluation on the care level of the elderly. And later, if any major changes happen to the elderly person's physical condition, the center will carry out continuous evaluations. Langli has an 18 page Elderly People Care Level Evaluation Form. According to this form, Langli will evaluate and rate the elderly person's physical and mental conditions, including self-care ability, cognitive ability, emotional behavior, visual ability and so on. Moreover, Langli will also evaluate the elderly person's social living environments, including living conditions, family conditions and so on. The result of the evaluation is the basis for the care center to determine the service content and frequency, as well as the service fee in the contract with the customer. It also highlights the issues that require special attention in the future service.

2. Daily management

Langli gives special attention to the new residents of their care center. The stuff need to fill in the New Resident's Adaptation Evaluation Form every day, pay attention to their psychological and physiological changes, and propose proper countermeasures. The personnel who fill in Elderly People Care Level Evaluation Form and New Resident's Adaptation Evaluation Form should be of no interest relationship with the resident or the caregivers.

During the daily care of the elderly, the most important thing is that the staff should always observe the condition of the elderly closely when taking care of them and discover any unusual behavior or occasion on time. Responsible and experienced personnel are the key to qualified service. Langli works hard to cultivate all-round abilities of its employees, improve their sense of pride in working and team cohesion, and ensures that all the employees fully understand the habits of each elderly person they serve. These make it possible for Langli to take preventive measures before the problems occur.

3. Making reserve plans

To prepare for the potential accidents, such as the loss of the elderly, violent behavior due to mental illness, and natural disasters like earthquakes, Chengdu Langli has developed a series of reserve plans based on its experience and lessons learned in the past, including Prevention and Emergency Plan for the Loss of the Elderly with Dementia, Reserve Plan for the Prevention of Violence of the Elderly and Emergency Service Plan. Among these plans, Prevention and Emergency Plan for the Loss of the Elderly with Dementia provides detailed and standard procedures to cope with the accident, from evaluation of the elderly person with dementia before residing, nursing details, guard system, to the reporting mechanism and specific searching plans when the loss occurs, and even the procedures to placate customers, find reasons, and communicate to the family members after the elder person is found. In case any elderly person is lost, the team can begin its searching work immediately according to the plan.

4. Whole process evidence recording

The community service center for the elderly has installed CCTV system to cover every corner. If any elderly person meets health problems or other unexpected problems occur, the CCTV system can record the video of the whole process of the accident. Even when any argument occurs between the family members of the elderly and the staff of the service center, the center will also save the video evidence for future use. In case Langli was evolved in any harassment, claims or lawsuits by the family members of its customers, these evidences can help Langli to protect its own rights and interests reasonably.

5. Communication and strength assurance

When Langli community elderly service center tries to set up new stations, it often encounters opposition from the community residents. This problem cannot be solved by Langli itself. Local governments and neighborhood committees must step forward. When local residents oppose their plans, the government and the neighborhood committees can coordinate in between, collect the residents' opinions and concerns, and organize meetings, through which Chengdu Langli can explain their construction plan and operation model in detail, answer the residents' questions and eliminate their concerns by giving successful examples and experience in the past.

The enterprise must be an expert in its own field. That is the key to persuade local residents. In Langli's 36 community elderly service centers, no elderly person they serve died during their residence. Langli's preventive measures and emergency plans make sure its community elderly care centers can take precautions before the emergencies, and send the elderly person to the hospital in case any emergency happens. These measures can prevent the residents from having bad feelings, and clear the road for the enterprise's future development.

Team Building

1. Professional team, young team

Qinghai Zhu once said, "I may not be a professional, but I must do business in professional way." Guided by this notion, Langli always recruits professional staff with high level and high standard. Unlike traditional elderly care providers and community service organizations, the founding team of Chengdu Langli is young, and its employees are young and professional too. Among the company's employees, post-80 s and post-90s accounted for 70%. Among 22 members of its core management team, all of them hold bachelor's degree or above. Among 153 members of its nursing team, 85% hold certificates—nine of them are certified national senior elderly care attendant, and five had received training in Japan. Among 43 full-time social workers, 31 of them had social work-related education background or hold related certificates, two of them are certified second-class psychological consultants, four are certified third-class psychological consultants, and three are certified lawyers.

Langli encourages its employees to receive trainings and continue learning. Many employees got both certificates of elderly care and social work during their employment.

2. Market based salary

The professional talents should be paid with proper market-based salaries, especially for the young people with individualities. In order to keep them in the elderly care service industry which is discriminated by the society, the company must give them competitive salaries, as well as the opportunities for their future development.

When the company was just founded, Langli recruited the only Asian who studied public health management in France by offering high salary.

Moreover, Langli's salary level for the staff is much higher than the average level in Chengdu, and also higher than that of the elderly care industry. For example, in 2016, the average salary of Chengdu Langli's nursing workers reached 3500 yuan (excluding insurance) per month, with free food and housing. In the same year, the average annual income of Chengdu residents in service, repair and other service industries was 34,847 yuan, which is about 2900 yuan per month. To some extent, it provides financial security to its employees.

3. Application of Siemens 3i management system

Chengdu Langli introduced Siemens 3i (ideas, impulses, initiatives) management system. The highest management of the company formed a management committee to systematically manage employees' submission of suggestions, evaluate these suggestions and give rewards. With this system, employees know what effective suggestions are, how to put forward effective suggestions, and the rewards for different types of suggestions. Employees can get encouragement and material rewards for their suggestions and improvements.

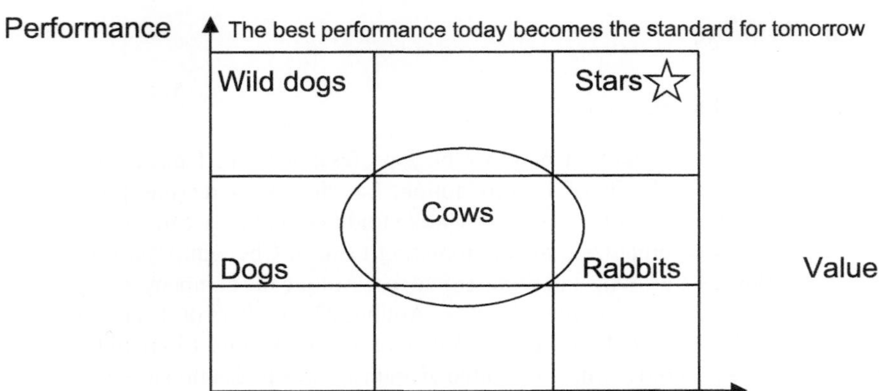

Fig. 5 Langli's performance appraisal system

4. Performance appraisal system with equal emphasis on performance and values

Langli's performance appraisal system includes two parts: achievement appraisal and value appraisal, each accounting for 50%. If someone fails in value appraisal, she or he will fail the performance appraisal. Langli used the graph in Fig. 3 to explain the relationship between the scores of achievement appraisal and value appraisal (Fig. 5).

Performance The best performance today becomes the standard for tomorrow

Key performance indicators (KPIs) are used for achievement appraisal of employees, among which 30% of the indicators are for the overall customer satisfaction on the department; 10% are for the customer satisfaction on the individual employee; only 30% are related to the service volume and order quantity; 10% are for the monthly tests and themed tests, including written test and simulation drills about enterprise management specifications and risk response (to daily and emergency events); the rest 20% are for daily evaluation, including the employees' suggestions on the improvement and optimization of products and processes.

In the value appraisal, Langli emphasizes the priority of the company's mission. "All the employees of Langli should work hard for the mission of 'improving the life quality of the elderly, and releasing the burden of their families'. We will always be kind. We will keep on making innovations and creating value for the society." "We promote our values through all the activities, including recruitment, training, personnel selection, performance appraisal, cultural construction and so on." "Human resources managers must avoid taking value appraisal simply as a "tool." They must fully understand the purpose of incorporating value appraisal into performance appraisal, make in-depth and careful observation and fair judgment on employees. The appraisal should be carried out not too rigid or too loose, so as to achieve the company's real purpose of promoting its values."(see Fig. 6).

Langli's Value system

Langli interpreted and explained each element of these values, and formed a practical appraisal system, to inspire its employees and help them reach consensus.

Fig. 6 Chengdu Langli's value system

5. Psychological assistance within the team

Employees working in elderly care industry face the elderly people and various sudden events every day, such as elderly people's illness, their family members' complains and even quarrels. It's difficult for the employees to work for a long time in such depressing working environment without a strong heart. High salary and sense of mission may not be enough. Even so, more than 80% of Chengdu Langli's employees have worked for more than three years.

Employees often say that "it's like a cozy home here." Led by the general manager, the employees gather together and give each other psychological guidance. The company also organizes team building activity every month. When employees meet problems in work, they can get comfort by talking to their peers, superiors and even the general manager and by participating team activities. Their problems can also be solved. Social workers in psychological counseling positions can be the psychotherapists for the employees in daily team communications. The trust and understanding between every member of the company, and the problem solving mechanism encourage employees to face problems at work. Complete emergency plans and frequent training and testing allow employees to be competent and confident in their daily work.

Financial Sustainability: Planning and Evolution

Farsighted Cash Flow Design

Chengdu Langli, who has a strong commercial gene, has been taking financial sustainability as the top priority for its elderly care business from the very beginning.

Before opening its first community elderly care center, Chengdu Langli had thought about scalable replication model. In order to improve the quality and professionalism of its services, the company paid a lot to hire professional staff including nurses, rehabilitation practitioners, etc. However, if the company only runs one or two community elderly care centers, these professionals' work load will be insufficient. And the profits won't cover the cost of the company's daily operation, let alone the cost of the management. Only by expanding the business scale, can the company realize its pursuit of high professionalism, build its advantages in specialization, and maintain its basic operation.

The community elderly care centers mainly provide full care and day care for the elderly. Their profits provide stable cash flow for Langli and guarantee its basic operation. Home-based elderly care services based on these centers provides extra cash flow over the cost. When it successfully duplicated 11 community elderly care centers in the first year, Chengdu Langli achieved financial balance.

Compared with community elderly care service, social work service does not require investment in fixed assets. Therefore, it can save capital for the company in its initial development stages, and generate continuous cash flow to the largest extend.

Elderly adaption products and platforms will be the most important sources of financial profit and cash flow for Langli in the future. Franchising model can not only help Langli increase its brand influence and expand the elderly care market rapidly, but also disperse its capital pressure and bring new cash inflow in the short term.

Market-Oriented Evolution of Revenue and Cost Structure

Chengdu Langli's earliest community elderly care centers mainly served for ordinary elderly people who can afford the service. With the development of its community business, Langli had more chances to cooperate with the government, especially in the field of social work services, and most by means of government procurement. Government procurement also helped promote its elderly adaption business, especially in the early stages, by setting good examples and increasing public awareness.

Currently, Langli's profit comes from three businesses—elderly care services, social work services and elderly adaptive transformation. For elderly care services, market purchase income accounts for about 70%. For social worker services, government purchase income accounts for about 70%. And for elderly adaptive transformation, government purchase income and market purchase income account for about half each.

During its development in the past, Chengdu Langli has got some financial support from the government, especially free venues for some of its community elderly care centers. But now, Langli is obtaining more and more venues by renting low-cost venues from the government or just by fair trade from the market.

Chengdu Langli reviewed the influence of government procurement and government support made on its financial state. The people that receive government procurement services are the most vulnerable groups in the society. Companies provide services for these groups and fulfilling their own social missions, which helps them win social trust at the same time. The recognition of the government is also necessary to promote the development of the elderly care service market and the concept of elderly adaptive transformation. In the long run, it is an important business of elderly care companies to undertake government procurement projects actively. However, if a company depends solely on the low-cost government procurement projects as its major source of income, or take the free venues and other resources provided by the government as the major way to reduce costs, these benefits may even hinder the company's development, innovation and progress on the contrary, or even lead to crisis in case of policy changes.

Therefore, for the future, Langli plans to strengthen the market competitiveness, especially to increase the social awareness of elderly adaptive transformation in more effective and efficiently ways.

Risks and Challenges

Since Chengdu Langli established its first community elderly care center in October 2011, the total has reached 36, providing elderly care and social work services for more than 3000 people. Thanks to its good name among the customers, the company has gradually formed its core ability of elderly care service. The company has been developing stably, and its goal of serving the ordinary elderly population has also become clear. However, as its elderly adaptive transformation industry chain develops, the company requires more resources, and is faced with greater challenges.

IPO or not?

During its expansion, Chengdu Langli has been using the investment of its founding team and the company's own funds to develop, without using any bank loans. However, how to provide more attractive income to the management team members and the employees who have followed them for six or seven years? That is the question Qinghai Zhu has been thinking about. In 2015, the company once considered listing on the new third board. This plan was terminated due to the structural problems of a large number of private non-enterprise organizations within the company and the problems of the new third board market itself.

Qinghai Zhu, one of the founders and general manager of the company, believed that the purpose of IPO should not be bringing funds or business expansion. He valued more about other benefits IPO may bring to the company One benefit is the social attention it brings to the company. The other is that IPO gives the company more opportunities for media exposure. Both of them can help the company realize fast expansion of its elderly adaptive transformation business and the promotion of its own brand. He also valued another benefit of IPO, that is, IPO can realize liquidity of enterprise value, so that its core team and employees can be rewarded as they deserve. However, the capital market investors introduced by IPO may have a different development model or performance orientation. And the benefits of IPO may not be practical or irreplaceable. All these makes Qinghai Zhu hesitate.

In order to improve the qualification of its franchisees, Chengdu Langli reduced its original franchise fee to allow social enterprises and social organizations to join in. At the same time, Langli also plans to open direct stores in other cities. All these bring financial pressure to Langli. So Langli may consider IPO or introduction of external strategic investment in the near future.

Qinghai Zhu is very confident about the company's future development. He believes that any difficulties that can be solved by market methods are not real difficulties. However, he hopes to be more careful about capital market. "It's not that important for me to control the company, but I hope we only introduce capital from investors who have the same value with us." he said. "I believe that 'people (will) attract capital from other people like themselves'. I'm not in a hurry. Such capital will appear someday."

Challenges of Standardized Management

Thanks to its rich management experience from previous business, Chengdu Langli is on the track of rapid development since its foundation. Although it has been standardizing its experience and management methods, Langli is not satisfied with the results, especially when replicating their services to new franchisees. For example, "product + service" model is the most important model used by Langli when selling and installing elderly care products. But this model is seldom implemented by the franchisees. The franchisees tend to adopt the ordinary product agency model. Even for the six evaluation systems that Langli thought have been standardized successfully, they had been carried out differently during operation.

In order to cope with this problem, Langli invited the former director of standardization and personnel training from Siemens in review the company's standards of personnel training, operation procedures and evaluation system, further expand the scope of standardization, refine the content, and even change the logic and structure of the existing six evaluation standard system. This will be a great challenge to the company's original management ideas and methods, information platform management system and employees' old habits.

Risks of Franchisee Management

Although Langli has made a careful design of its franchising system, and been controlling the expansion speed and recruitment standard, it still met some difficulties in operation, including: the protection of its intellectual property rights of the six evaluation systems; training and ability improvement of its personnel; management and control of new franchisees; negative influence of nonstandard operation of franchisees and other problems on the company's brand. Of course, when carrying out franchisee management, Langli have always been keeping an open mind, and ready to adjust its management mechanism whenever a problem is found. However, the recruitment of franchisees brings risks to the company, as well as accelerating its development as a platform.

The Future of the Platform

Chengdu Langli has just completed its transformation from a service provider to a platform. According to the company's goal, the biggest benefit of developing elderly adaption information platform management system is obtaining the big data of elderly care services. However, the collection and processing of these big data are still under slow progress by the company and its franchisees, together with their daily work in elderly care services, social work services or elderly adaptive transformation. For the Internet of things products that the company attaches great importance to, the market still needs more time to accept them. They can be easily replaced by other products on the market. They are quite different from the company's existing services and elderly adaptive transformation. They haven't formed their own brand effect yet. How to improve the company's platform? Can it expand its data volume as desired? How will these big data generate value? All these questions are still pending solutions.

Further Reading

Chengdu Bureau of Statistics Public Information Network (2017) Announcement of Chengdu Municipal Bureau of Statistics on the average wage of all urban employees in 2016. http://www.cdstats.chengdu.gov.cn/htm/detail_51951.html. Accessed 2 June 2017

Decision of the Central Committee of the Communist Party of China and the State Council (2000) Strengthening the work of elderly (ZF no 13)

Jun T (2014) Strange circle of elderly care service, effective demand and government subsidies. China Hum Resour Soc Secur 5

Research group of China Research Center on Aging, et al (2011) Research on situation of urban and rural disabled elderly. Disabil Res 2

Yushao W, Lili W, et al (2015) Research report on the development of China's Elderly Care Organizations. Hualing Press, Beijing

Yuetao S (2012) Beijing Geriatric Hospital: falls of the elderly and preventive. China Union Medical University Press, Beijing

Company Information

Chengdu L (year). Mighty talks about elderly adaption. http://cdlangli.com/news/newinfo/id/154. Accessed 31 Aug 2016

China Finance and Economics Report (2016) Different elderly care businesses. http://tv.cntv.cn/video/C10465/dd0ce5a0cc5e4d3a8aaf17feae3cddb1. Accessed 8 Oct 2016

Ideas and Focus, Sichuan TV. (year). Post-90s and the elderly. http://www.cdlangli.com/news/newinfo/id/159. Accessed 7 Oct 2016

Taiwan Strait Economy (2016) Interview with Qinghai Zhu, director of Langli elderly adaptive transformation. http://www.cdlangli.com/news/newinfo/id/158. Accessed 3 Oct 2016

DaddyLab: Let Good Money Drive Out Bad Money

Qiang Wang, Xiaoguang Li, Yanfang Xu, Zhuang Mi, and Shuo Zhan

Let's find out the invisible dangers in our lives together
Take science and laboratory tests as the weapon
Eliminate harmful products
Fight against vicious manufacturers
Expose dishonest advertising
Recommend qualified products
We may not be able to change the society, but we do the best we can.

—Wenfeng Wei, founder of DaddyLab

It All Started with Book Covers

In the spring of 2015, like all the other parents, Wenfeng Wei bought some stationery for his daughter for the coming new semester. But when wrapping the new textbooks, he felt a pungent smell coming from the plastic book covers. Wenfeng Wei had been working in laboratory testing field for more than ten years. He immediately knew something must be wrong these plastic book covers. For his daughter's health, he decided to find out where this strange smell came from. Therefore, he bought seven kinds of book covers from the stores near school gate randomly and sent them to Taizhou National Fine Chemicals Quality Inspection Center in Jiangsu Province. He paid 9,500 yuan for the center to give a comprehensive "examination" to these book covers. The testing reports showed that all the seven kinds of book covers he sent for examination contain a large number of polycyclic aromatic hydrocarbons and phthalates.

Q. Wang (✉) · X. Li · Y. Xu · Z. Mi · S. Zhan
Business School, Renmin University of China, Beijing, China
e-mail: wangqiang@rmbs.ruc.edu.cn

M. Zhao and J. Mao (eds.), *Social Entrepreneurship*,
https://doi.org/10.1007/978-981-15-9881-4_5

Wenfeng Wei, who majored in chemical industry, is quite familiar with these two substances. Among them, phthalate is a plasticizer widely used in industry. It is harmful to children and pregnant women. Polycyclic aromatic hydrocarbons are identified as strong carcinogens around the world.

After further investigation, Wenfeng Wei found that most of these book cover manufacturers previously were wallpaper manufacturers in Jiangsu, Zhejiang and Guangdong. They thought of book covers as smaller wallpapers, so they produced them with the same techniques and formula. But in fact, the standard of stationery is quite different from that of home decoration products: the stationery industry has higher and stricter requirements on the substances contained in the products. The wrong production methods and the lack of inspection lead to this situation together.

Wenfeng Wei immediately reported his discovery to relevant government authorities, but the respond was not so satisfactory. Driven by his love for his daughter and the sense of social responsibility, Wenfeng Wei decided to expose the issue of these book covers by himself. At his own expense, he made a small documentary about the toxic book covers, and published an article on his social media and We Media platform entitled "Is the book covers you bought for your children toxic?"

His documentary and article caused uproar in the society immediately. The articles were read over 100,000 times, and video was viewed over 15 million times in a short time. Many local media made relevant reports, and People's Daily also made reports on its official platforms. The social influence of book cover event brought Wenfeng Wei to the center of attentions by all walks of the society, as well as a large number of parents.

These parents gave Wenfeng Wei a nickname—"Father Wei." They gave him suggestions and asked him to test other products. They took him as the spokesperson for their interests and rights. Wenfeng Wei was deeply touched and began to realize that there were so many hidden dangers in the daily life of the children. Many common parents like him were not capable of solving these problems by themselves even though they wanted to. So he decided to do this for them.

In 2015, Wenfeng Wei organized "DaddyLab" team, and established Hangzhou DaddyLab Testing Technology Co., Ltd and its self-Media platform. They communicated with parents through WeChat and other social media, and carried out testing on products their children use every day. Gradually, DaddyLab found its mission during work—"Protect all the children from toxic and harmful products."

A Daddy's Odyssey

Old Hands Encounter New Problems

Wenfeng Wei graduated from the Department of physics, Zhejiang University. Then he entered Zhejiang Import and Export Inspection and Quarantine Bureau, doing electrical and chemical testing related jobs. After working for some time, Wenfeng

Wei felt he was fettered by the rules and regulations in his work, but no chance for innovations. His inborn entrepreneurship made him makes up his mind to leave the Bureau and start his own business.

Around 2008, Wenfeng Wei resigned from the Bureau to peruse his own business. That year, European Union just issued the Registration, Evaluation, Authorization and Restriction of Chemicals (REACH) to improve its chemical regulatory system. REACH stipulates that enterprises of the EU trading partner countries must meet a series of complex regulations to export to the EU. As soon as the regulations were issued, many domestic export enterprises were affected. The demand for advisory services related to Technical Barriers to Trade increased rapidly. Wenfeng Wei ceased this opportunity. He found like-minded partners, studied the REACH regulations in detail, and used his work experience in the inspection and Quarantine Bureau, to provide consulting services for China's export enterprises to the European Union, helped them transform their production methods to comply with the REACH regulations.

During this entrepreneur experience, Wenfeng Wei demonstrated outstanding entrepreneurship and business talent. He created and implemented his own "three major tactics": The first one is to provide as much exposure as possible to the enterprise. The second one is to hold as many training sessions as possible. By holding free training sessions on laws and regulations all over the country, they expanded the influence of their enterprises successfully. Wenfeng Wei remembered that they held 157 training sessions in just one year, and made his enterprise well known all over the country. The third one is the combination of telemarketing and door-to-door service. The "three major tactics" was quite effective. The company signed more than 2,900 contracts which brought in more than 30 million yuan of revenue.

"The book cover event" happened later made Wenfeng Wei realize that although he has been working in testing field for 15 years, but there are now even more new potential problems in this field He found that harmful products were just around him and his families and friends. As a veteran of testing, he couldn't identify all these products, let alone the public. Then, is there any way to change this situation? Wenfeng Wei decided to try independent product testing.

Difficulties in Product Testing

"Fake and shoddy" and "toxic and harmful" products have been pervasive on the market for many years. Although the government and enterprises have been trying hard to change this situation, the result is not very satisfying. Wenfeng Wei has a lot to say about this issue. "Currently, the mechanism of most national testing standards is to set up "blacklists" of banned chemical substances. However, there are so many chemical substances in the world. In order to reduce costs, manufacturers can always find other substances outside the blacklists but equally harmful to human. Besides, the number of products on the market is so huge, government authorities can only conduct sampling inspection. On the other hand, non-government testing organizations need to charge testing fees from private enterprises. The relationship of interest between them may affect the authenticity of the testing results. This is the case with toxic book covers. Manufacturers take advantage of the loopholes in testing standards to produce and sell unqualified products."

As a result, the problem of toxic and harmful products has always been a headache for the government and enterprises. With the development of China's economy and the growth of people' income, it is the goal of the whole society to improve the quality of consumption and the overall well-being of people. It is urgent to eliminate toxic and harmful products and create a good consumption environment for consumers. This is how Wenfeng Wei discovered the opportunities for starting his own business in independent testing.

A Father's Exploration

Since book cover event, Wenfeng Wei has been exploring a business model suitable for DaddyLab. When book cover event just happened, many parents came to ask Wenfeng Wei where they can buy non-toxic book covers. In order to help these parents, Wenfeng Wei found a factory in Shanghai and persuaded it to produce qualified book covers according to stationary standard. In the following September when the new semester began, his company sold 5,000 book covers, and was welcomed and supported by many parents.

Actually, the book cover event had provided a feasible business model for Wenfeng Wei—which is to combine testing with production. But at that time, he just didn't realize it. Or maybe, he was unwilling to do so.

Wenfeng Wei always believed that he was not selling products, but exploring the solution of a social problem—the toxic and harmful goods. Wenfeng Wei refused to sell products, because he just wants to serve for public welfare. The 5,000 book covers were produced just to fulfill the needs of the parents, rather than pursue profit. Even when later he was forced to sell products to maintain the operation of his company, Wenfeng Wei still felt uncomfortable to do so. Because he was not willing to sell products, he refused to promote these products. On DaddyLab's early online store Web pages, there were only a few words and some plain pictures of the products. Unlike other good online stores, the entire interface of DaddyLab online store had no design elements at all.

As a result, the company spent all their money by the end of 2015. Product testing is a highly invested business. From the first testing of book covers (which cost nearly 10,000 yuan), to runway pavement, chopping board, milk, and table lamp, DaddyLab spent more and more money on product testing. The revenue from selling just rubbers and pencils could hardly maintain the business operation any longer. Therefore, financing became the biggest challenge.

Wenfeng Wei, who was forty years old by then, wrote a business plan on the story of his DaddyLab testing, hoping to attract investments to continue the carrier that he loved. But unfortunately, he failed to attract any investors who were interested.

Some investors even told him directly that they would not invest for people over the age of 35. Wenfeng Wei had no choice but to try other ways.

Trying the New "Crowd Funding and Testing" Mode

At that time, his supporters stood up to help him. One night in January 2016, after learning DaddyLab was faced with financing difficulties, 112 parents raised two million yuan for them. Thus, the crisis was defused. Wenfeng Wei thought that he had found the right business model by combining crowd funding and testing. Crowd funding from the society would support the testing, and the testing results were fed back to the society. This business model could solve the social problem on the one hand, and maintain their business operation on the other. Therefore, DaddyLab began to motivate crowd funding by sending out small gifts and so on.

The crowd funding model might sound good, but it was not perfect. Crowd funding could only cover the cost of product testing, but DaddyLab also needed to support its own operation team of more than ten members. Meanwhile, as the number of projects and the frequency of testing increased, the testing fee for each product allocated from the crowd funding reduced. DaddyLab encountered serious challenges.

Inspired by the Parents

Once again, Wenfeng Wei began to question the existing model and think of new model. He considered several common profit-making models: the first one was to charge the enterprises with testing fees like traditional testing agencies; the second one is to put advertisements on its self-media platforms to transfer customer flow into advertising income; the third one is to charge the consumers who need testing services directly. The first two models would naturally affect the independence of testing results. And for the third one, how to charge consumers?

It was common sense that charging consumers directly would easily lead to consumer loss. Wei learned that the common practice adopted by western countries was to submitting reports to members how subscribed and paid, such as the "consumer report" in the United States. This model had been successful in the United States. But in China where consumers' copyright production awareness had not been fully established, the conversion rate of paid users was quite low. Therefore, it was difficult to obtain stable income. At the same time, this model required a considerable user base, which was not the case for DaddyLab. Wenfeng Wei made a rough calculation: "For an Internet celebrity with more than 10 million fans, when the conversion rate is 3%, there will be 300 thousand paid users; when charging 100 yuan on each user, the income will be 30 million yuan; when charging 200 yuan, it will be 60 million yuan. Our team needs about four million yuan per year, including bonus, salary, venue fee, etc. Testing fee will be about one million yuan. Considering all these factors, membership model is not suitable for us."

Finally, Wenfeng Wei found that all the existing models were not feasible. Once again, his supporters helped him find a new solution. A fan left a message to him: "You can't just say that this product is toxic and that one it is harmful. This just frightens us. You have to tell us which products are good and where to buy them."

These words struck Wenfeng Wei like a lightening. He began to make up his mind on the business model of "We Media and e-commerce in combination." Previous rewarding and crowd funding were also different ways of charging the consumers, while e-commerce was the most direct way. By selling goods that had passed independent testing, consumers could use healthy and safe products, and continue to make blood for the enterprise. Meanwhile, the company could obtain sustainable profit for its business operation.

Painstaking Transformation

Therefore, Wenfeng Wei established DaddyLab online store to sell qualified products they recommended. Meanwhile, he continued to work on social media and self-Media platforms, to expand their influence and attract more fans.

Wenfeng Wei summarized his business model as "online celebrity of testing and e-commerce." In this model, he published testing reports on We Media platform to attract more fans. And at the same time, he made profit by selling products through e-commerce platform. Actually, this business model was a transformation of charged service model that is to add the added value of the testing service into the price of the products, to support independent testing service, and provide qualified products to the customers.

Through e-commerce platform, DaddyLab realized financial balance in the second year of establishment. Wenfeng Wei estimated that DaddyLab would achieve a turnover of 30 million yuan in the year of 2017, which would be enough for the company's further development after deducting various costs.

The Way to Become a "Online Celebrity of Testing"

Fans Group—Where to Find the Customers of DaddyLab?

For DaddyLab, it's the most important thing to find the right business model that can support its sustainable development. When DaddyLab was just founded, Wenfeng Wei saw the company as a platform for public welfare. They did product tests using the fund partly from the money raised from their fans and partly from their own money. However, in less than a year, Wenfeng Wei found that they had invested too much time and money to continue the business any more. At that time, other parents who had been following his social media account and trusted him persuaded him to go on.

Wenfeng Wei admitted that DaddyLab's achievements today owns to these enthusiastic and loyal supporters. Looking back, he was deeply moved. "I didn't want to sell products at first. But as a result I spent all my money by the end of 2015. Then I told the parents honestly that 'we are not making money and we don't have any money left'. The parents said that 'you can't just give up. Money is not the problem. We can raise money for you'. Then some of them found my WeChat count, and transferred money to me. 3,000 yuan, 5,000 yuan, or 10,000 yuan."

The main customer group of DaddyLab is the parents of children in the first and second tier cities. They have the willingness and ability to afford healthy life for their children and themselves. At the same time, they also have a big heart. In the past three years, they have always been supporting DaddyLab. They came to them not just to buy products or enjoy services, but also to help and support them like friends do. During an interview, Wenfeng Wei recalled: "Once, a parent came to our company with her child to help us pack and deliver products during summer vacation. I wanted to pay them internship fee, but she refused to take it. We also have parent volunteers who often help us. A parent from Changsha was in trademark registration industry. He told me: 'Father Wei, you need to register your own trademark. This is just what I do. If you don't mind, I can help you'. I said, 'Sure, I'll pay you'. But he said, "No, you just need to pay the registration fee. You don't need to pay service fee to me'. We also have a lawyer team, including lawyers from Shanghai and Hangzhou. They are all parents too. They gave me a lot of support. They told me, 'Father Wei, you should pay attention to legal risks. I'm a lawyer'. This is: when you do the right thing, the whole world will help you."

There are a lot of stories like this in DaddyLab. This means social enterprises like DaddyLab can influence and unite people. When we communicate honestly with our users, users will trust us. Wenfeng Wei found this. So he continued to find new ways to interact with customers and win trust from fans and customers. Thus, he attracted a large number of loyal customers.

Wenfeng Wei and his father also make full use of We Media and set up a number of WeChat fans groups to interact with their fans. By June 2017, DaddyLab has established 13 WeChat groups, each of which was almost full (the maximum member of a group is 500). In every WeChat group, a DaddyLab team member will stay online and answer customer's questions. Wenfeng Wei explained that their WeChat groups have always been very active. The group members not only asked questions about testing to DaddyLab staff, but also discussed with each other about their children's health, household products and other topics. They would even consult other group members before buying products. The atmosphere in the group was very pleasant. Wenfeng Wei humorously called these groups "the clinic of shopping."

Meanwhile, DaddyLab continued to develop its crowdfunding platform. In proportion, the revenue brought by crowdfunding was far less than that of e-commerce. But Wenfeng Wei said he would continue with crowdfunding. He said, "we will continue crowdfunding, because it is a good way to interact with our supporters. Once, twice and more. The more we interact, the more the customers would be likely to buy from us. If customers forget us, our business would be over."

Increasing the Influence by Apparatus Circulation

In addition to interacting with customers through media, DaddyLab also launched apparatus circulation. Currently, they are circulating formaldehyde meters.

The idea of apparatus circulation was borrowed from book circulation. That is, to circulate expensive testing apparatus that ordinary families wouldn't buy between its fans. The formaldehyde meters under currently circulation worth about 10,000 yuan. Although most families can afford it, it's not worthwhile just for one test.

Therefore, DaddyLab purchased a number of formaldehyde meters for circulation. In order to avoid the damage of the meters during circulation, DaddyLab followed the advices of the fans and customized protective covers for the formaldehyde meters. The circulation activity was widely welcomed once it was launched (Fig. 1).

In August 2016, this activity attracted the attention of the Bill Gates Foundation. The Foundation forwarded articles on this activity, and made DaddyLab famous overnight. Wenfeng Wei recalls that, during that period, the number of new follower of their social media account increased by about 10,000 every day. A large number of users came to ask about their formaldehyde meter circulation activity. There was an anecdote happened during this time: One morning, the young girl in charge of online customer service woke up and found there were hundreds of new messages and requests on DaddyLab's WeChat account. So she just sat on the bed to reply the messages and requests for the whole morning, before she could take a break to wash up. You can guess how popular the activity was.

In order to make better use of the circulation activity and enhance customer viscosity, DaddyLab team designed a circulation diary. When the formaldehyde meter arrived at a new customer, he or she can write down his or her own using experience. Now there were altogether three whole books of diaries filled with users' experience.

Fig. 1 Formaldehyde meter and protective cover

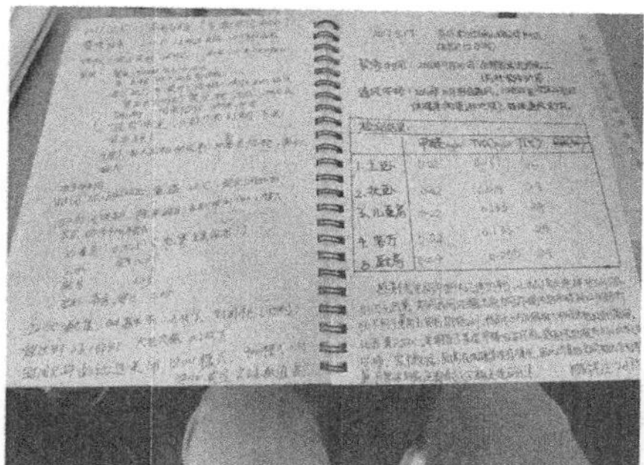

Fig. 2 Circulation diaries

In these diaries, in addition to users' testing records, some users even expressed their good wishes and gratitude for DaddyLab by pictures and words. In the information age, circulation and diary writing may seem out of date. But they helped draw the customers closer to DaddyLab. They were also effective advertisements and attracted more fans (Fig. 2).

In addition to formaldehyde meters, DaddyLab also carried out circulation activities for lamp light meters. All these activities were designed to allow parents to test the quality of the products around them and make sure the environment around themselves and their families were healthy and safe.

Sustainable Revenue Making—DaddyLab Online Store

After determining the business model of "online celebrity of testing and e-commerce," DaddyLab started to develop his own e-commerce business.

DaddyLab used WeChat Youzan Store as its major sales channel, supplemented with its WeChat public account and a dozen of WeChat groups to boost sales. They also have Tmall online store on Taobao. The company also set up e-commerce department to manage its e-commerce business, including supply chain, sales consultation and after-sale services (Fig. 3).

Currently, the commodities in DaddyLab online store on the mobile terminal include stationeries, maternal and infant supplies, kitchen supplies and household supplies, as well as other daily supplies such as food and fruits. All these products are qualified products that have passed DaddyLab's testing. Some of them are purchased by DaddyLab from third party suppliers after they tested them; and some are customized by DaddyLab. Most of the products are purchased directly from manufacturers at home and abroad. As DaddyLab put it, they purchase only the good products wherever they are from. For example, in the winter of 2016, many parents asked DaddyLab to recommend anti-smog masks. After a series of testing, DaddyLab selected a mask from Japan, and obtained sales right after negotiating with

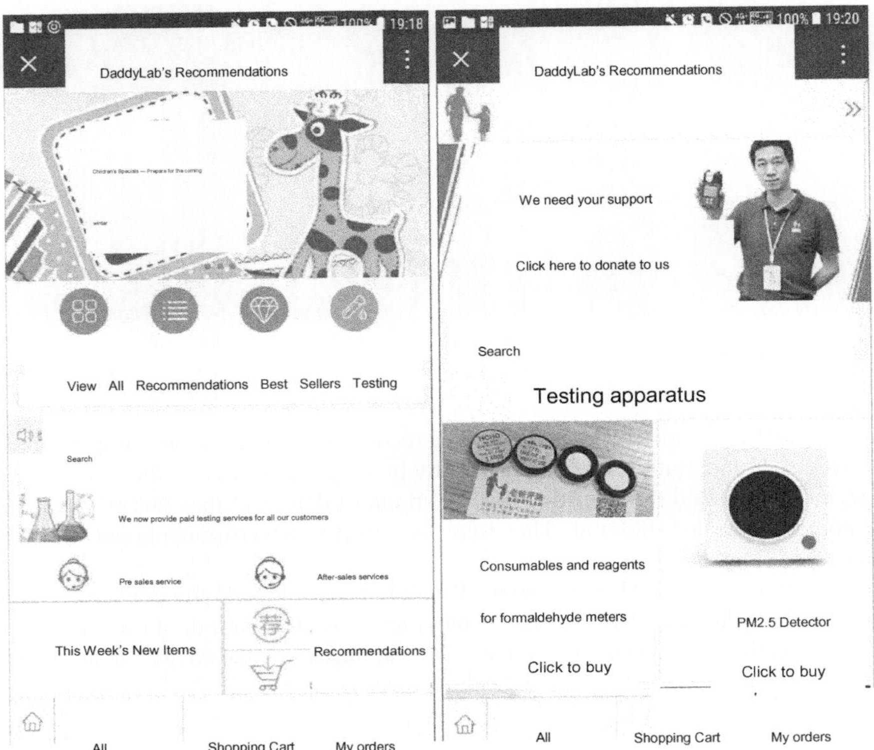

Fig. 3 DaddyLab online store interface

the manufacturer. Meanwhile, the online store also rents testing apparatus and sells related consumables. DaddyLab not only sells qualified products, but also provides tools for the customers to test product quality by themselves.

To ensure users' experience and loyalty, DaddyLab inspects every batch of food and contact materials it sells. For the non-contact products, it does annual sampling inspection. If any problem is found, all products of this batch will be recalled immediately. Wenfeng Wei remembered that once some customers complained that the qualification rate of the bulb of the lamp was below 95%. DaddyLab sent out notice to recall this batch of products and replaced with qualified ones. They also rewarded customers who found these problems to encourage more customers to supervise the quality of the products in their online store.

All the products in DaddyLab online store need to pass many tests and provide good after-sales service. Although the prices are usually higher than the average prices of similar products in other e-commerce terminals, they have a high reputation and stable sales volume thanks to DaddyLab's highly loyal customer group and excellent product quality.

DaddyLab estimates that the repurchase rate should be over 40%, and currently it is about 42%. Thanks to its high repurchase rate, DaddyLab achieves an average monthly sale of two million yuan with only more than 100,000 fans. This is impossible even for some platforms with millions of fans. Also, the product comments are mostly positive (Fig. 4).

The negative comments are mainly about logistics.

By its e-commerce platform, DaddyLab realized financial balance in the second year of establishment. Wenfeng Wei's predicts that DaddyLab will achieve a turnover of 30 million yuan in 2017, which will be enough to support its further development. Thus, DaddyLab does not need to cater to the investors. They just need to stick to their own values and devote themselves to their mission, which is to provide qualified, safety and harmless products to the customers.

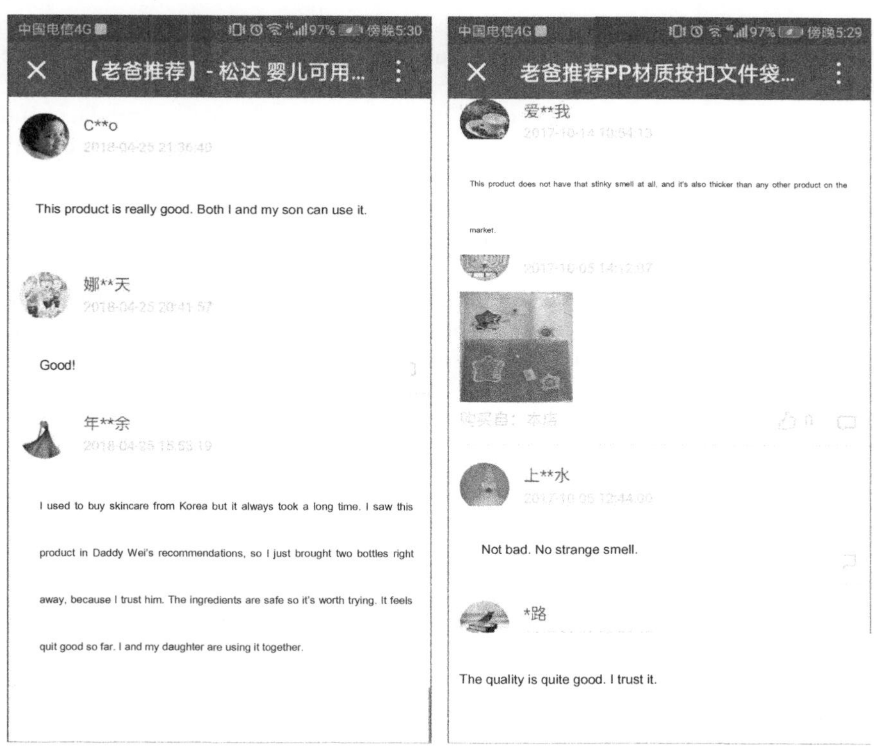

Fig. 4 Some comments on DaddyLab online store products

Quality Assurance—DaddyLab's Quality Control System

In order to select suitable testing products and ensure the quality of products in the online store, DaddyLab established his own quality control system—DaddyLab Quality Control System. The quality control system consists of four parts: DaddyLab standards, alternate sampling, cost sharing and parents' participation (Fig. 5).

In order to avoid the loopholes in the common "blacklist" inspection standards, DaddyLab established his own inspection standards—DaddyLab standards, which are even higher than the international standards for the selection of its products and suppliers. There are basically two ways to test: one is on the products' general physical properties, which can be conducted in DaddyLab own laboratory; and the other is on the products' complex physical properties and chemical properties, which will be done by professional laboratory. DaddyLab's laboratory is located in the company, which was built using the funds from the fans and customers. There are many tools and apparatus to test the product properties in the laboratory, which are capable of testing the general physical properties of the product (Fig. 6).

At the same time, in order to ensure the quality of each batch of products and user experience, DaddyLab invites customers from time to time to test the quality of the products they purchased. If the testing result does not meet their quality standards, DaddyLab will recall this batch of products after confirming the testing result. According to Wenfeng Wei, DaddyLab should be the first one to have a recalling system among all the e-commerce retailers.

In order to obtain sufficient testing funds to support the company's testing business, DaddyLab will draw a small proportion of crowdfunding testing fee from the revenue of its online store. Of course, users will be informed before they purchase the products (Fig. 7).

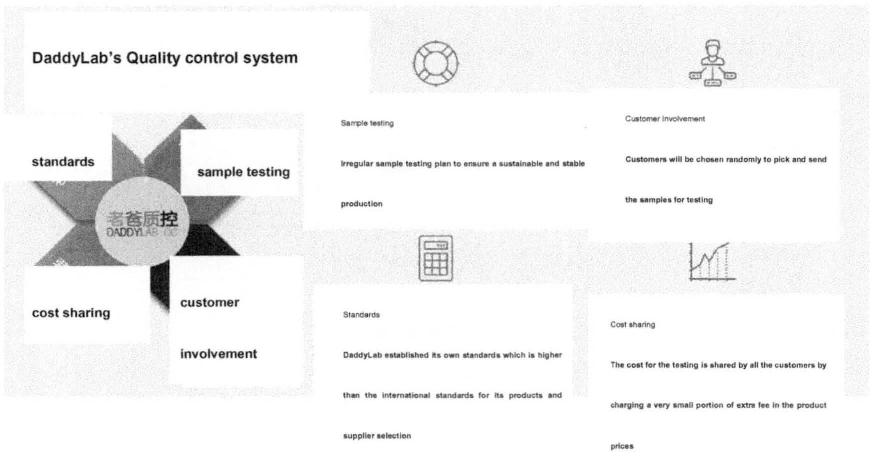

Fig. 5 Dad's quality control system

Fig. 6 DaddyLab's laboratory

Fig. 7 Crowdfunding testing fee

Enterprise Values—Love Cannot Be Traded

During daily operation, Wenfeng Wei always pay attention to convey the values of social mission and customer service that he has been believed into employees. And he has also been working on cultivating their team spirit. Once, a team member proposed that DaddyLab could copy the business model of paid knowledge service on some platforms, which means, customers pay for the professionals to answer their questions. Although this business model can increase the company's revenue, Wenfeng

Wei rejected this proposal right away. About this, Wenfeng Wei commented, "what does paid knowledge service mean? It means you give me money and in exchange I answer your question. What's this? It's a trade! Is Wenfeng Wei (DaddyLab) doing a trade? We are working for love! And love cannot be measured by money. People come to me and ask me questions, I will answer them if I can; If not, I will simply tell them your question is too complicated, and I don't know the answer. If I spend a lot of time on the question, people may reward me. That's acceptable and nice, because they are doing it voluntarily. But I can't charge people simple for answering their questions. That's not the way we do our business, because there's no love."

DaddyLab's distinctive values also brought them unexpected rewards. When DaddyLab was a start-up company, there were only a few members. All of them shared a small office, working on all kinds of jobs, from answering customer needs, making testing lists, contacting testing laboratories, to writing articles, and so on. It was DaddyLab's distinct values that helped Wenfeng Wei attract a group of outstanding and ambitions employees in short time. Some people originally working in testing institutions in Hangzhou were inspired by them and joined them after learning about their stories in detail. Wenfeng Wei made an example: "one of our members resigned from his previous job in a laboratory in the west area of Hangzhou city. At that time, he had already bought a house in the west area of the city. He just sold the house and bought another one in Binjiang Area. Our company was located in the south-east area of the city. He just moved to this area with his wife and children and joined us. This guy was so brave. The salary I offered him was even less than what he earned from his original laboratory."

As for equity, DaddyLab was jointly founded by Wenfeng Wei and some supporters. Currently, 90% of DaddyLab's shares are controlled by Wenfeng Wei (15% of which are options of the core team), and the remaining 10% belong to the supporters. These supporter shareholders fully trust Wenfeng Wei, and they grand him with their share of decision-making power, which also guarantees the stability of DaddyLab's corporate goals.

As for profit distribution, there is still no clear plan in the DaddyLab's company regulations. Wenfeng Wei said, "I don't think it's necessary to regulate whether a company should share 60%, 50% or 10% of its profit as annual dividend. The specific proportion doesn't make sense. The important thing is that we are still working on this … Profit distribution plan should be determined by the entrepreneur or the leader based on the enterprise's development plan and goal each year."

In fact, after paying for the company's daily expenses and staff salaries every year, most of DaddyLab's revenue has been used on testing. Currently, the company hasn't made enough profit for sharing.

Strong Enough to Help the Society

From Children's Products to Daily Supplies

With the development of its business, DaddyLab's business scope extended from children's products to daily supplies. DaddyLab also created a new slogan, which is "Keep dangers away from our lives. Let good money drive out bad money."

One way for DaddyLab to choose the products for testing is by the recommendation of its fans. DaddyLab evaluates all the products recommended by users during a period of time, and determines which products will be sent for testing. Therefore, as the number of its fans increases, the range of DaddyLab's testing also expanded, and is no longer limited to products for children.

Since its establishment in 2015, DaddyLab has tested nearly 100 kinds of products around us, including book covers, desk lamps, runway pavement, iron pans, chopping boards, floor boards, paints, etc. The products they tested include all kinds of products in daily life. DaddyLab also carried out special tests for products that were found suspicious in preliminary tests (Fig. 8).

Meanwhile, DaddyLab also keeps on exploring innovative ways to serve its consulting clients and consumers, such as the formaldehyde meter circulation activity which lasted more than one year. This activity was launched by DaddyLab after

Fig. 8 The products that have been tested by DaddyLab

Fig. 9 DaddyLab's testing apparatus circulation system

receiving a lot of consultation on how to remove formaldehyde from its customers. The company purchased more than 100 formaldehyde meters at its own expense, and lent them to its customers in different cities for free use. When the circulation activity of the formaldehyde meter was welcomed after running for some while, DaddyLab also launched circulation of TVOC (volatile organic compounds) detector, radiation detector and other apparatus that were also needed by its customers (Fig. 9).

Promote the Upgrading of Industry Standards and Drive Out Bad Money with Good Currency

DaddyLab's private testing also has positive externality in the economic sense, that is, promoting the upgrading of industry standards and improving the product standards of manufacture enterprises. This is also the goal that DaddyLab has been pursuing.

The book cover event in 2015 was not over yet. After DaddyLab became more famous, there was a sequel to the story. After the story of "Father Wei" became popular, many book cover manufacturers found DaddyLab to seek cooperate. Some of them suggested manufacturing non-toxic book covers for DaddyLab; and some sent their own book covers to DaddyLab for testing.

As a result, some book cover enterprises upgraded their manufacture standards. They abandoned the harmful PVC materials containing plasticizers and changed to PP or PE materials for production. Driven by these enterprises, the whole book cover industry was changed. On February 16, 2016, Shanghai Municipal Bureau of Quality and Technical Supervision issued the Early Warning Report on the Quality and Healthy Risks of Plastic Book Wrapping Film and Book Cover Products. The Bureau inspected 30 batches of plastic book wrapping films randomly, and 25 batches were found not meeting the standards on plasticizer. This kind of temporary random inspection for book wrapping films was very rare in the past. On the other hand, DaddyLab's own qualified and non-toxic book wrapping films have forced most of the unqualified products quit the market, which means good money has driven out the bad money.

It is safe to say that through this "book cover revolution," DaddyLab improved the general product quality of the whole industry. It not only changed the behavior of other enterprises, but also helped the government fix the loopholes in supervision. Another similar example was the toxic runway pavement incident. At that time, unqualified runway pavement materials in many schools were exposed to the public one after another. Ultimately, the overall standard of runway pavement materials used by schools was improved. Students' health and safety were ensured.

This is the positive externality of DaddyLab. And it is also the mission of social enterprise in Wenfeng Wei's understanding—social enterprise should not just make profits, but also make positive social influence through its operation and the realization of its social goals. This influence is not directly equivalent to the profits of the enterprise, but is beneficial to the development of the whole society. This is also the direction of DaddyLab's future development and its bigger social goal.

In December 2017, DaddyLab became one of the product quality and safety injury information monitoring stations established by Zhejiang Quality and Technical Supervision Bureau. The responsibility of this monitoring station is to provide product quality and safety injury information and help the government authorities to carry out product quality and safety risk assessment and recall defective products. Later, Zhejiang Product Quality and Safety Inspection Institute issued the risk warning of defective Magic Eraser products in January 2018, thanks to the contribution of DaddyLab.

Wenfeng Wei said in an interview that one of his goals is to promote "DaddyLab Standards" by increasing its social influence continuously, and use these standards to select products in DaddyLab's online store, so that consumers can trust any products that meet DaddyLab Standards. Moreover, he uses his social media and DaddyLab online store to promote healthy products to consumers, form a benign competition, and improve the general product quality of the whole industry, so as to drive out the bad money with good money, and keep toxic and harmful products away from consumers and the market.

Our Time Will Come

Although DaddyLab currently has achieved basic financial balance and was on the right track, it was still faced with some challenges, and even some objections to its business model.

Not Valued as a Small Business

The biggest problem DaddyLab met at the early stage of its development was that it was unappreciated, even though the problem it aims to solve is an urgent society problem.

During book cover event, Wenfeng Wei failed to get any response from relevant government authorities after reporting the problem for many times. So he was forced to choose another way. On the other hand, DaddyLab failed to obtain sufficient investment from any investors due to their prejudices at the beginning of its establishment. However, Wenfeng Wei and his team did not give up. Through their own efforts, they won the trust from a group of parent fans. By means of crowd funding and e-commerce, DaddyLab finally achieved sustainable development, which allowed it to carry out a large number of product tests and promoted the upgrading of some industry standards.

Unfortunately, up to now, DaddyLab cannot and is not allowed to release the testing results for some industries and products for various reasons. Some professional testing institutions at home and abroad are still unwilling to cooperate with them because of their concerns of offending some big clients in the industries. There's still a lot to do to promote China's social reform, and go on the right track where good money can drive out bad money.

Revenge from Those Who Suffered Loses

Although DaddyLab provides consumers with qualified products, what they have done also incurred hatred from the producers of unqualified products.

Wenfeng Wei recalled that once DaddyLab sent some diatom mud for testing and found that the products of several brands were unqualified. Therefore, it released the testing results in several articles to warn the customers. This action jeopardized the interests of relevant diatom mud manufacturers. Soon, Wenfeng Wei received a threat message from a diatom mud manufacturer, asking him to delete these articles, or else he will suffer. But Wenfeng Wei didn't panic. He refused to delete these articles because it was against his believes. On the contrary, after thinking a little bit, Wenfeng Wei sent these communication records to their WeChat fans groups.

His braveness and persistence in the face of threats was highly appreciated by these supports.

Dispute Over the Business Model

Although DaddyLab's business model of "online celebrity of testing + e-commerce" has been successful and attracted a large number of fans, it has been drawing more disputes too.

Wenfeng Wei mentioned in an interview that some people came to him and confronted him with their business model. They pointed out that DaddyLab was just making money under the guise of "public welfare" and "social enterprise," and criticized that his intention was impure. Many people also believed that with this business model, DaddyLab's testing results cannot be convincing enough. There have been a lot of similar criticisms like these. As a respond to them, Wenfeng Wei said, "I told my team to remove the two words of "public welfare." It will save the time and trouble. I don't care about the title. As long as the parent fans support me, why should I care about the title? Enterprises have social values. Every enterprise, which doesn't do bad things, has its social value."

Wenfeng Wei believes that he is trying to solve a common social problem—the elimination of toxic and harmful products. E-commerce is only one way to achieve this goal, which can support the operation of his business. Supported by this concept, Wenfeng Wei has found a sustainable solution. As for whether to take public welfare or social goals as the mission of his company, Wenfeng Wei said that he didn't really care about it. As long as DaddyLab is recognized and supported by its customers and can continue to develop, that is enough.

Peers and Potential Competitors

With the trend of consumption upgrading, people are paying more and more attention on how to increase the quality of products. There are also other similar companies in the same field as DaddyLab, such as "Youke Network" and "Consumer Report." These organizations usually promote themselves as third-party testing agencies. They recommend high-quality products to the consumers, but they do not sell any products directly. These companies may become DaddyLab's future competitors. Since 2017, these companies also launched their own e-commerce platforms after seeing DaddyLab's successful business model.

Besides, some e-commerce platforms that claim to sell high-quality products, such as Netease's Yeation online store and Taobao's Tmall online stores, are also strong potential competitors. Although these kinds of platforms do not provide testing services, which is different from DaddyLab, their business field is also selling high-quality products, which overlaps with DaddyLab, and therefore may threaten DaddyLab in the future.

The Vision of "Physical Mall + Laboratory"

Restrained by their limited resources in fund and staff, DaddyLab cannot cover all the commodities on the market by its testing. However, as for his vision of the company, Wenfeng Wei said, "In the future, DaddyLab should be a platform providing high-quality products, because this is just what people need. Just like what one of our fans said, 'don't tell me this product is toxic and that one is harmful. Just tell me which one is good.' People need an organization that they can trust to tell them which products are good. This is not easy and it's just what we need to do. Our vision is to operate a DaddyLab shopping mall and a DaddyLab laboratory and combine them together. Consumers can shop in the mall with their shopping cart. And behind a glass wall next to them will be our laboratory, where our testing professionals wearing white uniforms and masks are testing the products. That will be the innovative combination of physical mall and laboratory in our vision."

Further Reading

Ao P (2016) Why is online celebrity so popular?—Interpretation of and reflection on online celebrity phenomenon. Contemp Commun (4)

Research Group of State Administration for Market Regulation, Shuping Zhi (2011) Quality administration system and construction of government execution: based on the empirical analysis of AQSIQ. China Admin (12)

Shanghai Municipal Bureau of Quality and Technical Supervision (2016) Early warning report on the quality and healthy risks of plastic book wrapping film and book cover products. http://www.cqn.com.cn/ms/content/2016-02/15/content_2645434.htm. Accessed 15 Feb 2016

Standardization Law of the People's Republic of China, revised and adopted at the 30th Meeting of the Standing Committee of the Twelfth National People's Congress on November 4, 2017, and came into force on January 1, 2018

Wang W (2016) The logic, ethical reflection and normative guidance of online celebrity economy. *Qiushi* (8)

Company Information

CCTV-13 (2016) Wenfeng Wei: DaddyLab for testing. Interview with Newsweek. http://tv.cntv.cn/video/C10600/a9e2105a66bb44a4a90825fc12b4639d. Accessed 10 Sept 2016

Huang S (2017) Online celebrity "DaddyLab" and consumer's dilemma in protecting their rights. Caixin.com. http://china.caixin.com/2017-05-03/101085668.html. Accessed 3 May 2017

Liu Y (2016) A senior inspector's public welfare cause: DaddyLab and the leading troops. Southern Weekend. http://www.infzm.com/content/119785. Accessed 27 Sept 2016

BeBetter Education: Introduce Financial Education to the Young People

Yunxia Feng and Jinfeng Cai

> When I founded BeBetter Education, I took public welfare as its most fundamental gene. The future of BeBetter will be formed by the gene. Commercial companies can hardly evolve social genes even after a long time of development.
>
> – Sheng Wang, founder of BeBetter Education

Shanghai BeBetter Education Consulting Center (hereinafter referred to as BeBetter Education) was registered in Shanghai Pudong Civil Affairs Bureau in July 2009. It is the first non-profit public organization dedicated to financial education of children and young people. BeBetter Education is a member of the Child & Youth Finance International, World Innovation Summit for Education, and the Asian Venture Philanthropy Network. The beneficiaries of BeBetter Education are Chinese children and young people between the age of 3 to 25 from poor families, such as migrant workers in cities and rural families. BeBetter Education provides children and young people with a series of courses in society and finance, life skills and social innovation. It aims to promote and popularize financial education, and improve the economic quality of children and young people. Since its foundation, BeBetter Education has served more than one million people and has set up branches in Shanghai, Beijing, Guangzhou, Chengdu, Guiyang, Shenzhen, Suzhou and Hong Kong. In May 2015, Sheng Wang, the founder of BeBetter Education, also registered and established Shanghai BeBetter Technology Co., Ltd. (hereinafter referred to as BeBetter Technology). BeBetter Education and BeBetter Technology are collectively referred to as Shanghai BeBetter.

Y. Feng (✉) · J. Cai
Business School, Renmin University of China, Beijing, China
e-mail: fengyunxia@rmbs.ruc.edu.cn

M. Zhao and J. Mao (eds.), *Social Entrepreneurship*,
https://doi.org/10.1007/978-981-15-9881-4_6

Building the no.1 Brand Name of Financial Education

Since its foundation, BeBetter Education has been taking "financial education for children and young people" as its goal. It has gone through several stages of development. Although there have been ups and downs, its goal has never been changed. To pursue this goal, the company has been expanding its beneficiary groups continuously. Now, it has become No.1 brand of financial education for children and young people in China.

Foundation of BeBetter Education

Sheng Wang, the founder of BeBetter Education, had a rather tortuous work experience. He had never worked in any company for more than seven years. After several twists and turns, Sheng Wang finally found the career he loves: children and young people's financial education.

Sheng Wang worked in a state-owned bookstore after graduating from Ocean University of China in 1991, majored in physics. In 1997, he quitted his job and began his own business. In 2005, he returned to school and studied for a full-time Ph.D. degree in education following Professor Zhu Yongxin of Suzhou University. At the same time, he was appointed by Professor Zhu as the executive director of the well-known educational think tank "21st Century Education Research Institute," and began his research in education public policy following Yang Dongping, who was the president of the Institute and also professor of Beijing University of Technology.

In 2008, the corporate social responsibility department of Citibank (China) entrusted Sheng Wang to send out free financial readers to high school students. In the process, Sheng Wang met Zhang Wei and the two became partners and registered a private non-enterprise organization "BeBetter Education" in Shanghai in July 2009. Once it was founded, the organization obtained its first donation of 50,000 US dollars from Citigroup Foundation, which was allocated to carry out more financial education activities for high school students. Sheng Wang named this organization BeBetter Education was because he believed that being better is more important than being the best. And its Chinese name "Baite" means that education should not only help children get 100 points, but also have its own features.

In July 2009, Sheng Wang went to Cairo, Egypt, to attend the global annual meeting of the International Children's Savings Fund. He met the founder of the fund, Ms. Jeroo Billimoria, and brought back the Aflatoun (which means happy child) project for children's financial education to China. From 2010 to 2013, entrusted by Professor Zhu Yongxin, Sheng Wang undertook the work of Secretary General of New Education Foundation. Meanwhile, BeBetter Education was operated by his partner Zhang Wei and Wang Xiong. Aflatoun project was launched during this period. There are five modules in Aflatoun project, e.g. self-exploring, rights and responsibilities, saving and consumption, planning and budgeting, and children's entrepreneurship. The courses of the first two modules were easy to promote, but the coursed of last three modules about financial thinking were not so popular. Sheng Wang realizes that this was a very bad sign. Aflatoun project might have to quit China if this situation wouldn't change.

How to promote the three modules of the project – saving and consumption, planning budget and children's entrepreneurship? Sheng Wang believed that the only solution was by changing children's behavior. Through his effort, children's behavior did change: They began to keep their own accounts, save money, make plans, and even set up their own stalls. These were the factors to measure the changes. However, it was just about the measurement of these behavior changes, Sheng Wang and the operation team at that time disagreed with each other. The operation team could not provide the data of children's social and financial behavior change. At the end of 2013, the conflicts between them were so serious that they could no longer cooperate. Under this circumstance, Sheng Wang had to leave New Education Foundation and lead BeBetter Education team by himself.

Searching for the Fundamental Significance of Financial Education

When he began to lead the team by himself to implement the project, Sheng Wang realized how difficult it had been for his brother Wang Xiong. First of all, the project was not supported by the teachers. Primary school teachers didn't think financial knowledge was essential. Children would know it when they grew up. Secondly, children in poor areas were all from poor families and had very little pocket money. They lived on free lunch. It was impractical to teach them financial management.

Sheng Wang was in a dilemma. How should he do? He asked himself two questions repeatedly: one was why children should learn to manage money. One was why we should teach children financial knowledge and even as part of school curriculum? The other was why the poor children should learn it. Poor children didn't even have any money. How would they learn how to manage money?

Sheng Wang reviewed the past experience since the project was launched in 2009: most schools and teachers agreed that it was useful to teach children how to manage money. Learning how to manage money was not just about money itself. More importantly, it helped children development their way of thinking, which would benefit their whole life. After contemplation, Sheng Wang and his team started to form their own solution.

"Education in China is all about academics. We never teach children about sex, money, or the complicated relationships between people. Sex, power and money are the three topics we can't avoid in our life. They are invisible in our education, but they are around us in real life. People say children will learn little by little by themselves. Maybe it is true that children will know it as they grow up. But most of the time, the society will give them a lesson. There is a big difference between active learning and possible learning."

Money is related to a person's self-esteem. When a person does not have any money, his or her self-esteem is often low; however, it is also not true that the more money a person has, the higher his or her self-esteem would be. Nowadays, many young people from rich families are very rich, but that doesn't necessarily mean their self-esteem is high, or it doesn't necessarily bring them higher self-esteem or more meaning to their lives than ordinary people. However, when a child from urban or rural area earns just one yuan by selling goods in a community stall by themselves, their self-esteem will be greatly improved.

After in-depth thinking, Sheng Wang finally realized that associating money with people's self-esteem might be the breakthrough. There are both rich and ordinary people in our society. Aflatoun courses, or financial courses, or economical citizen courses, are open to the children from both affluent families and less affluent families. Our society needs not only exam oriented education, but also ability elevation education. And financial courses and related products can help Chinese children and young people learn such skills.

Sheng Wang's team learned that: Financial intelligence and financial education were helpful for improving children's money management skills, and they could also change children's behavior. They found the starting point to initiate financial education, and their "Aflatoun Concept School" also began to get on the right track.

Keep on Going

Thanks to the hard work of Sheng Wang and his team, many Aflatoun Concept School opened one after another. Currently, BeBetter Education has 52 full-time employees and 988 volunteer employees. Its economic citizenship education covers more than 40 cities, benefiting more than one million children and young people. BeBetter Education hopes to increase the number of their students to 10 million by 2020.

At the beginning of 2013, BeBetter Education submitted its strategic transformation plan to Citigroup Foundation. There are more than 200 million children from less affluent families in China, and the demand for financial education is huge. No matter how hard BeBetter Education works and how many resources Citigroup foundation invests, the number of people they could serve would still be very limited. In order to popularize financial education, and benefit more children, they must change their original working principles and methods. The strategic transformation plan BeBetter Education put forward is: the organization will transform from the one that carries out financial education to a platform that provides capacity building service on such education for other public organizations, which will carry out the education. They also plan to carry out more systematic research and promotion, to push policy reform, and make financial education become a part of school curriculum.

Strategic Transformation from a Project to a Product Platform

Like other typical public welfare project models, BeBetter Education went through a similar development stage in the first few years: It obtained donations and used them on the project, introduce courses from abroad, localized the courses, gave trainings to teachers in rural and urban schools after, and the teachers went back to their schools and taught these courses to their students.

Since its foundation in 2009, BeBetter Education has obtained financial support from several foreign foundations and foreign enterprises, including Citibank, Barclays Bank, and VISA. By 2015, the number of people benefited from their project reached about 500,000.

Although BeBetter Education had made remarkable achievements, and the source and amount of donations it received was quite admirable in others eyes, Sheng Wang still felt the crisis. From the perspective of project performance itself, "the cost of our teaching model was too high, and the process was too complicated. According to our experience, out of every 100 teachers we trained, only 20 of them would still be teaching our courses after a year. The conversion rate was only 20%. After another year, only five or six of these 20 teachers would continue the courses. The decline rate was very fast."

From the perspective of project funds, on the one hand, in order to obtain continuous donations, they had to keep on expanding the business scale. This required increasing investments in research and development, market expansion, and personnel. On the other hand, although the proportion of foreign funding used on personnel expenditure had been better than that of some domestic foundations, and could basically guarantee the stability of its personnel and continuous training, but this excessive proportion of donation funds was also a hidden danger in case the donation was unstable. If the size of donation fluctuates, the number of existing personnel may fluctuate too, which would be very harmful to the stable development of the organization.

If BeBetter Education continues to operate as a subsidiary of the donation organizations, "There will be no future for us. The only way to change this situation is to build a platform."

Platform Model and Products

"To operate as a platform means to cooperate with local NGOs or local government to carry out the project. We'll give them trainings and then they teach the courses." "To achieve anything, we need to use leverage. When we were carrying out the project by ourselves, the leverage is ourselves. When we are the platform, other social forces will be the leverage. Leverage can help expand our social influence."

"To be a platform, one of the most important things is to have our own products." At the beginning, we didn't have standardized products, so the promotion and replication process was very slow. Therefore, BeBetter Education established two standardized product lines. One was a series of children's financial education tools, developed and simplified based on Aflatoun products that they introduced from Aflatoun project, including children's readers (books), children's boxes (education kits), children's games (board games), etc. The other one was their own existing training courses and services, but they standardized them. If the first tangible products series were lightweight products, which would be used to enlighten and popularize the concept of financial education, then the other series of standardized services were heavyweight, in-depth and all-around.

(1) Self education of financial intelligence: simplified tangible products

As for the simplified tangible products, Sheng Wang's idea was that: "we didn't expect these products can make it (educating parents and teachers) all at once. The purpose is just letting them know about the concept. It's an enlightenment product, a primary product. They aim to realize the transformation from not knowing to knowing. Then the next steps will be the transformation from knowing to doing, and then from doing to getting used to do (Figure 1).

The simplified tangible products convey the rules of children's behavior, the rules of the market and the attitude toward wealth with its book contents and the rules of the games. Children can learn and practice these rules during reading and playing. Thus, children can receive financial education without relying solely on teachers. They were easy to popularize and apply, so the promotion of these products was quite effective. Their board games were adopted by some enterprises and NGOs for their community public welfare activities, and were highly welcomed by the children (Figure 2).

(2) Standardization of the service

BeBetter Education also standardized the processes in their original and new service products.

For example, for the service product of "Aflatoun Concept School," BeBetter Education helped the schools transform their original small flower mechanism into the bank token point mechanism. The school would be the head office and the class would be the branch. The tokens had different values, and could be earned in different activities in the school. Students could exchange their tokens for rewards. Students could also be the contractor of school cinema. They could sell tickets to other students. Some schools also set up campus markets, where students could earn more tokens by selling things they didn't use at home. Al these activities helped to develop children's financial intelligence and ability. During experiment stage, "Aflatoun Concept School" had been upgraded and optimized, and promoted in classes. The precious experience and lessons learned were recorded and later made into CD-ROMs. Thus, "Aflatoun Concept School" model was formed.

Another example was the "Youth Urban Survival Challenge Competition" product. It required mentors from enterprises and college student challengers to

Fig. 1 Magic Bunny product samples

Fig. 2 Funny Chicken product samples

cooperate and complete the task together. By this competition, college students had a better understanding. At the beginning of the competition, all the teams competed for the trip funds. Some teams could get round-trip funds, while some might get nothing at all. There was a special stage, where each team could get two hats. Each team could trade them with passers-by for money or free lunch. Then the teams would get to a library to answer some questions. Each question was worth two yuan. Finally, each team should buy some local products, and the team that bought more products with lower prices got the points. They could also make investments, including deposit, stock, insurance and donation. After one month, the final evaluation would be made based on the current value of their stocks and other investments. The competition was participated by up to 14 teams when it was held in Xi'an Province.

Two Different Ways of Scale Development

For scale development, BeBetter Education needed to cooperate with various social forces through different models in systematical ways. It made full use of two important models: giving online courses and cooperating with the government.

"You can communicate with children directly through the Internet without any school teachers." This year, BeBetter Education cooperates with hujiang.com, and launched online finance and business course on hujiang's education platform CCtalk. Currently, 120 schools in Gansu, Yunnan, Henan and other provinces are having their online courses. Most of these schools are primary schools in remote rural areas. The teachers of BeBetter Education teach lessons on the Internet in their offices using their computer. All the classes just connect to the Internet, and thousands of students in these classes can share the same lesson. Any student can raise their hands to speak during the lesson, and the teacher can see them. "I can't believe this can be done, but it is what we are doing now."

The successful cooperation with hujiang.com made BeBetter Education realize the importance of government support. They carry out online courses in Gansu Province with the help of Gansu Provincial Audio-Visual Education Center. But first of all, they must get the recognition and support of Gansu Provincial Education Department. "First we need to create a product model to promote social changes. Then we can provide information and research results to the government, and let the government know that it is feasible. Government support is a strong power."

Organization and Innovation During Strategic Transformation

"For public welfare projects, only those small-scaled and mature projects can be successful and sustainable. It would be very difficult for large-scale projects. Projects with large scale and was sustainable can hardly achieve high performance, while projects with good performance and large-scale can hardly sustain, due to large investment." In order to reduce its dependence on donation and clear the road for future development, BeBetter Education decided to transform from project model to product model. However, "when the decision was made, we found that the management of the whole organization is also changing significantly. We need different talents and different management models," because there are many differences between the people who work on public welfare projects and those on market-oriented products in their ways of thinking and their personalities.

How to solve the problems in culture and personnel during the transformation from project model to product model is the key to ensure the quality and influence of its public welfare activities and their sustainable development. Therefore, Sheng Wang decided to set up an independent company – BeBetter Technology. BeBetter Technology was registered in 2015. It focuses on the development of products for children from middle-class families and rich families. It makes profits through market sales. Public welfare organization BeBetter Education and market-oriented company Better Technology are collectively called Shanghai BeBetter.

Efforts to Integrate Corporate Culture

The strategic transformation of the enterprise is faced with the challenge of cultural integration. The new strategic transformation goal from 2016 to 2020 Shanghai BeBetter proposed is to transfer the organization into a platform. To achieve this goal, Shanghai BeBetter started to publicize and implement new corporate cultures. To unify the value of the employees, the first step is to unify the value of the senior management.

Sheng Wang's idea is to maintain the goal of public welfare. "Before BeBetter Education was founded, many people advised me to establish an ordinary commercial company. Mr. Yongxin Zhu's new education experiments are focusing on micro education reforms. President Yang Dongping of the 21st Century Education Research Institute focuses his study of education on the innovation and reform of macro policies. These two mentors have deep insights into the public welfare of education. After eight years of business operation, I can fully understand and also totally agree with the views held by the two mentors. I can't make my contributions to education innovation like them. But I can explore my own way of education innovation, starting from our courses. When I founded BeBetter Education, I took public welfare as its most fundamental gene, which will form all the features of the company. Ordinary commercial companies can hardly evolve social genes even after a long time of development."

In 2015, Sheng Wang shifted his focus from BeBetter Education to BeBetter Technology, and appointed Ms. Hong Chen as the executive director of BeBetter Education. Hong Chen previously worked in Shanghai Qingyi Social Work Talent Service Center (a public welfare organization), whose main responsibility was to improve the work ability of social workers, and carry out industry research. Meanwhile, she studied for her postgraduate degree in social service management from Hong Kong Polytechnic University.

Hong Chen said, "Mr. Sheng Wang and I are both in the public welfare industry and have known each other for a long time. Mr. Sheng Wang and I share the same values that are to maintain public welfare as the essence of our business. BeBetter Education needed me at the critical moment of strategic transformation, so I joined. Mr. Sheng Wang is good at divergent thinking. He has business background, as well as public welfare and social enterprise background. Mr. Sheng Wang and I have different advantages and can complement each other. I can find out the problems during the strategic transformation and solve them effectively. He trusted me with his team and stepped back to be my coach."

To ensure corporate culture integration, new members to the management team must have the same core values. Moreover, cultural integration should also be carried out among all the employees. BeBetter Education invested a lot of money in various trainings to improve ideological and cultural integration.

BeBetter Education is now in the early stage of strategic transformation. Some employees still cannot fully understand it. They think that BeBetter Education and BeBetter Technology are working on costs and profits now, while in the past

BeBetter Education just received donations from sponsors and spent them on the project. Through cultural integration training, the employees can gradually accept the strategic transformation and commercial operation. But it would take some more time for them to fully understand it.

For BeBetter Education, employees are its most important asset, especially the professional employees. Since 2014, the organization has been changing rapidly. Not only new employees need training, but also the original employees. The age span of the employees of BeBetter Education is wide, ranging from 60's to 90's. BeBetter Education carries out various forms of training to improve the integration. According to Director Hong Chen, "cultural integration must be done at all costs; otherwise the employees can hardly be united together. Strategic transformation will be impossible. Fortunately, employees now have adapted to strategic transformation."

Improvement and Construction of Organizational Capacity

BeBetter Education takes "Big Platform and Light Area" as the basic principle for its organizational transformation.

Before the transformation, the organizational structure was set according to the geographical location of "headquarters and regional branches." With this structure, the headquarters played the leading role. The regional branches followed the instructions of the headquarters. And they also copied the operation model of the headquarters. The focus was on the project rather than management. This structure was not good for the long term improvement of the organization's overall capacity.

After the transformation, how to improve the organizational capability has become the key issue. The company put efforts both on transformation and management construction. The efficiency and pace of the work of the regional branches depend mostly on the branch heads' interpretation of the strategic intentions of the headquarters. The goal BeBetter Education set for its organizational capacity is to build a flexible organization, that is, the headquarters provides strong platform support, and the regional branches coordinate effectively and flexibly.

Currently, BeBetter Education headquarter is located in Shanghai, and has seven regional branches in seven different provinces. These seven branches also have some offices and staff, which require extra operating costs.

The key of Shanghai BeBetter's organizational capacity building is to provide standardized product services and strong platform supports, to fulfill the requirements of different regions. The company will no longer increase the office space of its regional branches or make heavy asset investment. Instead, it will depend on its professional team to drive the market through projects. On the one hand, it will stay sensitive to customer needs and listen to their criticism; on the other hand, it will link to the headquarters' platform, integrate resources, and provide suitable and timely serves to its beneficiary groups. As a market-based social enterprise, BeBetter Technology operates as a commercial company. It will transform from the current cross functional product project system that fulfills the customer demands, to the business unit system with the product line manager as the main body of responsibility and rights, and then to the subsidiary and parent company system. BeBetter Education and BeBetter Technology maintain close cooperation in accordance with the corporate regulations.

Matching of Human Resources Management Policies

BeBetter Education always stick to the principle of "employees first, beneficiaries second, stakeholders third, council and board of shareholders fourth." In BeBetter Education, the Council is the highest leading unite. Employees also participate in democratic decision-making. The organization and its employees develop together. BeBetter Technology pays back to public welfare and encourages all the employees to participate in the corporate management. These are the essential competitive advantages of a social enterprise.

After setting its goal of building a flexible organization with "Big Platform and Light Area," BeBetter Education begins to strengthen its internal promotion system. It trains and promotes talented personnel. Meanwhile, it recruits new professional personnel to improve its professional capability. The recruitment principle of the headquarters is to recruit talents with professional abilities, such as brand management, training, R&D, etc., to create high-quality products. While the branches focus on building knowledge-based teams, enhancing their flexible corporative capabilities, and improving their adaptability to complex environments. The branches recruit their own staff and follow the remote supervision of the headquarters. Therefore, the branches need to be highly self-driven, which means: first, they should be in line with the strategy, business model, and the value of the headquarters; second, they should be capable of self-management and target management.

Xiang Li, graduated from Yantai Nanshan University, is responsible for the operation of BeBetter Technology. Since graduation, she had been working as a software engineer in several cities, and then she joined BeBetter Education. Talking about her career development in BeBetter Education, Xiang Li said, "when I was in Shanghai, I wanted to "learn more about social enterprises and innovative practice. BeBetter Education provided a perfect opportunity. After I joined BeBetter Education, I worked in many different functions including training, development, sales and project management. I was promoted from a business manager to business director, and now I'm the head of BeBetter Technology. The founder Mr. Sheng Wang has been guiding me all the way, and he led me to the position of general manager. He offered me enough space for self-development. I hope that I can lead BeBetter Technology to be the first brand name in the field of financial education in China. And I hope we can continue to make profits, and support the development of BeBetter public welfare."

He Ziyun, the project manager of BeBetter Education, has been working in BeBetter Education since graduation. He is responsible for two projects: one is the financial education project for children in communities and schools in Guangdong funded by HSBC; the other is the financial education project for high school students in 12 villages and towns across the country, also funded by HSBC.

In the interview, he Ziyun said, "I think the working environment is quite free in BeBetter Education. I can choose my position according to my own interests and specialties. Even though what I'm doing is not my major back in school, BeBetter Education still gave me the chance to try. The relationship between colleagues is quite harmonious. There is no office polity about promotions or interests. Most of the colleagues are working here because we believe in BeBetter Education's mission and value. Colleagues here are just like friends. We all think highly of Mr. Sheng Wang's personality, work ability, and philosophy. And we believe that he is a good leader we can trust."

Although BeBetter Education is a public welfare organization, it also needs to improve its efficiency and develop, and meet the requirements of the sponsors. If the project fails to meet the requirements of the sponsors, the sponsors may consider other public welfare organizations. When BeBetter Education was in its early developing stage, performance management didn't seem so important because the number of employees and projects were much fewer. But now it is a much bigger team with 52 employees, so it is necessary to introduce performance management system, to encourage the good behavior and punish the bad. After trial running for some while, the new performance management system is now accepted by the employees. As the organization grows stronger, its human resource evaluation system needs to grow too. BeBetter Technology is just in its childhood. Although the number of its personnel is not very big, it will continue to improve its human resource incentive system.

Strengthening Management Information System

The transformation from project model to product model makes the information and management of the whole value chain complicated. Therefore, Shanghai BeBetter strengthens its original management information system.

First, it strengthens its management of R&D. Shanghai BeBetter's production, R&D, and product R&D route design are all based on the needs of their beneficiary groups. BeBetter Education is responsible for exploring the in-depth demands of beneficiary groups, while BeBetter Technology carries out R&D at a higher level. Guided by market demands, Shanghai BeBetter carries out integrated management of R&D, design and supply chain. Its leading technology allows it to maintain its leading position in the field of public welfare.

Second, it establishes information support system. The construction of the big platform has very high requires on internal operation and management. The process and management information system is essential to improve the overall operation and management level. The process should be established according to business and R&D demands. The management information system runs through all functional departments horizontally and connects the headquarters and regional branches vertically, which can greatly improve the communication efficiency. At the same time, the company implements project information management, which can greatly improve the organizational capacity.

Third, it strengthens data analysis and research. Management information system strengthens the company's data collection and analysis ability and guides its strategic decision-making.

The Balance Between Public Welfare Goals and Business Goals

Internal Measures to Guarantee the Stability of Public Welfare Objectives

Fundamentally, BeBetter Education is a public welfare organization and BeBetter Technology is a market-based social enterprise. Both of them are clearly defined on legal aspect. This helps to maintain the stability of its social goals.

First, ensure the stability of public welfare objective through equity setting. After the transformation of its operation model and organization structure, BeBetter Education holds 20% of BeBetter Technology's total shares, while Sheng Wang, the founder, holds 58% of BeBetter Technology's total shares. According to this equity setting, 20% of the profits of BeBetter Technology will be assigned to BeBetter Education. Sheng Wang promised to donate part of his dividends, equivalent to 15% of BeBetter Technology profits, to BeBetter Education as employee development fund. Sheng Wang is also considering that in the future, BeBetter Technology should provide more support to BeBetter Education through donation and dividends. But this plan needs to be approved first by other investors of BeBetter Technology.

Second, define the functions of top management clearly. Sheng Wang is no longer responsible for the daily management of BeBetter Education. He is the president and legal person responsible for the company's development strategy and major decisions. Executive director Hong Chen is in charge of daily operation.

Third, define the tasks of every team clearly. The operation of BeBetter Education and BeBetter Technology is undertaken by two separate teams with completely no overlaps.

Fourth, define the brands and beneficiaries clearly. BeBetter Technology serves for children and young people from middle-class and high-end families, while BeBetter Education serves for children and young people from poor families. And they use different brands.

Fifth, implement independent financial accounting and clear financial settlement. When BeBetter Education and BeBetter Technology are involved in interrelated transactions or related production factors, the transaction shall be priced clearly and settled truthfully in systematic ways. Public welfare projects must go through bidding process. When the price and quality of products are the same, BeBetter Technology can have the priority (because it is a large donor). When the price and quality of products differ greatly, the best bidder will be the winner. For example, if BeBetter Education needs to entrust a third party to develop a product, it should go through the bidding process.

Mechanism Guarantee of Public Welfare Objectives

(1) Supervision by external partners

Foreign partners led BeBetter Education into the area of financial education. They provide BeBetter Education with the curriculum, professional resources, as well as the concept of sustainable operation. They also supervise BeBetter Education won't deviate from its social mission. These foreign partners include Citibank, HSBC, Barclays, etc. Domestic partners such as Nandu Public Welfare Foundation, Liu Hongru Financial Education Foundation, Shanghai Charity Foundation, Shanghai Lianquan Public Welfare Foundation, etc., are also supervising BeBetter Education.

(2) Setting up a scientific and reasonable cross subsidy model

Shanghai BeBetter fulfills its social mission by adopting the business model of "providing charging services for high-income people to subsidize similar but free services for low-income people." As regulated by corporate articles, BeBetter Technology should subsidize a large proportion of its profit dividends to BeBetter Education for its public welfare business. This rigid mechanism guarantees that the mission of Shanghai BeBetter will not drift.

(3) The inheritance of the organizational mission of BeBetter Education ensures that the social mission of Shanghai BeBetter will not drift.

For more than ten years, BeBetter Education's team has spent a lot of efforts to promote the financial education for children and young people. Wei Tang, the training director of BeBetter Education, is regarded as the spiritual leader by the employees. She describes her experience of joining BeBetter as follows:

"My major is not related to education. My first job was at China Poverty Alleviation Foundation. During the post-earthquake reconstruction of Wenchuan, I went there to give psychological intervention related works. I gave training to the teachers together with American experts. After leaving China Poverty Alleviation Foundation, I had a rest at home for almost half a year. Because I have been working in the public welfare field for many years, I read public welfare magazines from time to time. By chance, I saw a report about BeBetter Education. And I found that BeBetter Education was doing the same thing as I did in Wenchuan disaster area. So I was interested. And they were also looking for people who could give trainings. Through training, I learned that financial intelligence is not just a concept, or a product. It's more about values and ideas. BeBetter Education can help to improve children's abilities in economic thinking, time management and resource management. It can change the teaching concept of rural education and rural teachers. This gives me a sense of responsibility and great honor.

"Through rich work experience, I found that education and training is what I love and what I'm good at. I found that BeBetter Education is working on education wholeheartedly. Financial curriculum is the essence of BeBetter Education, but it is only a carrier. In fact, BeBetter Education is devoted to find the best way to implement education in China. So, to do the best education is what really attracts me."

Customer identification of public welfare objectives

BeBetter Education has always been sincere to its customers. It follows customers' needs to guide its product improvement, and takes brand building as the foundation of its survival. BeBetter Education divides its customers into channel customers, teacher customers and individual customers.

International Plan (China) is one of the important channel customers of BeBetter Education. From the beginning of their cooperation in 2014, their products have covered Yunnan, Shaanxi, Ningxia, Chengdu, Beijing and other places. The cooperation between BeBetter Education and International Plan (China) is mainly about a project called Youth Employment Project, which includes the development of life skills and social and financial curriculum materials, teachers' trainings, and youth entrepreneurship activity design. They visit the schools where their project is being implemented with the project team of International Plan (China), and provide professional guidance for teachers teaching life skills and social finance courses by attending their class and carrying out workshops.

Feng Liu is the director of the cooperation project between International Plan (China) and BeBetter Education. She believes that "BeBetter Education has significant professional and technical advantages and talent advantages in financial education, especially in financial education for children and young people. The company is the innovative model and industry leader in China. To International Plan, to entrust BeBetter Education with its Youth Employment Project is a wise choice, because the latter one can guarantee the quality of the project, as well as continuous technical update of the project module."

Gu Lianrong is a teacher from Hualin Primary School in Pudong New Area of Shanghai. She is also a volunteer teacher of BeBetter Education's social financial management course, and a loyal customer of BeBetter Education. Lianrong Gu began to teach social and financial management courses of BeBetter Education since 2011. She has been to Guangdong, Sichuan and other places to train teachers of public welfare education of financial intelligence. She said, "I organized many public welfare activities related to BeBetter Education for my students, such as "I'm Your Eye" distribution center charity sale, "Happy Competition" show, 200 yuan investment activity, American Investment Bank volunteer service day, museum public welfare day, and so on. I always believe that financial education can inspire students and parents' desire for financial education. More importantly, these activities can make students see that "life, money, happiness and sense of responsibility" are the essence of financial education!"

Future Challenges

Since its foundation in 2009, BeBetter Education has served more than one million children and young people, becoming the No.1 brand name of financial education for children and young people in China. At the same time, BeBetter Education is faced with great challenges.

The most important one is to prevent any deviation of its social mission. This can be ensured by the legal identify and system design of Shanghai BeBetter. BeBetter Education aims to cover 10 million children and young people by 2020 as its strategic goal. This is 10 times the number of people BeBetter Education has served in the past seven years since its foundation. This requires the joint efforts of BeBetter Education, as well as other public welfare organizations. Although there is supervision mechanism, it is still a very big challenge for a joint public welfare organization to prevent deviation of its social mission. BeBetter Education keeps on investing great effort and time in it.

Second, how to create products to meet the market demands is another challenge. There are also some problems in the implementation of financial education projects. For example, youth financial courses are usually not welcomed in vocational colleges; young students have little interest in financial intellectual education projects, although they easily accept the courses of employment and entrepreneurship. This is mainly because most of the college students are supported by their parents and don't need to worry about money, so they are more interested in career development courses, instead of financial intellectual education projects. Different from colleges, schools for smaller children care more about quality education and featured courses, so financial education courses is more successful in these schools. Sheng Wang pointed out: "financial education has just started in China, but there will be a big outbreak of demand in the future. The market space is enormous. At the same time, there are a lot of challenges, such as how to deal with the problem of insufficient capacity, and how to predict the demand trend of the beneficiary groups accurately."

Third, there are contradictions between the quality, and the depth and width of the customer coverage of the products. The strategies of its major sponsors sometimes conflict with BeBetter Education's objective of always making the best products. The sponsors require rapid expansion, but BeBetter Education cares more about the quality of its service, to meet in-depth market demand. If BeBetter Education does not follow the instructions of its sponsors, the sponsors may withdraw their funds. Although BeBetter has designed the plan of strategic transformation, the result of the plan is still unknown.

Fourth, there are challenges on the market. The financial education for children and young people is a sunrise industry. The threshold to enter and exit it is not comparative low. With the development and growth of the financial education industry, BeBetter Education has to face the complex dynamic situation of the continuous alternation between the Red Sea and the Blue Sea. BeBetter Education needs to keep on rebuilding its market boundary, pay more attention to the overall situation rather than specific figures, surpass the existing demands, and follow reasonable strategic order. Instead of defeating its competitors, BeBetter Education should focus more on creating value for its beneficiary groups, expanding new markets where there is "no competition," avoiding homogeneous competition, and creating its own blue ocean.

BeBetter Education is now considering establishing a scientific market performance evaluation system which can keep it always on the right track to create value for its beneficiary groups.

Further Reading

Bin H, Hao R (2009). Modular Design of Organizational Structure: Basic Principles and Model Construction. *Business Economy and Management*, 2009 (2)

Center for Civil Society Studies, Peking University. (2017). *All-in-One Book on Social Enterprise*

Jin M (2005) *Blue Ocean Strategy*. Commercial Press, Beijing

Zhiyang L, Quan L (2008). Analysis on the Strategy of Flattening the Organizational Structure of Enterprises. *Economic Management*, 2008 (2)

Company Information

Sheng W (2015). Sheng Wang: The Blue Ocean of Education Integrating Business and Public Welfare. http://gongyi.sohu.com/20150424/n411815709.shtml. Accessed 24 April 2015

Sheng W (2016). Sheng Wang's Parallel World: After Changing Five Jobs, He Chose to Promote Social Equity by Innovative Education. WeChat official account: Baitegongxue, 2016-09-27

Sheng W (2017). Recommended by Mr. Sheng Wang of BeBetter Education: "I Want to Talk with Myself About Money Philosophy." WeChat official account: Axinweiyan, 2017-05-31

Xiao W, Xu Z (2016) Sheng Wang: Another Kind of Return. *Chinese Philanthropists*, 2016 (12)

0Fenbei: Helping the Poor People

Yanfang Xu, Jiwen Song, Kangtao Ye, Meng Zhao, and Wei Wu

> Why does social poverty alleviation only take a small proportion among all social resources? One possible reason is that many organizations are doing poverty alleviation as public welfare with no returns. This model can hardly be sustainable. If we can turn poverty alleviation from a social activity into a profitable business activity, more social resources will join in this cause for interests. This is just what we want to do.
>
> –Li Wang, founder of 0Fenbei

Poverty has always been a worldwide issue. Although human beings have made great achievements dealing with this problem, the situation of poverty is still startling. Taking the living standard of $1.25 per person per day as extreme poverty, there are 836 million people living in extreme poverty around the world, most of them in developing countries.

China's poverty issue is also critical. In more than 30 years of reform and opening up, more than 800 million people in China have been lifted out of poverty, which made China one of the most effective countries in the world to eradicate poverty. However, by the end of 2013, there are still 82.49 million people in extreme poverty in our country. These poor people's minimum needs of food, clothing, housing, basic education and basic medical care have not been met yet. On November 3, 2013, during his visit to Shibadong Village in Hunan Province, General Secretary Xi Jinping first put forward the concept of "Accurate Poverty Alleviation," which became the basic strategy of the central government later. The essence of "targeted poverty alleviation" is to mobilize all the social resources and forces to help the truly poor households and populations to alleviate poverty by "implementing different policies according to their specific needs," so as to improve the effectiveness of poverty alleviation. To implement the targeted poverty alleviation strategy, from April to October 2014, 800,000 staff of poverty alleviation system went to the villages and households, and registered 128,000 poor villages and 8,962,000 poor people. They registered their information and gave them cards. From August 2015 to June 2016, national poverty

Y. Xu (✉) · J. Song · K. Ye · M. Zhao · W. Wu
Business School, Renmin University of China, Beijing, China
e-mail: xuyanfang@rmbs.ruc.edu.cn

M. Zhao and J. Mao (eds.), *Social Entrepreneurship*,
https://doi.org/10.1007/978-981-15-9881-4_7

alleviation system mobilized nearly two million people to "double check." They added another 8.07 million people in poverty, removed 9.29 million people with inaccurate information, and improve the accuracy of registration.

Although the central government has made great efforts on targeted poverty alleviation, there are still a lot of challenges in practice. On the one hand, due to the limited resources of the local government, it is difficult for the registered poor households to get the aids from the local government; on the other hand, due to information asymmetry, it is difficult for these poor households to get donations from social poverty alleviation organizations. Therefore, to develop a reliable information platform between the registered poor households and social poverty alleviation organizations, which can provide authentic and retailed information for various poverty alleviation organizations, help social poverty alleviation resources to find suitable poverty alleviation objects, and provide targeted assistance to the poor, is the key to improve the efficiency of poverty alleviation and achieve targeted poverty alleviation.

Beijing 0Fenbei Technology Co., Ltd. (hereinafter referred to as 0Fenbei) has made a useful attempt in this regard. The company cooperates with local governments at all levels, uses the Internet and big data technology to refine, classify and process the information of the registered poor households provided by local governments, so as to connect the poor households with social poverty alleviation organizations. Thus, it hopes to improve the targeted poverty alleviation and help the poor population by commercial means.

Getting Involved with Poverty Alleviation

Getting to Know Poverty Alleviation by Accident

0Fenbei's poverty alleviation business all started from an accidental experience of its founder Li Wang. Li Wang was born in Zhenxiong County, Zhaotong City, Yunnan Province in 1989. After graduating from computer major of Agricultural University of China in July 2011, Li Wang joined the head office of Industrial and Commercial Bank of China and became a white-collar. Although the benefits and working environment of the bank were both favorable, Li Wang was not satisfied. Deep in his heart, Li Wang hoped to start his own business. In November 2014, Li Wang resigned from the head office of ICBC and established his first company. The company was in Internet finance "blockchain" business. Although the company's operation was good, Li Wang had bigger ambitions and wanted to achieve more.

During the Qingming Festival in 2016, Li Wang returned to his hometown in Yunnan to visit his relatives. A local poverty alleviation officer posted the information of a child in his WeChat circle of friends to ask for help. The child was suffering from severe hearing impairment. His family was impoverished because of his illness. Li Wang saw the help information after it was reposted several times. Li Wang happened to know a public welfare project which could provide such help. Therefore he gave the information to the child, and helped him join the public welfare project successfully. In the few days at his hometown, Li Wang chatted with some relatives and friends who were civil servants in local government and found that they had the same problem.

Li Wang's hometown, Zhenxiong County, is located on the border of the three provinces of Yunnan, Guizhou and Sichuan. It is in Wumeng Mountain area. It was a national poverty-stricken county and one of the poorest areas in China. It had poor natural resources, and large population. Poverty had been a historical problem for years. There were more than 80,000 poor households and nearly 300,000 poor people, out of the county's total population of 1.6 million. In order to implement the targeted poverty alleviation strategy, the local government called on local officials to take charge of poor households. Each officer was in charge of several or dozens of poverty-stricken households. The officials were responsible for visiting these households, collecting the information of these poor households and finding ways to help them out of poverty. However, the officials were met with many difficulties. Some of them couldn't find any solutions or resources to help these households, so they had to subsidize them with their own salaries which were already very low.

In order to help his hometown out of this problem, Li Wang decided to use his expertise to develop a net-based poverty alleviation information platform to help his hometown to find social public welfare resources for poverty alleviation. Therefore, Li Wang visited the Secretary of the local county Party Committee. The Secretary thought Li Wang's idea was very good. By the end of the day, he called on the Poverty Alleviation Office of the county to arrange related jobs. Thus, Li Wang entered the field of poverty alleviation.

Developing Poverty Alleviation Platform Free of Charge

After Qingming Festival, Li Wang returned to Beijing and immediately invited his friends from the Ministry of Civil Affairs and public welfare organizations to discuss this matter. They all agreed that it was feasible and were willing to help. Later, Li Wang discussed with his staff. Everyone thought it was a good thing and decided to develop the platform as soon as possible. On April 8, 2016, the project was officially launched. All six employees of the company began to work on the development. One was responsible for the product, one for design, one for back-end technology, one for front-end technology, and Li Wang and another colleague for the coordination of all the resources.

The first problem they must solve was which kind of platform should they develop? APP, WeChat official account or computer web page application? After discussion, the team abandoned APP first, because the development, upgrading and promotion were all complicated. And they all preferred WeChat public account over computer web page application, because local officials were not so good at using computers, and it was more convenient to input information by mobile phone.

The second problem was how to obtain the data of the poor households? After discussion, they decided to obtain the data of the poor households in the registration system of the county's Poverty Alleviation Office. The county's Poverty Alleviation Office would support them. The company's technicians could write scripts to read all the data and corresponding relationships, and store them in the company's database and process them. The local officials could verify the authenticity of this information when they register on the platform, and then the data of households they were responsible of would be linked to them automatically.

The third problem was how to obtain the information of public welfare organizations? There were tens of thousands of public welfare organizations registered in Civil Affairs Departments in China. The information they published were of different levels and with no consistent standard. Members of the project team decided to write a crawler program to obtain the data of these foundations and public welfare projects from the Internet, and then clean, classify and archive them for future use.

The fourth problem is how to match the data. The members of the project team planned to label and classify the poor households according to the reasons of poverty, then label and classify the foundations according to the project types of the foundations, and finally, match the poor households with the foundations according to their labels, and recommend suitable foundations and projects to the local officials in real time.

The plan seemed perfect. So, they drew the working chart and made the schedule. They worked six days a week, and 12 h a day. Everybody devoted all their efforts to the development of the platform with enthusiasm. However, when they started, they found so many unexpected difficulties and problems were waiting for them.

First of all, the information of the registered poor households could not meet the requirements for matching. When they analyzed the data, they found that the poverty reasons entered in the registration system of the county's Poverty Alleviation Office were limited to only 12 fixed options, which could not support accurate matching. They had to collect more detailed information of poverty reasons. Therefore, members of the project team created a new poverty cause category of nearly 100 options. They also added a poverty reason collection module to the registration page, and required local officials to fill in detailed reasons for poverty when submitting the information of the poor households.

Secondly, there were a lot of mistakes in the matching of local officials and the poor households they were responsible of. When they were testing the platform one day before launch, members of the project team found that some officials had hundreds or even thousands of poor households matched to them. And the information of poor households was updated only until 2014. After consulting the Poverty Alleviation Office of the county, they learned that some villages only registered the information of the poor households, but not the offices that were responsible for them. So their staff just put all the poor households under the name of the village head. Moreover, the data in the system was only updated to 2014. Although the county had accurate information collected by each villages and towns within the last year and a half, this information had not been entered in the registration system. So the team members decided to do it by themselves. These unexpected problems increased their workload dramatically. They had to work overtime and stay up late. Sometimes they even didn't have time for meals (Fig. 1).

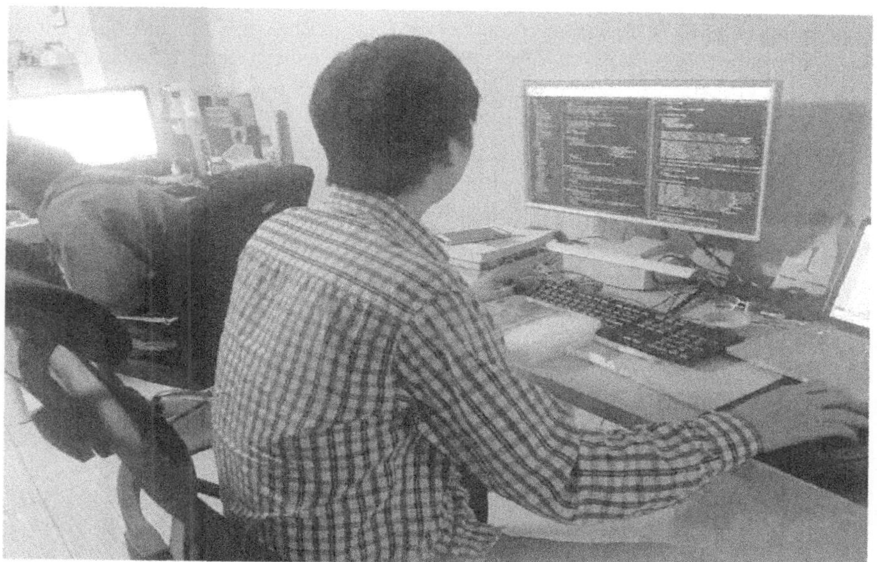

Fig. 1 A project team member is developing Poverty Alleviation Platform

On April 24, the Poverty alleviation platform went online. On April 25, Li Wang contacted the county's poverty Alleviation Office and they agreed to provide trial access to three offices first. But what happened next disappointed all the members. Within one week after the platform went online, only 35 civil servants submitted information of less than 10 poor households. They interviewed some officials by telephone and learned that they were not motivated about this job because their daily work was quite busy already, and the May Day holiday was coming.

On May 4, Li Wang contacted the Secretary of the county's Party Committee. The Secretary of the county Party Committee attached great importance to this issue. The county government immediately issued a notice asking all the officials to register poor households on the platform as soon as possible. Under the supervision of the Secretary of the county Party Committee, by May 15, more than 1200 local poverty alleviation officials registered and linked up to 13,000 poor households on the platform. Soon, public welfare organizations began to match these poor households. Within one month after the poverty alleviation platform was launched, more than 20 poor households were matched with public welfare organizations. The platform became good assistant for local poverty alleviation officials.

On the morning of May 22, team member Jingping Yi published an article of their story about the development of poverty alleviation platform in the past one month.[1]

In the article, he wrote: "the photos of those poor households provided by local officials broke our hearts. We never knew that it is so hard for some people to just

[1] A group of programmers did a cool job. WeChat official account: nulishehui, 2016-05-22.

live. My hometown is Ganzhou, Jiangxi Province. Although I am not rich, I have never seen poor families like these. At the same time, we felt that we were not doing the job just because we were "brainwashed" by Mr. Wang, but because we could help these families."

Only half a day after the article was posted, it was read by tens of thousands of people. Soon, the company received dozens of e-mails from public welfare organizations, local governments and media to express their intentions for cooperation. People's Daily and other media made special interviews with 0Fenbei. Some individual volunteers expressed their willingness to help too.

Li Wang received attention, goodwill and apparition from all sectors of the society and felt the power of public welfare and enthusiastic people. From then on, Li Wang and his team began to think about how to upgrade their poverty alleviation platform and create more social values.

Innovative Products

Feelings Lead the Company's Vision

At the end of June 2016, Li Wang and his team decided to took poverty alleviation as their major business. In August, 0Fenbei Technology Co., Ltd. was officially registered in the Industrial and Commercial Bureau. Li Wang was the founder, and Jingping Yi and Junsheng Ji were the co-founders. As to the reason why they didn't register a non-profit organization, Wang replied frankly: "it's very complicated to register as a non-profit organization, and we don't want to use it to apply for subsidies. So far, we haven't taken anyone's money for nothing. In addition, being a non-profit organization will also constrain our future operation."

The company's name "0Fenbei" also has deeper meaning. The two Chinese characters "fen" and "bei" together will make the character "pin," which means "poverty." And "0Fenbei" means "eliminate poverty." This is also the vision of the company. As China's first social poverty alleviation network platform dedicated to providing information services for targeted poverty alleviation, 0Fenbei has set its goal as "helping the poorest people in China and ultimately eliminate poverty" since its foundation. By using Internet and big data technology, the company aims to make data portraits for the rural poor population in China, and provide information support for poverty alleviation organizations and rural market participants (from e-commerce, financial industry, tourism industry, etc.) to help the poor populations more efficiently and accurately.

When talking about the establishment of 0Fenbei in an interview, Li Wang said, "I established my first enterprise just to make profits. After helping my hometown establishing the official account of poverty alleviation, twenty or thirty poor households received aids in May. Many media reported on us, even People's Daily. After that, many people contacted me. There were poverty alleviation offices of local governments, public welfare organizations and media. I began to think if I can help more people. 0Fenbei was born with a social mission. The people we help are the poorest people. I just serve them."

Leverage Poverty Alleviation Resources by Innovation

Since its establishment, the company has developed four major innovative products (see Table 1), to leverage more social resources to join targeted poverty alleviation, so as to help the registered poor households in rural areas and realize the company's vision of zero poverty.

0Fenbei Poverty Alleviation Matching Platform

This is the first product developed by the company, aiming to use the Internet and data technology to link the poor population and social poverty alleviation resources effectively. From their past experience when developing the poverty alleviation platform for his hometown, Li Wang knew that there was the problem of information asymmetry between the poor population and poverty alleviation organizations. On the one hand, the rural poor need all kinds of external help; on the other hand, the poverty alleviation institutions have to spend a lot of costs to find the poor people who really need help. And this platform can solve the problems of both parties.

The development of this product was a complicated task. The first step was to develop the database of the poor people's needs. First of all, they obtained the data from the local governments' poverty alleviation system and formed the background government data. Next, they developed the civil servant terminal, where local poverty alleviation officials can register from the backend by their real names, and complete the detailed information of the poor households that they help, such as seasons for poverty. If the reason was illness, the system would collect specific information such as the name of the disease, diagnosed or not, treatment time, treatment status, name of the hospital, treatment cost, etc. And finally, they combined the information entered by the local officials with the data in the local county's poverty alleviation system, and then clear up, classify and refine them, to build a detailed and dynamic demand database. The second step was to develop the database of the poor people's needs. First, the company cooperated with public welfare organizations and used reptile technology to collect detailed information of the public welfare poverty alleviation projects and public welfare institutions, such as whom and where these organizations would help, what were the projects and what was the status of these projects. Then, they wrote data analysis script, extract key information from these data, and built supply database. The third step was to label and classify the poor households according to the poverty reason of the poor people, label and classify the public

Table 1 Main products of 0Fenbei

	0Fenbei Poverty Alleviation Matching Platform	Poverty Data Analysis Report	Basic credit and risk credit rating system of the rural poor population	Fenbeichou Student Assistance Platform
Problems to be solved	It is difficult for public welfare organizations to obtain authentic and accurate information of rural poor households	Low efficiency of poverty alleviation by local governments and public welfare organizations	High credit cost of financial institutions for the rural poor population	Rural poor children drop out of school because of poverty
	0Fenbei Poverty Alleviation Matching Platform	Poverty Data Analysis Report	Basic Credit and Risk Credit System of the Rural Poor Population	Fenbeichou Student Assistance Platform
Solutions	Establish poverty demand database and poverty supply database; connect poor households and public welfare organizations	Carry out data exploring, modeling, analysis and visualization for poverty data and generate Poverty Data Analysis Report	Carry out big data analysis, and provide financial credit information of the rural poor population to financial institutions	Attract the public to donate school expenses and living expenses for poor children
Target customers of the product	Public welfare organizations and public welfare projects of enterprises	Local government and public welfare organizations	Financial institutions providing services for the rural poor	Individuals
Ultimate beneficiary	Poor rural households in need of help	Poor rural households in need of help	Poor rural households in need of financial services	Rural poor children aged 6–14

welfare institutions according to their project types, and then match the information of the demand database and the supply database (see Fig. 2).

Once the matching was successful, the company would automatically push matching information to local officials and organizations and help them connect with the poor. Matching models included single household matching and package matching of households with the same poverty reasons. 0Fenbei not only provides the exiting data of poor households to local poverty alleviation cadres and public welfare institutions, it also matches projects with more poor people. For example, they find other poor people outside the government's system, and then contact public welfare institutions to design new public welfare projects for these people (Fig. 3).

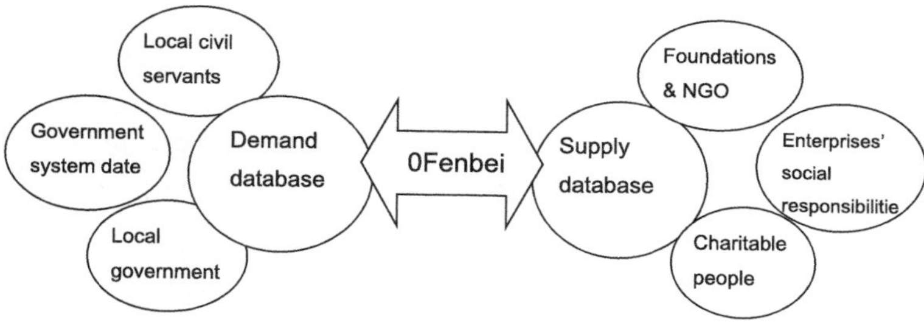

Fig. 2 Operation model of 0Fenbei Poverty Alleviation Matching Platform

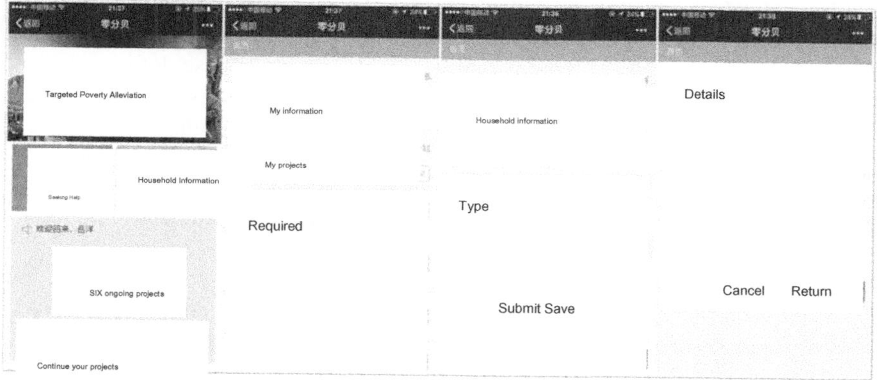

Fig. 3 Screenshot of backend system of 0Fenbei Poverty Alleviation Matching Platform

This product helps poverty alleviation organizations to reduce their cost of collecting information of the poor, and connects the demand side and the supply side. It attracts more social resources to participate in poverty alleviation, and improves the efficiency and accuracy of poverty alleviation.

Poverty Data Analysis Report

This is the second product developed by the company, which aims to make better use of the huge poverty data collected by local poverty alleviation cadres. With the deepening of their cooperation with local governments after their first product was launched, Li Wang found that the demand for poverty alleviation was far greater than the supply. There were a lot of poor households in need of help in a lot of places, and public welfare institutions alone could not meet the demands at all. Li Wang also found that plenty of poverty alleviation resources were controlled by the local governments. However, the data collected by local cadres hadn't been fully used by local governments in their poverty alleviation decision making. A lot of decisions were made randomly, resulting in waste of resources and low efficiency. To solve these problems, the company classified the data in its poverty demand database into categories of different gender ratio, age structure, education level, regional distribution, disease type and so on, then further explore, model, analyze and visualize these data, and finally generate the Poverty Data Analysis Report, which could provide data support and references for the governments, public welfare organizations and enterprises for their poverty alleviation projects, and improve the overall efficiency and accuracy of poverty alleviation. For example, if a hospital will be built in a poverty-stricken area for the poor, the analysis report will give detailed information for reference: the location to build it, the medicines to store, the types of doctors, the training for the doctors, and so on.

Although this product can provide data support for poverty alleviation institutions for their decision-making and has important social value, it is now being suspended. There are two main reasons. One is that the local governments seldom need it and public welfare organizations barely know it. The other reason is that the products can hardly be standardized and the development costs are too high.

Basic Credit and Risk Credit System of the Rural Poor Population

Peter F. Drucker said, "only by converting social needs and social problems into opportunities for profitable business, can this social problem be completely solved." Li Wang totally agrees with this view. He believes that poverty alleviation requires far more than social public welfare organizations' support and government investment. If poverty alleviation can be converted into something that can create business value, more and more people and resources will participate spontaneously, and the issue of (extreme) poverty eradication can finally be addressed. He said, "We are thinking about why there are only a small proportion of social resources devoted to social poverty alleviation? One possible reason is that many organizations are doing poverty alleviation as public welfare with no returns. This model can hardly be sustainable. If we can convert poverty alleviation from a social activity into a profitable business activity driven by interest, more social resources will participate. This is just what we want to do."

Therefore, the company developed basic credit and risk credit rating system of the rural poor population. The purpose of this product is to reduce the cost of financial services provided by traditional financial institutions for rural poor households, to help the rural poor who lack credit information to obtain financial services, and the financial institutions to make profits. In Li Wang's view, because of the poor traffic conditions, low informatization level and low education level in the rural areas, the customer acquisition cost and the credit rating cost of financial institutions in the rural areas are too high, and the risk control is very difficult too. These make it difficult for financial institutions to extend their business to the rural areas, especially the registered poor households. The company has collected a large amount of data in its poverty demand database during its past work. If it process these data and provide reliable credit rating and blacklists and whitelists to financial institutions to reduce their cost of financial services to poor households during customer acquisition and credit investigation processes, more financial institutions will be willing to provide financial services for poor groups. Furthermore, it will enable the poor people with good credit to get loans with lower interest rates and help them to get rid of poverty on their own.

Li Wang was very lucky to find a financial institution that recognized this idea and the two parties established a strategic partnership. In November 2016, the company launched this exciting project. Based on its multi-dimensional data (including basic information, production and living conditions, assets and liabilities, etc.) of millions of poor people in its Poverty demand database, 0Fenbei used the Zest Finance big data technology which is used by financial technology companies in the United States to serve the poor people, built three models (repayment ability, repayment willingness, stability), and developed this product successfully.

By April 2017, 300,000 poor households in Yunnan Province had obtained loans through this credit system. Although it takes time to accumulate data and improve the credit model, Li Wang believes that in the near future, 0Fenbei credit system can help more and more rural poor people get credit from financial institutions, and then get loans and become rich. Li Wang said, "There are countless reasons why the poor people became poor. If we provide loans to the honest and hardworking poor people, they will be able to get rid of poverty and become rich quickly. The government's poverty alleviation fund aims to help the poorest. Our product mainly focuses on helping those people who are at the edge of poverty and who have not yet get rid of poverty. They just need a hand from others to help they pass the poverty line and leave it behind forever."

Fenbeichou Student Assistance Platform

This is the fourth product of the company. It aims to build an Internet public welfare platform that everyone can use, to connect urban and rural people through mobile phones, and allow urban people to help poor rural children go to school. Different from the poverty alleviation platform which provides support for government and public welfare organizations, decibel fund aims to help the ordinary person participate in poverty alleviation and express their love. In fact, shortly after the company was founded, many people found Li Wang and asked him questions like "I want to help the poor, but I don't know what I can do." or "I want to sponsor a student. Can you help me to contact?" However, Internet applications for individual users requires high costs to develop and operate, and the company only has a small team who are already busy with other products, so the development of this product has been postponed. Even so, the company never forgets this project.

After the Spring Festival of 2017, the company cooperated with Aiyou Future Foundation, a public-raising foundation registered in Civil Affairs Department, and launched the project. Li Wang believes that it is a meaning deed for individuals to sponsor poor children on education. Therefore, the company started this project with "one-to-one education and living sponsorship."

In order to help these people fulfill their wishes of "sponsoring a poor child," and build mutual trust which has been a headache in traditional public welfare activities, the company stuck to the following principles in its product design. The first principle is to make sure they only sponsor the truly poor children. All the children they help are from the poor families registered in the system of Poverty Alleviation Office. Their information is collected and uploaded by local officials responsible for poverty alleviation in the villages. Decibel fund conducts secondary audits and gives them different priorities according to their situations, such as if they have single parent, if they are left behind by their parents, if their parents suffer from diseases, and if there are more than one child. The second principle is the company won't handle with money directly. All donations go directly to Aiyou Future Foundation's account and are distributed by the Foundation.

In order to attract more donors, the company made a lot of efforts in improving user experience. First, the platform provides various choices for matching, such as age, gender, birthday, etc. so that sponsors can choose the children they want to sponsor by seeing the photos and descriptions of these children, which gives the sponsors the freedom to choose. Second, donors can "add decibels" for the children they want to help. The higher the decibels, the higher the children will rank, and the more likely they will be sponsored. Third, the platform uploads photos and even videos of the children after they receive the donations, to let the sponsors know the changes their donation have made on the children and their families. Fourth, sponsors and the children being sponsored can communicate through the platform, so that the sponsors can feel the joy of helping these children.

The company is also careful about protecting the privacy of every poor child in its product design. It hides their specific school names. It only shows the name of the towns where they live. And it does not provide the contact numbers of the two parties to each other. In order to avoid making the children to depend totally on the donations and forget to work hard, the company also limits the amount of donation. The donation for each child is limited to 25 yuan per week or 100 yuan per month.

On March 21, 2017, Fenbeichou went online for trial operation. It achieved very good results without any promotions. In Li Wang's opinion, Fenbeichou undertakes an important mission. He said, "Making others happy is a demand. It's a very good spiritual experience. If you want to help the children, we can provide the best way. The fundamental purpose is still to help these poor children. If it wasn't for helping them, it wouldn't make any sense."

In the future, the company will expand its service to the children aged from 15 to 18. Li Wang and his team wants to build Fenbeichou into a "poverty alleviation weapon," which allows all the people who are passionate about public welfare help the truly poor children without worrying about being cheated, and all the poor children who drop out of school because of poverty go back to school and change their own lives with knowledge instead of struggling in poverty generation after generation (Fig. 4).

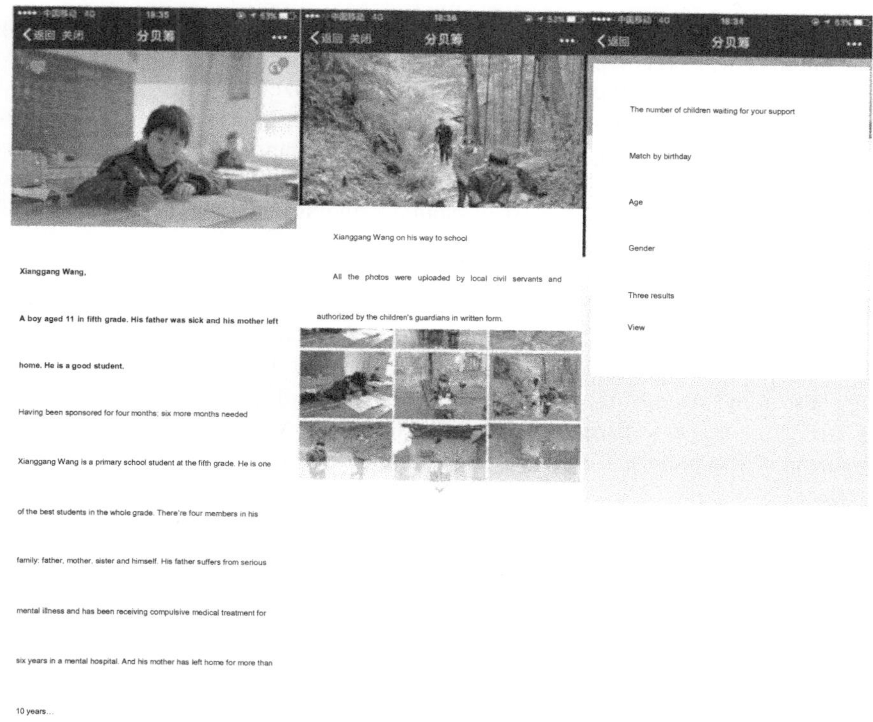

Fig. 4 Screenshot of Fenbeichou website

Financial Sustainability

As an innovative enterprise committed to promote targeted poverty alleviation, 0Fenbei is not like the ordinary public welfare organizations that achieve the sustainable development through external donations or funding, nor the ordinary commercial enterprises which take making profits as its only goal. 0Fenbei aims to contribute to social poverty alleviation. Its ultimate beneficiary is the poor households registered in the system of Poverty Alleviation Office in rural areas. It serves many different customers, including local governments, public welfare institutions and individuals, and financial institutions. Therefore, 0Fenbei adopts different charging policies for different products and customers. This charging strategy can help the company obtain stable cash flow and achieve financial sustainability, as well as make sure the company's mission won't deviate.

Product 1: 0Fenbei Poverty Alleviation Matching Platform. This product provides information of the poor population to local governments, public welfare institutions and enterprises. As this product mainly serves the government, public welfare institutions and other special groups, it was designed as a free matching platform.

Product 2: Poverty Data Analysis Report. This product mainly provides poverty alleviation analysis reports to local governments and public welfare organizations to improve their working efficiency. It needs to be customized according to customers' demands. It takes more manpower and costs to develop. In order to maintain financial sustainability, the company adopts traditional commercial pricing mode for this product, where customers pay the prices higher than the cost. Currently, the demand for this project is still very low, so it cannot bring substantial cash inflow to the company yet.

Product 3: basic credit and risk credit system for the rural poor. This product mainly provides financial credit information to financial institutions that operate in rural areas. It provides data query service to financial institutions, and charges one yuan per query through transaction charging mode. The revenue of the product depends on the scale of the database and the number of queries. At the beginning of 2017, one strategic partner invested 800,000 yuan to 0 decibel as the advance payment of the project. Currently, the company's main revenue comes from this product.

Product 4: Fenbeichou Student Assistance Platform. This product is a one-to-one student funding platform, connecting the students from poor families and people who are passionate about public welfare. Currently, the product is free. It might charge in the future to obtain stable cash flow for the company and enhance its financial sustainability. Li Wang said that there are three options for this product to make profits in the future. The first one is to cooperate with the insurance company to allow the donors donate insurance to the students, where the company can charge insurance company slotting allowance. The second one is to cooperate with e-commerce companies and allow the donors "buy" donation services, where the company obtains "premium profit" by charging the donors. And the third one is advertising revenue from public welfare advertisements on the platform.

The cost structure of the company is relatively simple. The total cost per month is about 200,000 to 300,000 yuan, of which the rent takes about 40,000 yuan, and the rest is mostly labor cost. In the short run, its revenue can cover the cost and achieve basic financial balance.

Li Wang and his team are confident about the future. They believe that the company's reputation can be converted into business value. In other words, poverty alleviation and profitability is not an "either-or" issue. There can be a win-win solution.

Mechanism Guarantee

In order to ensure the company's social goal of promoting targeted poverty alleviation will not deviate, 0Fenbei established a series of prevention mechanisms.

Always Follow the Lead of the Correct Values

Li Wang fully understands the importance of correct values to a company. At the end of June 2016, when Li Wang decided to shift the focus of his work to 0Fenbeis, he established the company's basic values, which are righteousness (the morality), efficiency (the methodology), fun (the attitude toward work and life), and value creation (the goal).

Righteousness means never harming the interests of the poor households and the partners. Efficiency is to develop more products and services to enhance the effectiveness and accuracy of poverty alleviation. Fun is to make poverty alleviation an interesting thing, not a tough job. Value creation means the company provides information for both sides of supply and demand, solve the problem of information asymmetry in poverty alleviation, realize business value by serving the society, and maintain sustainable development of the company.

About "righteousness," Wang said, "we agreed to put righteousness as our first principle during our discussions. 'Righteousness' means we can never infringe the interests of any stakeholders, especially the poor people. We must not harm the interests of the poor or our partners for any purpose, such as profit or good reputation."

In Li Wang's view, there are contradictions between social value and commercial value, but they are not completely contradictory. "In fact, it's hard to distinguish between social value and commercial value. Sometimes, commercial value can become social value," he said. "The last thing we can afford to compromise is poverty alleviation. All the four things (the four products) we did are about poverty alleviation. The reason we developed the later three products is that after we finished the first product, we found that the supply was far from enough. We had to continue."

Improve the Organizational Structure

The source of the company's capital directly determines the leaders of the company, as well as the operation concept and overall route of the company. When 0Fenbei was just founded, Li Wang, an idealist who was passionate about poverty alleviation, held 85% of the total equities (partly on behalf of others), Jingping Yi 10% and Junsheng Ji 5% (see Fig. 5). In April 2017, the company adjusted its ownership structure according to each member's contribution. Li Wang held more than 60%

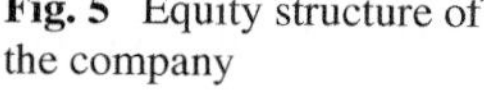
Fig. 5 Equity structure of the company

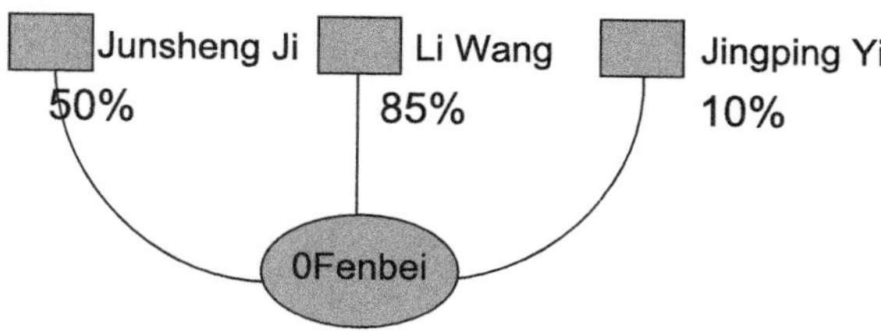

of the total equities and remained the actual controller of the company, leading the operation of the company.

Currently, there are six members in the founding team. Two of them are idealists passionate about poverty alleviation, and the other four are pragmatic realists. But concerning poverty alleviation, there are very few disagreements among the team members. As Li Wang said in an interview, "One of our team members and me are more of idealistic. We want to work on something with social values even though it makes less money. Others want to make more money, because people of our age don't have the concept or the social resources to do public welfare. Actually these two purposes are not contradictory. As long as a company can create social value, it can make money. They are inseparable. It is just this belief that unites us together to continue our business."

The company is very cautious about financing. In the early stage, they contacted some public welfare investment institutions, because they didn't want to introduce external capitals to influence their decision-making and the overall development direction of the company. However, public welfare investment is not practical enough. So it is not an ideal partner. The company plans to cooperate with commercial organizations in the future. Li Wang believes that commercial organizations recognize the 0Fenbei's business model, and understand its operation model. Therefore, it is easier to cooperate with commercial organizations. Even so, Li Wang said that their mission of poverty alleviation will not change.

Fruitful Achievements

Remarkable Achievements

The 0Fenbei Poverty Alleviation Matching Platform is the first product developed by the company, and also one of the most effective one of all its poverty alleviation products. In just three month after the platform went online, it was linked to more than 300 public welfare institutions and registered by more than 8000 local officials in Zhenxiong County, Yunnan Province.

Yinxia Wang, from Chahe Village, Chishuiyuan Town, is among the first poverty alleviation officials who registered on this platform. She entered basic information of herself and the poor households she's responsible for into the platform for a try. Only a week later, Yinxia Wang received a phone call from the platform, asking her to visit the poor households to reconfirm the information and take some photos of their actual living conditions to upload to the platform. Yinxia Wang came to Kaichao Luo's home to confirm the information, and helped them apply for three types of public welfare assistances including education, health care and medical assistance. After the reconfirmed information was approved, 0Fenbei sent a message to Yinxia Wang. Yinxia Wang followed the instructions in 0Fenbei's short message. She went to the county's Poverty Alleviation Office, got one-year living allowance of 1200 yuan for Kaichao Luo's family, and sent it to Kaichao Luo's home.

Runjiao Liu, a 20-year-old young woman from Gangou Village, Wude Town, Zhenxiong County, suffered from severe epilepsy for five years and was unable to live a normal life or go to school. After taking medicines for several years, she didn't get better at all. Her family used to live a decent life, but now it was heavily indebted. It was a typically example of returning to poverty due to illness. In August 2016, after learning about the situation, Xing Wu, who was responsible for this family, registered her information on the 0Fenbei Poverty Alleviation Matching Platform. Three months later, Xing Wu received short message from the platform and learned that a public welfare project of China Social Assistance Foundation called "Yinuoqianjin" could provide Runjiao Liu with free surgical treatment. Soon later, Runjiao Liu received operation in Tiantan Hospital and the lesion was removed successfully.

In December 2016, Phoenix TV's poverty alleviation program "Promise 2020" visited and interviewed a poor household that had been helped by 0Fenbei. The man lost his spouse in 2015. He had to take care of his daughter and son who were still young by himself. He could not leave them behind to work in cities. So he could only make some money by farming and doing some random jobs near the village. The family lived in extreme poverty. 0Fenbei raised education and living fund of 100 yuan per month for each of his two children through its "Wumeng Hope" project. During the interview, when the reporter asked about the children's study, pride appeared on the shy man's face. One of his children just got the best grade in the final exam (Fig. 6).

As of May 2017, 0Fenbei's poverty demand database and poverty supply database were large enough to cover most of the poor populations in Yunnan and Guizhou provinces. By data screening and analysis, in less than a year, 0Fenbei has helped more than 7,000 poor households (about 25,000 people) to connect to public welfare projects in medical, education, poverty alleviation and other areas, and more public welfare projects are being connected with poor households now. Currently, 0Fenbei

Fig. 6 Interview with a poor household by Phoenix TV

has built cooperation with Ordos Municipal Government in Inner Mongolia. Other municipal governments in Guangxi, Hebei, and Shaanxi have also expressed their willingness for cooperation with 0Fenbei.

Fenbeichou is the latest product developed by the company and also the most popular one. Poverty alleviation cadres only need to take about 10 min to fill in the information of the children of school-age in the poverty-stricken families they are responsible of with their mobile phones, and raise financial aid for them. This product went online for trial operation on March 21, 2017. In the first month after its launch, it received 110,000 hits, 6.6% of which turned into donations, and 3.9% repeated donations. This great achievement was made without any promotion.

Yutian Guan is among many children who received donations from Fenbeichou. She was born into a poor family in Zhenxiong County, Yunnan Province. When she was in the first grade, her mother died of illness, so she was forced to quit school because of poverty. The village's poverty alleviation cadres registered Yutian Guan's information in Fenbeichou's platform. And in just a few days, they successfully raised education and living fund of one whole year for her.

The donor left a message saying, "I have a daughter just like you. And today is her birthday. I hope you can receive as much love and blessings as possible as you grow up, and become a kind and generous girl who loves to study. No matter what your life is like, always try to read more books. Books can give you a different world."

Ms. Li is a cadre of the Disabled Persons' Federation of Zhenxiong County. Of all the poor families she helped, three of them had difficulties to support their children's education. When she learned that Fenbeichou could help these children, she immediately got the approval of their guardians and uploaded their information on the platform. Through her efforts, she helped them raise living fund of a year in only five days. In late May 2017, these children received education fund of 300 yuan for the first quarter of the year. The funds were received, managed and distributed by a public-raising foundation registered in the Civil Affairs Bureau, and directly transferred into their guardians' bank cards every quarter. After their families received funds, Ms. Li went to their families and passed the donors' messages to the children. Meanwhile, she updated the latest situation of the children and expressed their gratitude to the donors.

Through the efforts of more than 700 poverty alleviation cadres, more than 1000 children in Zhenxiong County received one-to-one donations from the individuals in just two months since the launch of Fenbeichou, which was worth more than 500,000 yuan in total. Some of these donations came from the circle of friends of poverty alleviation cadres, and some from people living in big cities thousands of miles away. More than half of the donors hope they can sponsor a child continuously.

For this innovative poverty alleviation model, Section Chief Jiang of Zhenxiong County Party Committee, who was responsible of eight poor households, said, "Poverty alleviation has always been my job. In the past there was not much I can do to help these poor households except filling in some forms. But now, I just need to take some photos and collect some information of these families, and then they can connect with the donors and get substantial aids. It is very convenient. And I feel that I am actually helping them, so I'm motivated too. Sometimes I don't have time to visit the children and take photos for them. Then I will ask my colleagues to help me do it, and feedback the children's latest information to the donors. These poor children are very lovely. Every time I visit them, they are shy. But I can tell that they are very happy because they know someone cares about them. In the past, when we visited the homes of the poor people, we weren't welcomed because they thought we weren't helping them. After we helped the poor children get education donations, the villagers' attitude to us is much better. I feel that my efforts not only brought money to the poor households, but also positive energy."

Innovation Changes the Society

0Fenbei's innovative model of targeted poverty alleviation through commercial operation also attracted the attention from all walks of life.

In May 2016, People's Daily published the first report on 0Fenbei. In August 1, 2016, Xinhua News Agency Kunming branch published a featured article entitled *Yunnan Zhenxiong: '0Fenbei' official account helps with targeted poverty alleviation.* The report said, "I didn't expect that an APP we use to chat with friends and colleagues and post photos could also be used on poverty alleviation."

Wang Hua, deputy director of Poverty Alleviation Office of Zhenxiong County, said, "as a network platform for targeted poverty alleviation, 0Fenbei effectively makes up where the government cannot cover and improves the investments, channels and strength of poverty alleviation."

In June 2017, China Poverty Alleviation published a featured article introducing Fenbeichou's innovative ways of poverty alleviation. Shengyun Pan, a local poverty alleviation cadre, commented on the Fenbeichou: "through Fenbeichou, the public can be "paired" with the poor students who are registered in the governments' poverty alleviation system and provide one-to-one educational support. It can greatly ease the financial burden of these poor households, and improve the living and educational conditions of the children."

That's exactly what 0Fenbei wants to do. 0Fenbei hopes to use Internet and big data technologies to help the poorest people in China and give them the opportunity to change their lives.

In order to recognize Li Wang's contribution in poverty alleviation, in October 2016, Yunnan provincial government awarded Li Wang "Innovation Award for Poverty Alleviation."

Three Major Challenges

The Profit Model Is Not Clear

At present, only the third one of the four products can bring in relatively stable cash flow, and the profit model of the fourth product is still under exploration. In the future, the first challenge faced by 0Fenbeis is to find the profit model as soon as possible and obtain stable profit. If it can't find a suitable profit model as soon as possible, the financial sustainability of the company will be affected, and even the future development of the company will be harmed.

Source of Data Is Uncertain

The second challenge for companies is the updating of poverty data. Now, the company mainly obtains the information of the poor households from local governments. On November 25, 2015, the central government held a poverty alleviation meeting, which stipulated that all poverty-stricken areas and the poor population must be lifted out of poverty in an all-round way by 2020. When the national poverty alleviation task is ended by 2020, the information source of the poor households will be another challenge for the company.

Increasingly Fierce Competition

The third challenge faced by the company is that more and more financial institutions begin to pay attention to the huge market of rural finance, so there are more and more competitors in this field. For example, CD Finance, a branch of the Poverty Alleviation Foundation, aims to provide service for new rural areas (new farmers), which is about 20% of the agricultural population. Although it serves the new farmers in rural areas, not the poor population, the space of rural financial market is definitely getting smaller in the future, and the competition is getting fiercer.

One year has passed since the foundation of 0Fenbei before everybody knew it. In response to the doubts about 0Fenbei's work on targeted poverty alleviation, Li Wang said, "I don't care what others think of me, I only care about the value we create. We created value not only for the poor, but also for the public welfare organizations. For example, our business more or less impacted the public welfare industry and accelerated its innovation and development. Through our efforts, 300,000 people in Yunnan Province got loans. This is great social value. We didn't help them by ourselves, but they got loans through our service, and the interest rate was very low. We also help a financial institution obtain 300,000 high growth users. We created value for all parties working with 0Fenbei."

Currently, the company aims to become “the most reliable information platform for poor households and the initiator of poverty alleviation projects.” In the future, 0Fenbei plans to develop some in-depth projects. Based on complete data, it will initiate some longer-term and in-depth projects, such as industrial poverty alleviation, e-commerce poverty alleviation, training on agriculture, forestry, and animal husbandry technologies, and migrant workers training. Ultimately, the company hopes to gather the power of government, social organizations, enterprises and individuals together to improve the efficiency of poverty alleviation and make substantial changes.

As a group of programmers, Li Wang and his team members hope they can continue this significant cause. They want to make their own contributions to the poor people, the public welfare industry, the government and the people around them as programmers, and make the world a better place. This is the ideal of these young programmers!

Further Reading

Center for Civil Society Studies, Peking University, Yunus Center for Social Business & Microfinance, Renmin University of China (2017) China Social Enterprise White Paper Project

Chen E, Dong J, Hou X (2017) A serious commitment, a historical leap. http://www.spp.gov.cn/zdgz/201705/t20170522_191128.shtml. Accessed 22 May 2017

China Talking, SETV (2017) Poverty eradication, a commitment of a nation. https://v.qq.com/x/page/c0504zt6m5n.html. Accessed 19 May 2017

0fenbei (2017) Fenbeichou, solving the big problem of poverty alleviation. WeChat official account: zhongguofupin, 2017-06-27

Laowang (2017) An idealistic story of a group of programmers. WeChat official account: nulishehui, 2017-04-07

Qin B (2017) New exploration on targeted poverty alleviation using big data technology. China Poverty Alleviation (14)

Xiaoping (2016) A group of programmers did a cool job. WeChat official account: nulishehui, 2016-05-22

Company Information

Fanfan (2017) He claims to be a villager, but he makes products that BAT can’t even imagine. http://mb.yidianzixun.com/article/0G6bQqB9?s=mb&appid=mibrowser. Accessed 13 Apr 2017

0Fenbei website: www.0Fenbei.com

0Fenbei WeChat official account

Fenbeichou WeChat official account

Tencent Foundation (2017) Fenbeichou: raise money only for the real poor. http://gongyi.qq.com/a/20170418/023275.htm. Accessed 18 Apr 2017

Zhang T (2016) 0Fenbei: targeted poverty alleviation by means of big data. http://epaper.21jingji.com/html/2016-09/08/content_46395.htm. Accessed 8 Sep 2016

Dream Cycling: Guardian of the Spiritual Journey

Jingyue Xu, Jianying Wang, and Yuyu Liu

> They struggle through the journey. Their buttocks are red, but they are singing happy songs. They are just like boiling teapots.
>
> —Shuhe Li, founder of Dream Cycling

Chengdu Dream Cycling Club (hereinafter referred to as "Dream Cycling") was founded in 2013 and registered as a non-profit organization in Chengdu Civil Affairs Bureau in April 2014. It is the only professional organization providing rescue and security services for travelers entering Tibet, and the first non-profit organization in China providing outdoor self-rescue and urban safe cycling training camp. From the beginning of its establishment, Dream Cycling defined itself as "the promoter of safe cycling and the guardian of Heaven Road," and set its main business as "providing outdoor self-rescue training, implementing rescue service, and issuing certificates and medals for cyclists entering Tibet." In the past four years since its establishment, Dream Cycling has trained and helped more than 10,000 cyclists reached Tibetan safely, provided direct security services for more than 100,000 Tibetan travelers, and carried out public welfare publicity to more than one million travelers. In addition, Dream Cycling has long been committed to organizing cyclists to participate in environmental protection, education and other public welfare activities, and has played an important role in strengthening the friendship between Han people and Tibetans and improving the cultural environment in Tibet. And all this started with the Sichuan-Tibet Highway, which is known as the "Landscape Avenue of Chinese People."

J. Xu (✉) · J. Wang · Y. Liu
Business School, Renmin University of China, Beijing, China
e-mail: xujingyue@rmbs.ruc.edu.cn

M. Zhao and J. Mao (eds.), *Social Entrepreneurship*,
https://doi.org/10.1007/978-981-15-9881-4_8

Where the Dream Began

Sichuan-Tibet Highway is the combined name of Chuankang highway and Kangzang highway, which was known as the ancient Tea-horse road in history. Built in 1930s, Chuankang highway was the interprovincial highway between Chengdu and Ya'an, the capital of Xikang province at that time. In 1951, the Kang Zang highway from Ya'an to Lhasa was built. After Xikang was withdrawn from the province, the two roads were collectively called Sichuan-Tibet Highway.

As a part of national highway 318, Sichuan-Tibet Highway has been given the name of the "Landscape Avenue of Chinese People" by Chinese National Geographic magazine. On both sides of this 2,154 km highway, there are 12 mountains over 4,000 meters high above sea level, including Dongda Mountain of 5,130 meters high and Mira Mountain of 5,013 meters high. Because of its special geographical location, this famous highway is surrounded by mountains and valleys, and countless scenery that are awesome, dangerous, unique, beautiful, grand and majestic. The landscape along the way is full of changes and surprises. Traveling along the way, you can experience "different weathers in different mountains, and four seasons in the same day." Therefore, this road is the first choice for all the outdoor sports lovers to travel to Tibet no matter by hiking, cycling or driving. It is also the best route to appreciate various natural landscapes in China, including glaciers, hot springs, snowy mountains and forest. However, Sichuan-Tibet Highway is also recognized as the most dangerous and difficult highway in China. It crosses the Hengduan Mountains in the east of the Qinghai Tibet Plateau. This mountain and canyon area has the most complex and unique topography in the world. Geographers from China and overseas call it "the road to death." When people travel on this road, they often have this feeling that "their souls are in heaven, but their bodies are in hell" (Fig. 1).

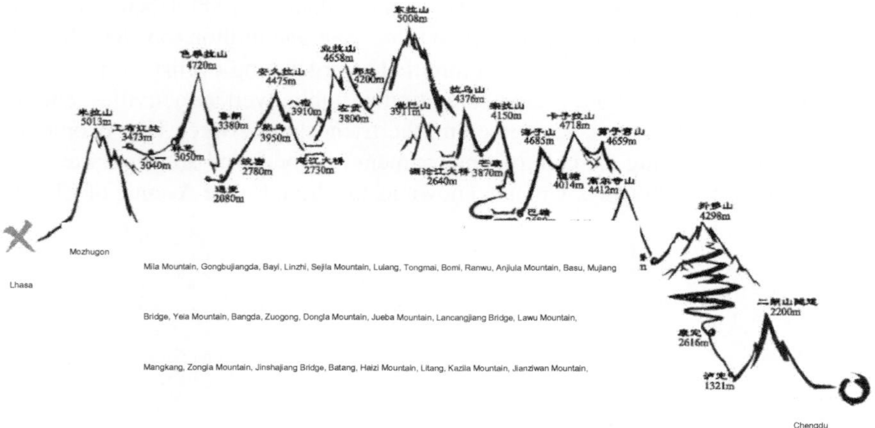

Fig. 1 Route from Chengdu to Lhasa (Photo provided by Dream Cycling)

Despite the difficulties and dangers in the road, the number of people who hike, cycle or drive into Tibet by Sichuan-Tibet Highway is still increasing every year. According to the data from Ganzi Tourism Bureau, Sichuan Minzu University and the inspection stations along the way, the number of cyclists was up to 250,000 in 2014 and 320,000 in 2015. The number dropped to 270,000 in 2016 because the road was destroyed in August. In 2017, the number was basically the same as that in 2016, but the total number of travelers entering Tibet by hiking, cycling and driving exceeded 2.8 million. With the rapid growth of the travelers, the problems of how to ensure the safety of travelers and protect the environment along the Sichuan-Tibet Highway has become increasingly prominent and even became social problems pending to be address.

However, this social problem can hardly be solved by government or commercial means. Because from the prospect of the government, Sichuan-Tibet Highway is 2,154 km long and runs through many administrative areas, and the range of each administration's authority is not very clear. Moreover, their administrative measures are not very effective. Therefore, it is difficult for the government to organize relevant resources to carry out effective road rescue and environmental protection measures. In addition, the governments at all levels undertake various functions and have many urgent issues to handle. They have very limited energy to take care of the travelers on Sichuan-Tibet Highway. From the commercial point of view, it is very difficult for a company to establish a commercial security and rescue system along the Sichuan-Tibet Highway, which can bring in enough profits to maintain its operation. Therefore, since the Sichuan-Tibet Highway was officially opened to traffic in 1954, hundreds of thousands of travelers are traveling through this road every year; there is still no commercial organization to solve this problem successfully. It can be said that the problems of safety rescue and environmental protection on Sichuan-Tibet Highway is a typical issue of government and market "double failure."

Of course, social problems of "double failure" are not completely unsolvable. In recent years, with the rapid development of economy and society, social enterprises that solve social problems through entrepreneurship are getting increasingly active around the world. Peter Drucker (2007), the master of management, predicted that "social enterprises adopt innovative ways to solve social problems of "double failures" of government and market. They will become an important force for future economic development, even the real growth force in the developed economic system in the post capitalist era." on Sichuan-Tibet Highway, Shuhe Li, a Chengdu native, and the Chengdu Dream Cycling club he founded demonstrate Drucker's prediction with their actions. It can be said that in the face of Sichuan-Tibet Highway that is both loved and hated by people, and that is full of beauty and danger, as well as opportunities and risks, Shuhe Li embarked his cause to solve the problems by means of social enterprise. His decision seems random, but actually it is inevitable.

Heading on the Road Alone

Born in a family whose parents are both geologists, Shuhe Li moved to different places since his childhood because his parents' work relocated all the time. He changed five schools during his six years of primary school, two schools during junior high school years and two schools during senior high school years. After graduating from University, Shuhe Li worked in China Inspection and Certification Group and Fuert Technology Service Co., Ltd. He was on business trip for about 290 days out of a year, feeling displaced. By and by, he began to desire for a stable life. In 2013, Shuhe Li felt lost about his work. He felt that he had to stop and gave a serious thought about what he really wanted to do.

In an interview, Shuhe Li said, "At that time I felt that I couldn't go on like this, so I asked for three months' leave. I wanted to go out and have a look. I wanted to know what it would be like if I'm not working. I wanted to challenge myself and think about what I should do next. I knew something about the Sichuan-Tibet Highway, so I wanted to see if I could do some stable jobs on Sichuan-Tibet Highway. I started off just one week after I made the decision."

Unfortunately, his partner changed his mind and quitted just before they were going to set out. He was all on himself. However, it did not stop him. He decided to start off by himself. That year, he was 33 years old.

Meting New Friends

Although he had no companion, there were a lot of other travelers on Sichuan-Tibet Highway. During his first 30 days of cycling from July 17 to August 15, 2013, Shuhe Li met many different people. There were energetic college students, successful business men who wanted to stop and think, people who wanted to adjust themselves for better development, and young people who want to prove themselves after graduating from high school. Shuhe Li found later that these people basically cover the main types of travelers on Sichuan-Tibet Highway. It complied with the result of customer type survey conducted by Dream Cycling.

During his travel on Sichuan-Tibet Highway with different kinds of people, Shuhe Li realized that cycling along the Sichuan-Tibet Highway plays different roles in the hearts of different people. It's the rite of passage for senior high school students, the training ground for confused people, and a reflection space for successful business men. Thus, he had a precise understanding of the people he would serve in the future and their needs, although he did not realize it at that time. Later, Dream Cycling defined its customers as three types: innocent young people who pursue the dream of entering Tibet; social backbones who meet setbacks in feelings or career and loves exploration; and elderly people who never give up. Although these people have different backgrounds, purposes and physical strength, they have one thing in common: they all want to pursue their dreams and prove themselves, and they all love cycling. They have the courage to challenge themselves and a strong sense of honor.

In addition to the different needs of these cyclists, Shuhe Li also found many problems among them. For example, they are not fully aware of the challenges on the road before they start off. They are not well prepared both psychologically or physically. They don't have the proper knowledge and ability in self-rescue and vehicle repair and maintenance. They don't have enough clothes with them for unpredictable weather, or enough supplies and regular medicines. For many people, cycling on Sichuan-Tibet Highway is an adventure. They exaggerate the romance of the adventure, but underestimate the hidden dangers and challenges on the road. However, according to his own experience, Shuhe Li believes that the first priority of cycling is safety. It must to be guaranteed. The cyclists can't deal with all these dangers and challenges on Sichuan-Tibet Highway by themselves.

Protecting Heaven Road

In addition to meeting various people, Shuhe Li also saw countless beautiful scenery that took his breath away during his 30 days' cycling. Out of his love for photography, he frequently stopped along the way to take photos. He took a large number of field photos. These photos became the first-hand materials for his training later. Besides the beautiful sceneries, Shuhe Li also encountered many landslides along the road. The journey is indeed a challenge for all the cyclists. In addition, he was deeply impressed by the wildness of Tibetan areas. People there had very limited resources of living materials and education (Fig. 2).

What bothered him most was the garbage along the way. Most of the garbage was water bottles everywhere. They ruined the beautiful sceneries along the Sichuan-Tibet Highway. No one reminded the cyclists to take away their own garbage. And nobody was organized to clean them up. There was basically nobody to maintain or manage the environment along the Sichuan-Tibet Highway. Just at that time, the idea of being the protector of Heaven Road was born in Shuhe Li's heart, because he loves this beautiful Heaven Road so much. In the interview, Shuhe Li said, "To tell the truth, I love this road. When I first walked on it, I fell in love with this beautiful road. There was a popular saying at that time, that if a man had never walked on this road, he would not be called a real man, because this road is so long, beautiful, and challenging. In 2006, Sichuan-Tibet Highway was granted with the name of the Most Beautiful Landscape Avenue in China by Chinese National Geographic magazine. We are obliged to protect this road and maintain its beauty. It is our responsibility."

Fig. 2 Beautiful sceneries along Sichuan-Tibet Highway (Photo provided by Dream Cycling)

Foundation of the Business

Beside all these dangers in the natural environment, there were also other risks along the Sichuan-Tibet Highway. Some of the hotels along the road were dishonest. The quality of accommodation was not guaranteed, and the food was poor and pricey. As a result, the cyclists could hardly get sufficient supplies or proper rest, which made their journey even more difficult, and degraded their overall experience. Recalling the situation at that time, Shuhe Li said, "Each year, from June to August, there were about 10,000 people cycling on the 2154 km Sichuan-Tibet Highway. (That was) a very big traffic volume. Can you imagine? These people's physical condition was not the same. Some people cycled fast and some very slowly. As a result, some people might not find any place to sleep at night. So what should they do? They could only ask those who rode faster to book rooms in advance, and give them a phone call after they got rooms. (Because) at that time, nobody played by rules. If you called the hotel to book a room, when you got there, nobody remembered your call. Why? Because who arrived there first, who got the room."

In addition to food and accommodation problems, sometimes roads would be blocked due to landslides and other reasons. Cyclists couldn't be informed in advance, and would only be left in anxiety and helplessness. Shuhe Li said, "We have encountered landslides during our journey. When we were halfway, Tongmai Bridge was broken. The price of goods along the road went up immediately. However, nobody knew the real condition of the road and when it would be back to traffic. There was no official information. Would it be back in a month, or ten days, or a week? Nobody knew. That was the situation (along the Sichuan-Tibet Highway at that time)."

What's more, when Shuhe Li and his partners arrived at the terminal after 30 days of arduous journey, the milestone marking the end of the Sichuan-Tibet Highway disappeared. This made them really upset. Taking photos besides the milestone had been the best way for the cyclists to prove that they have completed the Sichuan-Tibet Highway. It was the proof of their great courage and effort, and their great honor. Later, they learned that the milestone had been taken home by some cyclists as souvenir. Shuhe Li said that at that time, the four of them lied on the ground, totally disappointed and depressed. They talked about what they could do on Sichuan-Tibet Highway. One of them said he wanted to sell bicycle equipment. Another one said he wanted to open a Youth Hostel with standardized operation. And the third one said he wanted to sell Tibetan beads. We also asked Shuhe Li about his idea.

Shuhe Li said, "At that time, I didn't fully understand the concepts of profit-making and non-profit organizations. I replied: 'I heard there are non-profit organizations. I want to set up a non-profit organization. What shall I do? I will give trainings to people like us, and let them know more about the Sichuan-Tibet Highway. Secondly, I want to persuade Ping An of China to provide insurance for these people. Third, drinks are very expensive along the way. Sometimes there are even no drinks to buy. (Moreover,) a lot of water sources along the way are polluted and the level of metal is high. So I said I'm going to provide clean water and sports drinks to these people. And most importantly, when they have an accident, I will arrive at the scene quickly to rescue them. In addition, this is a fantastic and unforgettable journey. Only the warriors can accomplish this challenge. I want to design the Medal of Warrior for thousands of ordinary people like us to honor their great efforts.' The others all said that I must be mad. They said I couldn't do it, (because) the workload was too heavy; and that it was a mission impossible, especially for a non-profit organization. In a word, I was ridiculed and questioned."

When asked why he didn't give up even so, Shuhe Li said, "At that time, I came up with the idea of providing drinks, insurance, rescue and certification for the cyclists, and I wanted to establish a non-profit organization. The idea didn't just pop in my head. I had run many marathon games. When others were just running, I was thinking about how to operate a marathon game and how to get so many people to participate. I thought about borrowing the whole marathon operation system to Sichuan-Tibet Highway, including its operation, guarantee, publicity, and so on. I even thought about charging 50 yuan for each person just like a marathon. 2014 is the 60th anniversary of the Sichuan-Tibet Highway. People were traveling on the road since the 1980s, but the problems on the road had never been solved. What was the reason for that? I hoped I could solve them, even though I hadn't accounted the cost."

Guardian on Sichuan-Tibet Highway

Dream Cycling decided to enter this blank market due to its wish to guard the beautiful Heaven Road, as well as help hundreds of thousands of cyclists on Sichuan-Tibet Highway. However, how to turn a good wish into action and carry it on? Where to start? Where to get the resources required? Everything seems far beyond the ability of one person. However, Shuhe Li didn't give up.

Designing the Medal and Pamphlet

On August 17, 2013, Shuhe Li returned to Chengdu and started to set up the non-profit organization providing Sichuan-Tibet Highway rescue service immediately. He decided to begin with the designing and production of the medal first. When asked why he chose to begin with medals first, Shuhe Li explained: "It's very rare for ordinary citizens to win rewards or social recognition (of high level). For example, "May 1st Labor Medal," "March 8th Red Flag Bearer" and "May 4th Youth Medal." Very few people can be awarded with such medals. We just want to give these people a chance to win honor and recognition through their own efforts to enhance their sense of honor. Therefore, we want to help them realize their dreams in this way. There has never been such an organization or commercial enterprises along this road before. We are the first organization that can record the whole process of their hard journey. This medal is like a certification, which can make people proud."

The friends he knew from Sichuan-Tibet Highway helped him with the designing and making of the medals. He said, "I spent four months looking up historical materials and designing the medal. The friends that I knew from the journey contributed a lot too. Some of them were working in the industries of designing, manufacture, and painting. They helped me design the medals. And some worked in the library. They helped to look up the historical information about Sichuan-Tibet Highway."

Then how to persuade these people to help design the medal? Shuhe Li said, "When I decided to do this, these people's faces just appeared in my mind. This person could design, and that person could paint, although I had never talked about it with them when we were on Sichuan-Tibet Highway… First, I called the designer and said, "I want to do this, but I don't have much money. Can you help me with the designing?" She said my idea about giving medals made sense. She could help me, only if she could get the first medal. Just like that, she helped me with the design. When the first batch of medals was made, everybody participated were deeply moved, because the medals reminded them of the difficulties they experienced during the journey. This medal was the proof of their honor and dream. I still remember this girl named Yanqi Xu. At that time, she was still a college student of Sichuan Academy of Fine Arts. She was one of the major creators of the TV series *Galsang Flower Along the Way*. Now she is learning in Japan. She said, 'when I got the medal, my heart was pounding. My aunt read the words on the medal slowly - 2,154 km long and 5,130 meters high. Each drop of sweat and smile of yours, Sichuan-Tibet Highway never forgets. My tears rushed out immediately. Only those who have completed the journey can understand it!'"

There are two kinds of medals: one is the Medal of Warrior, the other is the Medal of Galsang Flower. Cyclists, who cycled all the way to the terminal without taking any vehicles, are real warriors. Besides getting the Medal of Galsang Flower, they are also awarded the Medal of Warrior. Those who accomplished the journey with the aid of other transportation tools for some reasons were awarded the Medal of Galsang Flower. For them, the Sichuan-Tibet Highway is a big challenge. It takes great courage to step on the road to Tibet. The journey is very tough, so they should be rewarded. In order to distinguish these two types of winners, Shuhe Li designed the pamphlets in traditional style. There are nine historical and cultural relics along Sichuan-Tibet Highway. The cyclists must arrive all of them and collect a stamp from each site. At the terminal, only those get all the nine stamps on their cards can be granted with the Medal of Warrior.

The design of the medals is exquisite and the making is excellent. This owes to the support of his brother, who specializes in numerical control milling machine. With this special technical support, their medals cannot be imitated by anybody. Currently, they have applied for patent protection. Shuhe Li believed that their medals and pamphlets both represent the highest honor of the cyclists on Sichuan-Tibet Highway. Therefore, they are also Dream Cycling's biggest competitive advantage (Fig. 3).

Establishing Service Stations and Rescue Teams

Service stations and rescue teams are the foundation of the business operation. Shuhe Li was clear from the beginning that these must be achieved by means of cooperation, instead of him. Therefore, Dream Cycling cooperates with the existing inns along the Sichuan-Tibet Highway. These inns became his service stations, and their staff work as part-time rescuers for him. In order to ensure the stability of these service stations and rescue teams, as well as to contribute to the economic development of Tibetan area, Dream Cycling prefers to cooperate with the inns run by the local Tibetans. These service stations have the following functions: first, providing paid food and accommodation for the cyclists; second, providing free functional drinks for the cyclists who bring their own bottles, to encourage cyclists to bring back their own garbage; third, cleaning the garbage and protecting the natural environment along the Sichuan-Tibet Highway; fourth, providing rescue service when there is an accidents.

In return, Dream Cycling can bring more stable customers to the service stations, and the rescuers will be paid for each rescue. Dream Cycling does not provide

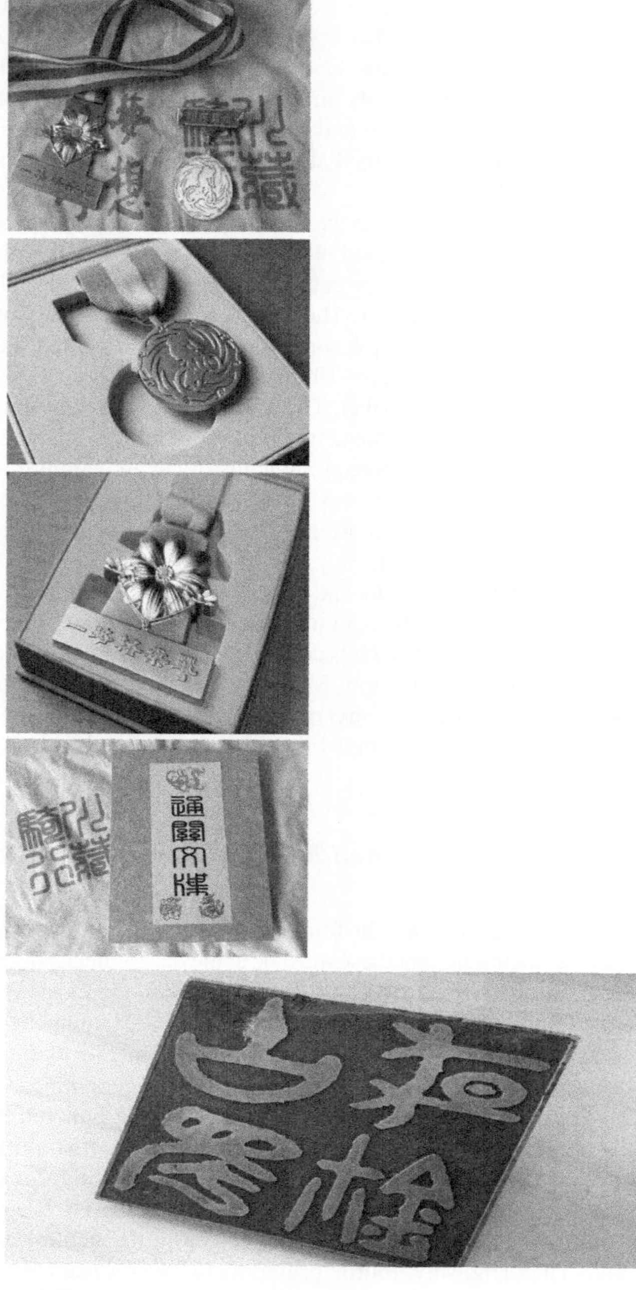

Fig. 3 Medals, pamphlets and certificates (Photo provided by Dream Cycling)

other financial support for these service stations. However, in order to reward the service stations and improve their service, Dream Cycling invites the operators of all the service stations to Chengdu for a three-day training every year. The training content includes hotel management and rescue skills. The trainings are carried out by the strategic partners of Dream Cycling, including International Youth Hostel, mountain rescue teams and cooperative hospitals. These trainings can help the service station operators to improve their rescue skills, as well as their service concept and management level. In addition, during daily operation, the service stations can also receive free consulting services from the International Youth Hostel.

In the aspect of rescue team construction, Dream Cycling cooperates with the Communist Youth League along the road to provide targeted training to the rescuers, to improve their overall quality and rescue skills. In addition to providing training to the rescuers at the service stations and their own volunteer teams, the Communist Youth League can also provide some financial support for the rescuers. Thus, it helps to form and expand a group of professional and stable rescue teams, and improves their capabilities. When an accident happens, the Communist Youth League can call on rescue teams and act in short time, which supplements the rescue capacity of the service stations. In addition, Dream Cycling also cooperates with the Communist Youth League to clean up the garbage on Sichuan-Tibet Highway on a regular basis, to protect the beautiful Heaven Road together.

In addition to the service stations, Dream Cycling prepares four shuttle rescue vehicles on Sichuan-Tibet Highway, equipped with medical staff, medical equipment and medicine. The rescue vehicles can provide riding service for the exhausted cyclists, and can also provide functional drinks for cyclists at any time. Only the drivers and a small number of assistants on the rescue vehicles are from Dream Cycling. All the medical staff is volunteers from Chengdu or the hospitals along the road. The medical bags for the cyclist and the medicine on the rescue vehicles are all donated by these cooperative hospitals. When talking about the cooperation with the hospital, Shuhe Li said, "Rescue needs medicine, as well as professional support from the doctors and nurses. At the beginning, I asked my friends for help, but it was not a long-term solution. Then I contacted the hospitals. The first one is Ping'an Hospital in Chengdu (Fig. 4). They are very good at orthopaedics. Later, I contacted many other hospitals. I found that many hospitals are willing to do public welfare. Currently, we have established cooperative relations with 12 hospitals. This medical system is still expanding, and is joined by many hospitals along the Sichuan-Tibet Highway."

Meeting All Material Needs Through Public Welfare Donation

One of the important strategies of the Dream Cycling is to meet all material needs by means of public donation. Currently, except for a small number of assistants on the rescue vehicles and some staff in the offices, all the professional personnel and materials are from public donations (see Table 1). Medical rescue teams, medicines,

Fig. 4 The operator of the service station became a member of the professional rescue team (Guofu Liang, owner of Litang Guofu Youth Hostel) (Photo provided by Dream Cycling)

Table 1 Public donation categories and cooperative organizations

Donation categories	Materials donated/professional support	Cooperative organizations
Medical supplies and capabilities	Free medicine packages	Cooperative hospitals
	Medical equipment in ambulances	
	Doctors and nurses in ambulances	
Clothing	Staff's clothing, raincoats, etc.	Hylaeion Outdoor Supplies, Hillcrest, Jeep Xtreme Performance, Shengyulan Outdoor Supplies
Insurance	Accident insurance of 1.5 million yuan for 100,000 person times	Ping An Insurance, Guangdong Yuhua Extreme Sports Aid Foundation
Vehicles	Four shuttle rescue vehicles and three other vehicles	Jeep, Ford, PetroChina, etc.
	Gasoline cost of the vehicles	
Functional drinks	Hi-Tiger functional drinks and food	Dali group
Training service	Training on inn management	International Youth Hostel
	Training before setting out	Cooperative hospitals
Volunteer services	Rescue volunteers and environmental protection volunteers	Provincial committees of the Communist Youth League and local government departments
Navigation system	1,000 navigators	Jiuzhou Beidou Group
	A set of monitoring system	

Source of information Surveys and interviews, as of October 2017

functional drinks, insurance, rescue vehicles, rescue equipment, and even the Beidou navigator provided to each cyclist and the monitoring system are all from public donation. Shuhe Li said, "Our mission is to serve all the travelers to Tibet, and the majority of this group is not very rich, so our charge is very low, only 298 yuan. This includes training before setting out, insurance, free medicines, raincoat, functional drinks and 26 days of rescue service. This price is far lower than the total operating cost. So we must obtain the materials through public donation. Of course, for some high-end customers who require full-time escort, the charge will be higher. But most of the customers are ordinary customers, and the charges are very low."

As for the reason why these enterprises are willing to donate to Dream Cycling, Shuhe Li thinks that's because many enterprises and even some institutions (such as hospitals) have a strong sense of social responsibility and are willing to support public welfare activities. Of course, that doesn't mean that all of them will donate to Dream Cycling, because they have many other choices. According to Shuhe Li, the main reason why these enterprises choose Dream Cycling is that they recognize its mission of "protecting the Heaven Road and saving lives." Another reason is that they believe making donations to Dream Cycling helps them to build the positive image of corporations with social responsibility. In addition, Shuhe Li thinks that another important reason that it can win the trust of the sponsors and get long-term support from them is that Dream Cycling can take the initiative to communication with them and submit reports on the latest news of Dream Cycling and the use of donated materials regularly to the donors.[1]

Establishing Strategic Partnership

The cooperation between Dream Cycling and its sponsors is not one-off, but a more stable strategic partnership, which has gradually become a strategic alliance system. And this alliance system is expanding with the development of Dream Cycling. As mentioned above, the number of hospitals cooperating with Dream Cycling has increased from 1 to 12, and it is likely to keep on growing. The same is true for the cooperation between Dream Cycling and Ping An Insurance LTD. At first, Ping An provided 3-month insurance worth 150,000 yuan in total for Dream Cycling, charging 10 yuan for each person. While in 2017, it provided five-year free insurance with the insurance amount of 1.5 million yuan per person for 100,000 persons. In addition, Ping An Insurance also provided team building funds for Dream Cycling. Through this cooperation, Ping An Insurance can obtain 100,000 valid customers. It is a sustainable win-win partnership.

The cooperation between Dream Cycling and Jiuzhou Beidou Group is another typical example. The navigators and monitoring system of Jiuzhou Beidou Group is

[1]Dream Cycling was approved to issue donation invoices after three months since its foundation in 2014. Currently, only five non-profit organizations in Chengdu have such qualifications. This is also one of the reasons why these enterprises are willing to sponsor it.

a satellite based navigation and positioning system with advanced technology and wide coverage. As a military enterprise, Jiuzhou Beidou Group began to explore its development in the field of civil application in recent years. It had been looking for suitable partners and channels for its transformation from military to civil application. On the other hand, it has been a headache for Dream Cycling to find a stable and reliable navigation and positioning system. Without the navigation and positioning system, the rescue action can only be initiated after the accident happens. Moreover, communication on Sichuan-Tibet Highway is usually very weak. And road signs are not available at the site of the accident. Problems like these have also brought great difficulties to the rescue. It can be said that because there is no navigation and positioning system, the rescue on the way to Tibet has been in a very primitive state.

Accidentally, Jiuzhou Beidou Group got in touch with the dream of riding, and the two sides established a formal cooperative relationship in March 2017, immediately after they learned about each other's demands. According to the agreement, Jiuzhou Beidou Group provides 1,000 navigators and one set of monitoring system, which worth more than two million yuan in total, to Dream Cycling free of charge. In return, Dream Cycling is responsible for trial use, display and promotion of the products. It also helps to improve the map along the Sichuan-Tibet Highway for Jiuzhou Beidou, adding the location of hospitals, clinics and medical vehicles into the map and the monitoring system.

With this rescue system, Dream Cycling is like a bird with wings that can overlook the routes around Sichuan-Tibet Highway freely from above. Because each cyclist is equipped with a Beidou positioning and communication (SMS + voice) device, the monitoring personnel of Dream Cycling can see the location of them through the monitoring platform. It can also delimit dangerous areas with electronic fences and send early warnings. Since it can receive feedback from the cyclists in real time, dream cyclists can learn about the rescue needs and organize rescue in the first time. For cyclists, they can use this device to contact the monitoring personnel any time they want, which greatly improves their sense of safety and riding experience. It is worth mentioning that Beidou navigation system is based on the Map World geography database platform, so its accuracy is very high—the error range is only 10 meters. In case of emergency, the rescuers can find the site of the emergency in short time. It is just like that the Beidou navigation system gives a pair of magic eyes to Dream Cycling, as well as the most effective security guarantee for cyclists. Currently, Jiuzhou Beidou Group has established exclusive strategic partnership with Dream Cycling on its positioning and navigation system (Fig. 5).

Besides Ping An and Jiuzhou Beidou, Dream Cycling also has a lot of other strategic partners, including hospitals, government departments along the road, and sponsors of vehicles, clothing, functional drink, etc. Shuhe Li believes that expanding strategic partners and maintaining a stable cooperative relationship with them are the fundamental guarantee for the implementation of its strategy. When asked how to expand the strategic partnership, Shuhe Li said, "Before you anything, you should always consider the needs of the related stakeholders first. Only when we can think from their perspective can we establish a sustainable cooperative relationship with them and achieve win-win results."

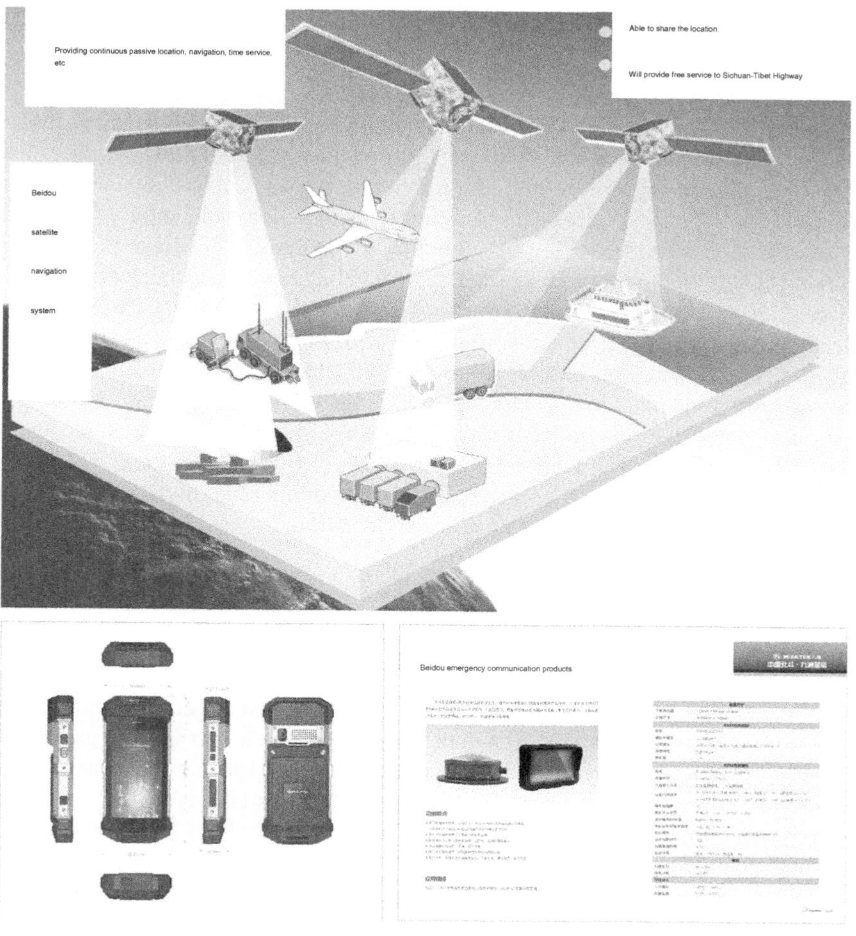

Fig. 5 Beidou satellite navigation system and navigator (Photo provided by Dream Cycling)

In order to maintain healthy strategic partnership, Shuhe Li pay special attention to maintaining proactive communication with the partners. He said, "we pay regular return visits to our sponsors, and issue regular (influence) reports to inform them what we have done recently and how do we improve the influence of their enterprise and institution."

Stepping to Standard Commercial Operation

In the past four years since its establishment, Dream Cycling has established an all-rounded offline rescue and guarantee system along the Sichuan-Tibet Highway, including 25 service stations which can provide accommodation, catering and supplies, 25 bicycle repair stations, 13 vehicle repair stations, 56 container service stations, 10 free supply stations, 12 county hospital medical support stations, four shuttle service vehicles, and one Beidou navigation full coverage positioning command center. In the past four years, Dream Cycling has also won a lot of honors, including "Top 100 Social Innovation Projects" by the 4th China Charity Fare, "Excellent Award" for the public welfare short videos by the Public Welfare Video Festival, "Top 10 Excellent Exhibitors" by the 4th Charity Exhibition, and "Top 20 Most Valuable Organizations to Donate" by Mingshan Public Welfare. Its unique "Four ones" public welfare project won the "Chuangqi Jiujiu Innovation Star" award from the British Council in China. However, Shuhe Li won't stop there. He hopes Dream Cycling can operate in a more standardized commercial model, to send it on the right track for healthy and sustainable development.

Standardizing the Business Procedures

Currently, Dream Cycling's major business is to provide rescue services and related supports on Sichuan-Tibet Highway. Other businesses include carrying out green and safe urban cycling activities, providing security service for sports events, etc. Shuhe Li believes for every business, standard procedure is the foundation for good customer service. Therefore, in the past four years, Dream Cycling has been summarizing and improving its operation procedures. Currently, it has formed a relatively clear and complete procedure and regulation system. Taking its main business of rescue service for an example, the operation procedure includes three phases: before the journey, during the journey and after the journey. Each phase has detailed procedures and service rules. Briefly, it includes the following contents:

(1) Before the journey

- Provide free travel training (updated constantly), physical tests, blood pressure and heart rate test for all the travelers to ensure that they are fully prepared before setting out.
- Provide high-quality raincoats for the travelers to cope with the changeable climate in Tibet. Provide free drugs of altitude sickness for the travelers to ease their altitude sickness.
- Make exquisite pamphlets to record their journey. Nine historical and cultural sites along the way to Tibet were printed on the pamphlets. Staff at Dream Cycling service stations chops artistic seals on these pamphlets, which adds humanistic value to them.

- Print the contact information of all the service stations and Safety Manuals for the travelers, so that they can contact the nearest service station when they need help.
- Provide five years of free insurance of China Ping An worth 1.5 million yuan in total to the travelers, which covers medical treatment for accidental disability and injury, plateau insurance, medical transportation, relatives' visit compensation, third party liability, etc.

(2) During the journey

- 25 service stations provide accommodation reservation, catering allowances, online payment and other services to the travelers, allowing them to have a comfortable and clean environment to rest. In addition, these 25 service stations also provide energy drinks every day to support these travelers to complete their challenge.
- Service stations' rescue vehicles and Dream Cycling's shuttle rescue vehicles provide 24-hour road rescue and can arrive at the site of the accident within one hour after receiving the request for rescue. 12 hospitals provide emergency medical services at any time. The shuttle rescue vehicles provide energy drinks to the travelers free of charge.
- Interact with the travelers on WeChat at real-time. Opened dream ride service account on WeChat and assigned dedicated responsible person to provide real-time information of road conditions, weather forecast, accommodation booking, supervision and customer complaints, early warning of dangerous road sections and other practical services for the travelers.

(3) After the journey

- Dream Cycling rewards a certificate and a Medal of Galsang Flower to all the cyclists who finish their journey to Tibet in Lhasa, to honor their achievement.
- For those who cycle all the way to the terminal without taking any other vehicles, it will also award them a Medal of Warrior and a Medal of Galsang Flower, to honor their courage and persistence.

Realizing Financial Self-reliance

For entrepreneurs, cash flow is always the problem. Dream Cycling is no exception. The start-up fund of Dream Cycling comes from Shuhe Li's personal savings, as well as his friends' investment, totaling 600,000 yuan. With the development of the company, its demand for capital also grows. Dream Cycling has encountered many financial difficulties. Shuhe Li recalled and said, "We did meet many problems during the implementation of this project. Many friends and organizations have given me a lot of support when they learned that we had difficulties to run the business because of financial pressures. At the toughest time, I even had my property mortgaged. My family turned against me because of this. They didn't understand what I was doing.

I told them I wanted to find out what I'm doing when I'm still young. Although I'm not sure what it will turn out to be, I know that I have worked hard for it. Even if I might fail one day, I won't regret."

It is grateful that after four years of operation, Dream Cycling has achieved financial balance. Currently, there are mainly five sources of revenue:

- Basic service fees for travelers cycling along Sichuan-Tibet Highway, including the full service before, during and after the journey, which is 298 yuan per person.
- Organizational fees charged on organizations for the green and safe urban cycling activities, which is 100,000 yuan every time, for about six times a year.
- Funds from public welfare donations, such as the funds from Beijing Aiyou Foundation of 100,000–300,000 yuan per year.
- Fees charged for providing security services for sports events or leasing equipment.
- Advertising charges on rescue vehicles, containers, etc.

Although its revenue is not very high, it is enough to support the sustainable operation of the company. This is because all the personnel are part-time and all the materials are sponsored. So the only expenses need to be covered by the company are its daily operating expenses, the costs of medals and pamphlets, and part of the rescue costs. It can be said that Dream Cycling is self-reliance. It has achieved financial balance and built a good foundation for its further development.

Of course, that doesn't mean the road ahead is all clear. With the expansion of its business, the shortage in personnel is worsening. Currently, the company has a total of 12 personnel, who are all overworking, especially in the peak season. Shuhe Li thinks it is unacceptable to exploit employees especially in public welfare industry. The company must recruit more employs. He hopes to support its business growth by improving its profitability.

Launching "Joint Brand" Products

In October 2017, Dream Cycling took some new measures by expanding its revenue sources and marketing channels. The first breakthrough it has achieved by now is to launch "joint brand" products by cooperating with outdoor sports brands and establish a marketing linkage mechanism. Its first partner is Hylaeion Outdoor Supplies, an outdoor supplier in Guangdong Province that has supported Dream Cycling for four years. Although it is a local brand in Guangdong Province, it has more than 450 stores in China. Shuhe Li said, "I talked with them to see if we can launch a joint brand. For example, we can put the logo of Dream Cycling on their T-shirts and storm suits, and sell them in their stores. The original price of a coat is 600 yuan. After adding our logo, the price will still be 600 yuan. But if people buy the clothes with our logo, they can enjoy our service for Sichuan-Tibet Highway worth 298 yuan. That is to say, customers can get our basic services free of charge if they buy our product."

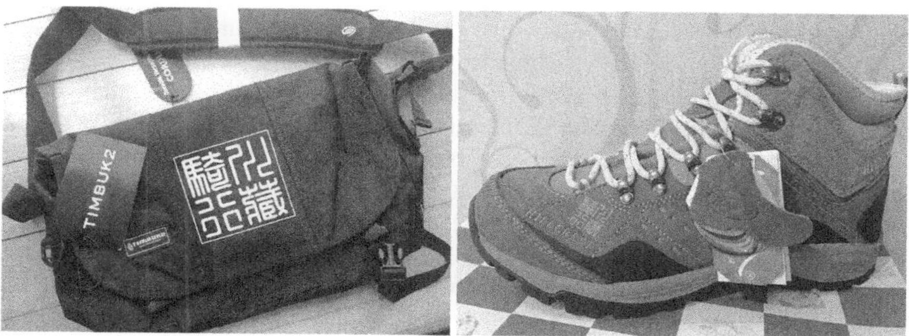

Fig. 6 Some of Dream Cycling's co-branding products (Photo provided by Dream Cycling)

According to the agreement, Hylaeion will pay 298 yuan to Dream Cycling out of the 600 yuan, and will provide the sales data to Dream Cycling. Then Dream Cycling will issue a donation invoice to Hylaeion, which can be used for tax deduction. Through this operation model, Hylaeion can increase its sales without using additional resources or investments. For Dream Cycling, this operation model can bring in more revenues, and expand its marketing channel at the same time. Dream Cycling used to spend a lot of energy on marketing. Through this cooperation, Dream Cycling can focus on providing services for cyclists on Sichuan-Tibet Highway. In addition, with the help of the sales data, Dream Cycling can predict the number of people heading out to the Sichuan-Tibet Highway. By far, Dream Cycling has released co-branding storm suits with Hylaeion, outdoor shoes with Hillcrest, and outdoor bags with UTC (a sub brand of Swiss Army). In the future, Dream Cycling will also develop more co-branding commodities, such as bicycles, goggles, helmets, etc. (Fig. 6).

Public Welfare Footprints

Dream Cycling has become a successful social enterprise because of its contributions in social activities, including providing cyclists with outdoor self-rescue training, implementing rescue, issuing certificates and medals to the cyclists, and its long-term commitment to organizing the cyclists in Tibet to participate in public welfare activities in environmental protection and education. It is the promoter and practitioner of protecting the Heaven Road and safe riding, the promoter and practitioner of environmental protection and green riding, the promoter of Han-Tibetan Friendship, and the improver of the cultural environment in Tibet.

In the past four years since its establishment, Dream Cycling has carried out a series of public welfare activities, including: building 81 service stations along Sichuan-Tibet Highway and Xinjiang-Tibet highway; carrying out the "Four ones" public welfare project and setting up vertical publication stations for green and safe cycling with 127 universities across the country; working with 100 Youth Hostels to set up Dream Cycling bulletin boards; working with ALI Tourism Development Committee of Tibet and responsible for the design and planning of Xinjiang-Tibet cycling campaign; working with the Communist Youth League of Ganzi Prefecture to establish the "Youth of Holy Land" bookstore to connect Han and Tibetan young people; working with the most influential event on Sichuan-Tibet Highway "Tibet Challenge" to build a professional cycling service platform for Tibet.

Among them, the "Four ones" public welfare project initiated by Dream Cycling is a typical project aiming to "transfer the friendship between Han and Tibet, improve the cultural environment of Tibet," which has won the "Chuangqi Jiujiu Innovation Star Award" of the British Council in China. The purpose of the project is to advocate the public welfare concept of "I serve everybody, and everybody serves others as they can," to make the public welfare simple and practical for everybody. This typical project demonstrates Dream Cycling's enthusiasm and devotion for public welfare. The "Four ones" advocated by the project refer to:

- One dream of arriving at Lhasa successfully: Dream Cycling helps every cyclist realize their dream of cycling to Tibet, and encourages people to start off to find the pure land they dreamed of.
- One kilogram of teaching materials: Dream Cycling invites every cyclist to be the dream postman, and deliver one kilogram of teaching materials to primary schools that are in need of them in Tibet.
- One outdoor interest class: Dream Cycling encourages every cyclist to give an outdoor interest class to the children after they deliver the materials to schools in Tibet. The class can be PE, martial arts, football, handicraft, art, music, etc.
- One kilogram of garbage: Dream Cycling requires cyclists to pick up one kilogram of non-degradable garbage and send it to Dream Cycling's service stations for disposal by reusing the package bags of the teaching materials (Fig. 7).

Heading Towards a More Beautiful Landscape

After more than four years of development, Dream Cycling has made great achievement. But there are also some challenges. According to Shuhe Li, the challenges mainly come from the following four aspects:

(1) Inadequate government recognition and support

Government recognition and support are indispensable for the development of social enterprises. However, government departments will not take the risk to recognize organizations like Dream Cycling easily. Dream Cycling still needs to prove its determination and ability by time and word-of-mouth. By now, Dream Cycling has won the recognition and support from some local Communist Youth League and local government along the way. But it is not enough.

(2) Large time and labor cost required for the expansion of public welfare donation and communication with the donors.

Fig. 7 "Four ones" public welfare project (Photo provided by Dream Cycling)

To support its high operating cost, as well as ensure its social goals of saving lives and providing social services, Dream Cycling must rely on public donations to support the operation. Therefore, Dream Cycling needs maintain its channel to obtain continuous donations. Moreover, it needs to establish long-term strategic alliances with more partners to serve more people. It takes a lot of time and manpower to communicate with public welfare organizations. Currently, this task is carried out the founder Shuhe Li, and he often feels short of time and energy.

(3) Lack of funds for continuous development

When Dream Cycling was initially founded, it mainly relied on Shuhe Li's savings and the funding of 600,000 yuan donated by five of his friends (30,000 yuan each) as the start-up fund. They registered non-profit organizations in Chengdu Civil Affairs Bureau. Later, Shuhe Li had his house mortgaged and borrowed money from the bank for the development of the enterprise. Currently, all the materials are provided by its sponsors. And its cash revenue mainly comes from its service income, small amount of subsidies from foundations and cash donations from enterprises. Shuhe Li said that the biggest cost of Dream Cycling is the cost of medals, the salary of its personnel, the subsidy for shuttle rescue vehicle drivers, and the cost of food and accommodation for the volunteers. Its service revenue can cover these expenses above, but not enough for its rapid business development.

(4) Low stability and ability of personnel

Shuhe Li thinks that the biggest problem at present is about the personnel. Both its stability and capability level has space for improvement. To ensure the stability of the personnel, Dream Cycling provides competitive salaries. The basic salary is 5,000 yuan, with complete social insurance, housing subsidies and free lunch. In addition, employees can also enjoy one and a half months' paid vacation during the Spring Festival. However, it is still difficult to maintain a stable team. Employees always have higher expectations. Back in the earlier years of Dream Cycling, once the employees asked for a raise of salary all together. According to Shuhe Li, that event almost bankrupted the company. As for the improvement of employees' ability, it requires continuous training, where Aiyou Charity Foundation can provide some help. At present, Dream Cycling is an "Aiyou + Maker" partner of Aiyou Foundation, so it can get Aiyou's support in training and capital resources, including the training for its employees. This is the largest and most effective support from the Foundation.

When asked if he could use ideals and values to inspire the employees, Shuhe Li said, "I see employees as my partners, so I often discuss work progress with them. Ideals and values were conveyed to them during these discussions. But I don't think it is enough. I must provide them with satisfying salaries and development opportunities too. They are the preconditions for ideals and values."

In spite of all these challenges, Shuhe Li said that Dream Cycling will keep on pursuing its dream. Dream Cycling defines its long-term vision as "building the largest safe cycling platform in China based on Beidou Navigation and Positioning System," and the short-term goal as expanding business to Xinjiang-Tibet line and Yunnan-Tibet line. At present, Dream Cycling has started to expand its business in Xinjiang-Tibet line in cooperation with ALI local government. In 2017, it served more than 3,000 travelers on Xinjiang-Tibet line, covering half of the total travelers. Yunnan-Tibet line is a big challenge, so the business hasn't began yet. In the future, Dream Cycling hopes to cover more travelers with its services, including rescue, monitoring, real-time rescue scheduling, etc. At that time, Dream Cycling will adopt an open way to cooperate with more cycling clubs or local governments, and output its management mode and provide technical support, as well as become an agent of Beidou Navigator and Monitoring System, to build a more mature business model through the expansion of these businesses. In the interview, Shuhe Li said, "I hope that one day someone can remember what we are doing. When the platform is built, our ability will be greatly improved and the rescue business will expand a lot. We can also provide security service for outdoor projects. In a word, there will be more business opportunities, including becoming the agent of Jiuzhou Beidou products. I also hope to improve the business value of our company. Ideal and spirits alone won't support the company."

When talking about his expectation for the future, Shuhe Li said, "My personal idea is to allow more people to travel safer on this road. Let the cyclists love traveling along the Sichuan-Tibet Highway. Let more local residents open inns for the travelers and improve the employment rate. Advocate environmental protection and keep the road clean and beautiful to attract more people, so as to change the industry. In the future, when people talk about traveling on this road, they'll remember that some man (Shuhe Li) has made his contributions!"

Company Information

Sina blog: Chengdu Dream Cycling Club, serving dream. http://blog.sina.com.cn/u/5223358186. Accessed 23 July 2014

Sina blog: Dream Cycling's Blog. http://blog.sina.com.cn/u/5223358186

Sina Weibo: Dream Cycling. https://weibo.com/u/5223358186?is_hot=1

DreamCycling (2017) Dream Cycling rescued a man in his 50s who suffered from altitude sickness in a rainy night. Sohu. http://www.sohu.com/a/138759214_492578. Accessed 5 May 2017

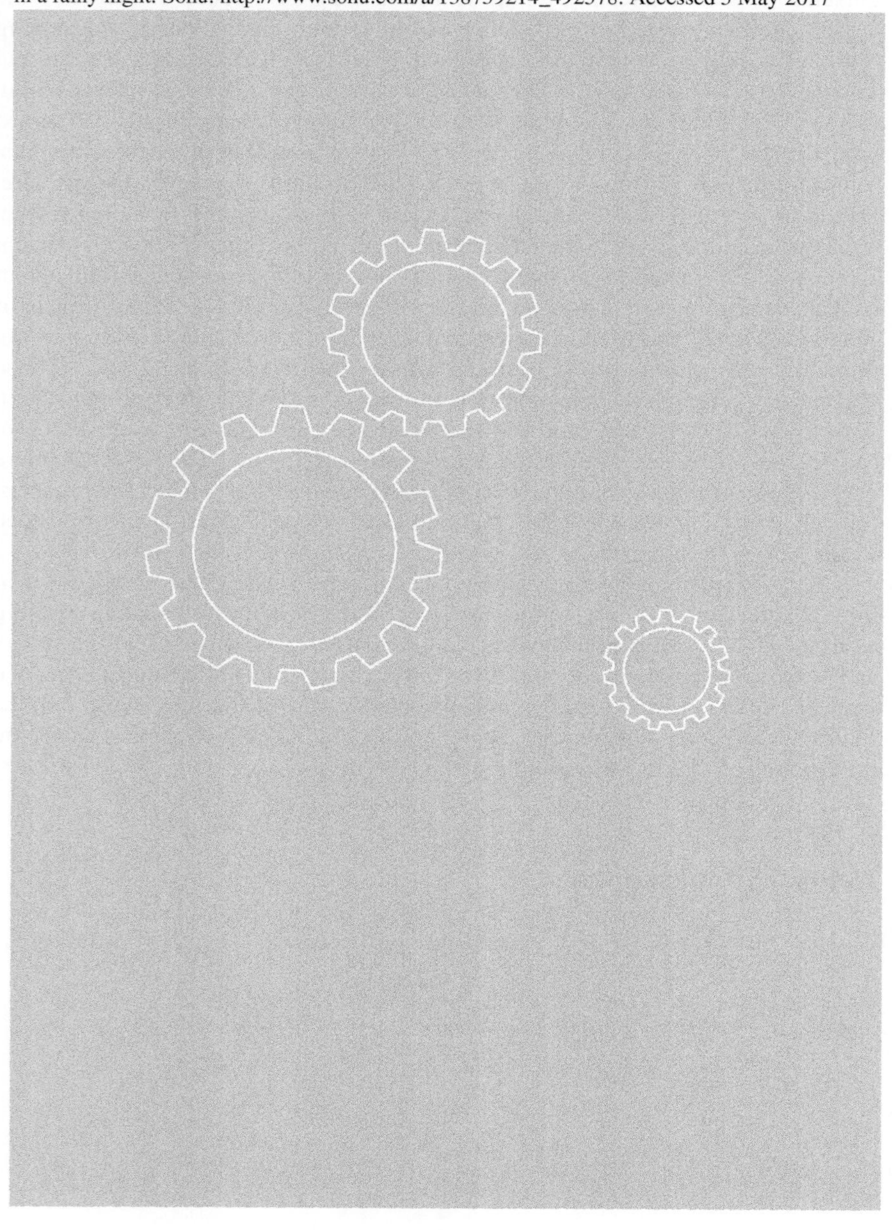

Rice Donate: Good Behavior Leverage Public Welfare

Qiang Wang, Shuo Zhan, Yanfang Xu, and Zhuang Mi

> Public welfare industry is not a rigid demand. In this sense it is simple enough because it does not attract or create demand. Instead, it should create value, to meet the demand of its users for self-growth, and to help them improve their influence while making contributions to the society. This is the only way for public welfare to go on.
>
> —Zi Wang, founder of Rice Donate

In May 2017, it was just the early summer in Beijing, when everything was growing and the branches of willow trees hanging down like hair. A group of social enterprise interviewer from Renmin Business School of Renmin University of China came to a business park near Dazhong Temple and visited Rice Donate.

This company was one of the three representative social enterprises invited by China Youth Social Entrepreneurship Project Exhibition held by the Social Innovation and Entrepreneurship Forum of Renmin University of China on February 26, 2017. Professor Yunus, Nobel Peace Prize winner, commented on it during the exhibition. On April 13, 2017, Forbes, a well-known financial media in the United States, released the list of "30 under 30 Asia." Zihao Mo and Zi Wang, the founder of Rice Donate, were selected. How did Rice Donate achieve such achievements and win the public recognition?

Inspired by a Painting

1. **Teaching experience in the countryside**

In October 2012, Zi Wang and Zihao Mo, senior students of Sun Yat-Sen University, thought of doing something special to give back to the society. This thought was inspired by a past experience, and eventually grow into Rice Donate like a seed.

Q. Wang (✉) · S. Zhan · Y. Xu · Z. Mi
Business School, Renmin University of China, Beijing, China
e-mail: wangqiang@rmbs.ruc.edu.cn

M. Zhao and J. Mao (eds.), *Social Entrepreneurship*,
https://doi.org/10.1007/978-981-15-9881-4_9

Zi Wang once went to a primary school in the countryside as a volunteer teacher to teach the children drawing. When he got there, he found that the children didn't even have markers. Zi Wang asked the leader of the team if he could buy some markers for these children. But the leader turned him down. He said that many volunteers had such idea before, but some of them failed to fulfill their promise. Even if they did bring the markers, it was just for once. The children were disappointed when the markers were used up. Then Zi Wang asked: how should they draw if I don't buy for them and they don't have any markers?

Nobody could answer his question. In fact, they didn't have the ability to change the reality at that time. This made Zi Wang realize for the first time that it is not an easy thing to help others. Later, Zi Wang realized that maybe the fundamental problem is the operation mechanism of public welfare. Individual's strength is too scattered to fulfill the demands of public welfare. One person's temporary compassion can hardly provide stable and reliable support. Is it possible to change this situation? Is there a better way to match the supply, the demand and the executor of public funds? Zi Wang had been searching for the answer.

2. **Fundamental problems of the industry**

In fact, problems in public welfare industry are far more than the matching of supply and demand. Back to school, Zi Wang and his classmate Zihao Mo sorted out the major events in public welfare industry nationwide from 2011 to 2012. Because of the low transparency, scandals happened from time to time in public welfare industry, which caused trust crisis in the whole industry. Most typical event was Guo Meimei event in 2011, which caused strong public discontent, and damaged the credibility of the Red Cross Society. On March 15, 2012, CCTV "3.15" Evening Gala exposed that Chinese Students Eye Care Project made profits by commercial means in the name of charity and public welfare. Many public welfare organizations handled charity funds by means of black box operation. According to a news report, some public welfare organizations "raised only 8,000 yuan of funds a year, but spend 620,000 yuan." In addition, there were also many cases of fraudulent donations.

Why was public welfare industry in such a disorder? Zi Wang and Zihao Mo carried out a survey and found that in China, public welfare industry runs in a chain operation mode, which means enterprises or individuals donate money to the foundations and then the foundations allocate it to public welfare organizations. However, these public welfare organizations have some problems during their implementation, such as low salary level, insufficient personnel, and low professional level of the personnel. As a result, they could not implement public welfare projects effectively and therefore could not be granted with more funds. In addition, the whole process was not connected to the public, which left space for corruption and dishonesty.

Enterprises don't have channels or intentions to learn about the exact use of their funds after they donated them. For many enterprises, donation was just a task. It was a series of figures in their social responsibility reports. As for the actual use behind these figures, whether to support poor children to go to school or help poor old people to spend the winter, they seldom cared.

Gradually, the two young men realized that the improvement of the efficiency and credibility of public welfare organizations was a "double failure" issue that neither the market nor the government could solve in short term. On the one hand, public welfare was regarded as a kind of public product. This public product was born with a natural defect, which is called the "free riding" phenomenon. In pure market economy, people tend to take a free ride to get their own share from the benefits that public welfare brings to the whole society. On the other hand, public welfare was not covered by the government's public services. As a result, public welfare industry fell into the area of "double failure" of market and government.

In fact, there were quite a number of people working in the front line of China's social work, who had professional ability and quality, as well as the willingness to do public welfare. However, they did not have enough resources to do this well. Then why these people could not get proper resources, while people with resources were not capable of doing such work? Zi Wang and Zihao Mo believed that there should be a new organization or resource allocation solution to straighten out public welfare process. What was this innovative and optimized solution?

Zi Wang and Zihao Mo were determined to find out the right path of public welfare innovation.

"Partners from Sun Yat-Sen University"

1. **Starting from campus**

Zi Wang had been interested in mobile Internet and had entrepreneurial experience. He is one of the founders of the popular mobile game "Fisherman." And Zihao Mo had a lot of experience in public welfare. After many discussions, they finally found a possible solution to tackle the problems in public welfare. That has become the core concept of Rice Donate: to introduce the thinking of mobile Internet into public welfare.

In fact, the two young men were already influential figures on the campus of Sun Yat-Sen University at that time. Zi Wang was selected as "The Person of the Year of Sun Yat-Sen University in 2012." He went to Aarhus Business School in Denmark as an exchange student. Zihao Mo won scholarships for many times during his four years of college, and went to Miami University as an exchange student. They had respectively been admitted to Tsinghua University and Peking University as graduate students without examinations. Zi Wang said, "At that time, I was well connected on the campus. So we organized a team of more than 20 people in more than two months. These people were basically elites in their own college."

Thanks to their influence on the campus, Zi Wang and Zihao Mo successfully put together an excellent team of more than 20 people. The members were the best talents in each college of Sun Yat-Sen University, who had professional backgrounds in different fields such as finance, technology, publicity, etc.

"After the team was built up, it conducted a large number of preliminary investigations. It also visited some NGOs to know their practical needs. For example, many toys donated by children's hospice care institutions were out of battery power. So we contacted battery manufacturers to see if they wanted to donate. We introduced the projects of public welfare organizations to them through mobile app. The name of the manufacturer would be put on the app. When users click the games, they would get virtual 'rice,' which could be accumulated and converted into materials. Volunteers would send these materials to public welfare organizations regularly."

The then newly established Rice Donate team, made an in-depth analysis on the public welfare market. After a lot of research and brainstorming, they concluded that: "One big problem in this industry is that the work is not divided in specialized way. It should be divided into several specialized stages. Any industry should be divided into many stages from upstream to downstream. Even a very small part may represent a specialized stage. But the degree of specialization in public welfare industry was very low. Basically, works of all stages were undertaken by one organization, from project planning, advertising and sponsorship, enterprise service, recruitment of volunteers, training, to implementation and feedback. And members of this organization probably only earned a salary of 2,000 yuan a month. The industry could not develop healthily in this way… Our solution is to carry out specialized division of tasks. There should be various professional institutions in this industry, which can make full use of the best service resources, and provide reasonable benefits for the professionals to give their best performance."

Meanwhile, as for the continuous operation of this model, Rice Donate public welfare paid attention to the individual users. They said, "Take ourselves for example; we know that we want to do public welfare. But it's still hard to keep on doing it. This is the case for most young people around us. This group has the willingness and ability to do public welfare, and its number is increasing. But their attention to public welfare might fall to the bottom when they graduate, and then it would grow back later, such as at their 30s or 40s (see Fig. 1). We found that the same is true for all the users. There will be discontinuity. As soon as they graduate, they will be busy buying a house, getting married and dealing with other social pressures. During this period, they would pay less attention and time on public welfare. So it's difficult for many people in the society to keep on doing something that is not directly related to their personal lives. We want to make it easier for everyone to participate in public welfare activities, and to keep on doing it… If users don't want to donate money but they still want to keep on doing something charitable every day, then can we let the enterprise pay for it instead?"

Rice Donate team thought of a three-in-one business model, which links individual users, public welfare organizations and enterprises together, and forms a triangle. The enterprises pay the money, the public welfare organizations undertake the work, and the individuals pay their fragment time to grow together with the public welfare community. Zihao Mo and Zi Wang introduced: "Among a dozen of public welfare organizations nationwide cooperating with Rice Donate, many of them are small-scale organizations dedicated to serving a special group of people, such as Butterfly's Home Children's Care Center in Changsha, Hunan Province, and Irene Qingdao

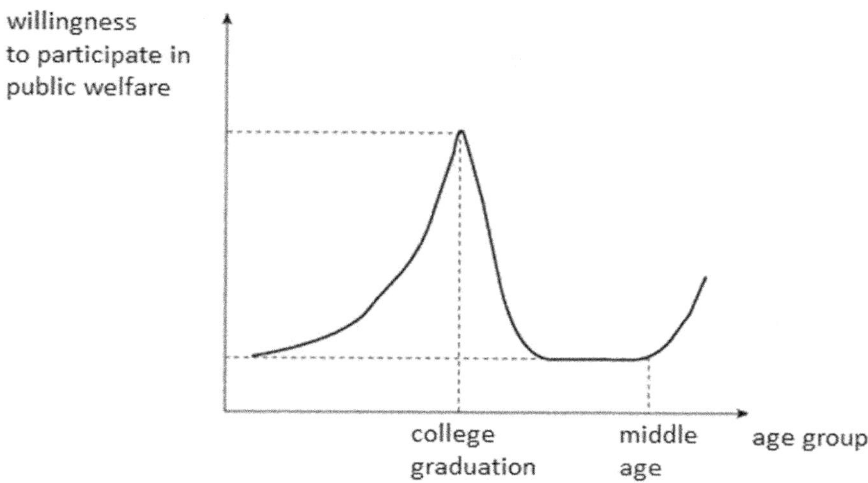

Fig. 1 Life cycle of public welfare willingness

Autism Research Association for autistic children. These downplaying grassroots NGOs need more exposure."

2. **Launching the app**

The two founders led the team for 15 days' of closed work. They carried out business planning and design, and completed all the preparation works for the foundation of the company. The model app was launched after the closed work. The mobile app was refreshing. Figure 2 is one of the advertisements on the app. It shows the app's slogan "Making donation easy for everybody," and five small functions, including Rice stretch, Rice aerobic, Rice twist, Rice knowledge and Rice mom.

The "rice" is the general equivalent of public welfare circulation defined by Rice Donate. Public users can participate in the activities on the app to win Rice. For example, user can get 20 Rice for answering a question in "Rice knowledge," or get 10 Rice for doing a shoulder relaxation stretching exercise in "Rice stretch." The materials donated by the enterprises are labeled with price in the app. For example, a pencil is priced five Rice. Users can buy this pencil with their Rice and donate it to the cooperative organizations of Rice Donate. Users can participate in public welfare activities as easy as that. These five functions Rice Donate developed in its early stage (Rice stretch, Rice aerobic, Rice twist, Rice knowledge and Rice mom) focus on people's daily activities like life, health, etc. They were widely participated and highly rated by a lot of users.

Zi Wang recalled and said, "It took us half a year to get the demo product online since we thought of it. We got in touch with several enterprises as our first funders, all through our friends in college. In June 2013, we were reported by all the major media in Guangzhou on their front pages."

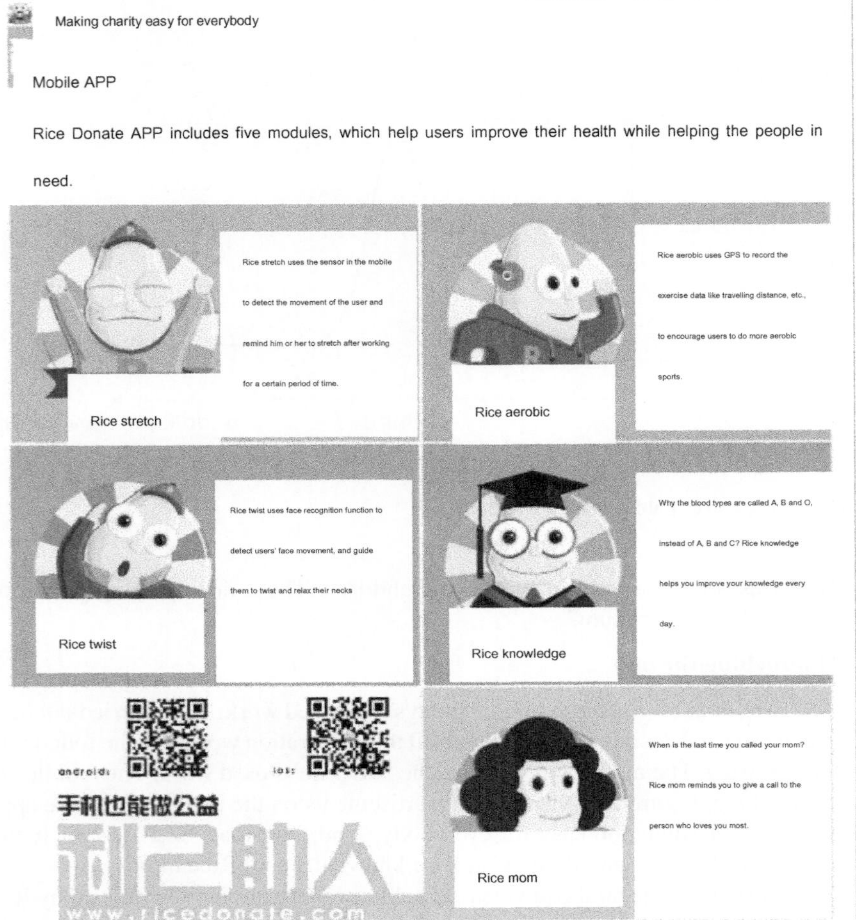

Fig. 2 Rice Donate's mobile app in 2013

Just overnight, the media were surprised by Rice Donate's innovative public welfare. They were quite curious about this new form of public welfare. Rice Donate appeared on the headlines of major newspapers in Guangzhou. It became the focus of public attention.

Back in 2013, Rice Donate was still in its exploration stage, but its debut was quite successful for sure. The team of Rice Donate was compared to the partners in the film "Chinese Partners" at that time. People called them "Campus Partners."

In that year, a report on Netease Finance about Rice Donate represented the typical view of the media at that time: "Combining public welfare with people's daily life, to lower the threshold of charity, and make it go to the public. That is exactly what these 'Campus Partners' is doing."

Never Give up

1. Twists and turns

At that time, Rice Donate operated mainly in Guangzhou, and the team members were all students of Sun Yat-Sen University. Although they were faced with many challenges in funds and publicity, they were still solvable. Therefore Rice Donate developed rapidly in the first half a year. However, this growth trend stopped abruptly soon after that.

In the second half of 2013, many problems began to merge. "The key for its success is also the cause for the challenge." The first problem was with the team. Rice Donate's members went together because they were school mates of the same University, but they had to separate when they graduated. This is also a common problem faced by many entrepreneurial teams of college students. When graduation season comes, team members go to pursue different goals. Some of them continue their studies in China, some go abroad, and some find jobs in different cities. The team may break apart. When the founder Zi Wang recalled this experience, he sighed: "Everyone has their own destination after graduation. When Rice Donate was just in fast development, the team suddenly broke apart, because we agreed from the beginning that this was just a temporary team for half a year. Afterwards, everybody could go to study or work as they planned. The number of team members plummeted from more than 20 to 5. A lot of work has to be suspended."

Even for Zi Wang himself, he had to spend less time on this project after he went to Tsinghua University for master's degree. Due to the shortage in manpower and funds, as well as his own busy study schedule, the team could no longer input enough time and energy to Rice Donate. The development of the whole project was slowed down. Zi Wang said, "At that time, we were new in Beijing. We needed to get familiar with the new environment. So the work slowed down. That means no one went to contact the enterprises. No one raised funds. And no one worked on product promotion. There were just hundreds of existing users went online every day."

In addition to the problem with the team, Rice Donate was also faced with a typical problem for all the social enterprises—the problem of funds. Generally speaking, for a start-up enterprise like Rice Donate that has a team of strong executive capability and perspective, as well as the business model that is subversive for the industry, it won't be a problem to attract investors. Bike sharing pioneers Mobike and OFO are good examples. However, it was not the case for Rice Donate. Although it has excellent team and advanced concept, it is a public welfare company. Can a start-up company like this make profits? How to balance its social attribute and commercial attribute after it can make profits? These are the fundamental problems that hamper Rice Donate from obtaining investment.

In order to support Rice Donate's development, Zi Wang began to work hard to look for investments. Fortunately, Zi Wang's innovative operation model attracted an investor. He was enthusiastic about public welfare and thought high of the business concept of Rice Donate. He invested one million yuan of angel capital and provided additional funds for Rice Donate to maintain its daily operation. The problem of funding was solved for the time being.

2. **Just learn it if you don't know it**

When development was formally started, technical problems soon emerged. Zi Wang hired four technicians for the development of the mobile client application. However, two month passed without much progress. Zi Wang suspected that these technicians did not put in all the efforts. But he knew nothing about programming, so he could do anything. Once again, Zi Wang was in a difficult position.

"We hired four employees in our Beijing office. All of them are programmers. The application needed to be rewritten. It was done by outsourced team before. One month passed and there was no achievement with the development work. And two months passed. It was still the same. We realized a serious problem – we don't know anything about software development."

After this experience, Zi Wang and Zihao Mo began to study development knowledge. They also invited an old classmate working in a famous technology company for help. This classmate helped Rice Donate "supervise" the work of their programmers, and developed a strict management system to let employees know that although Rice Donate was a new enterprise, it had clear rules in management and technology. Since then, Rice Donate established its way to solve technical problems, and kept on with it.

In 2014, difficulties in personnel, funding, technology and other aspects forced Rice Donate to slow down. Starting a business is like sailing upward the stream. If you stop moving upward, you will flow downward. When Rice Donate slowed down its development, user stopped using the app or even unloaded it. This made it more difficult to promote its cooperation between public organizations and enterprises. When solving these problems, Rice Donate also began to re-examine the old three-in-one business model, and seek ways to improve it.

The Three-in-One Business Model

1. **Continuous improvement of the three-in-one business model**

Rice Donate was just like a seed when it was founded. Now, it has grown into a big tree. Rice Donate has a clear idea about its business model from the beginning, and has been stick to it till today.

"Our business model is generally the model of users, public welfare organizations and enterprises. In short, the roles of each participant on this platform are different. Public welfare organizations are responsible for implementation. For users, they don't need to spend money. They just need to spend some fragmented time every day, by which they can get a sense of achievement, satisfaction, identity and a series of spiritual satisfaction. This will make them keep on doing public welfare and using our products. For enterprises, they need to donate to public welfare every year. This might be a rigid demand for some enterprises. And at the same time, they also hope to improve their influence by doing so."

With the interaction of the three parties, a closed-loop public welfare cycle is formed (see Fig. 3).

The funders, including enterprises and foundations, have different needs, such as charity, public relations and team building, to perform their social responsibilities. Many enterprises have special funds for their social responsibilities every year. Some large enterprises even have designated teams to implement donations or hold other activities. They can achieve both goals of social dedication and enterprise development by these activities. But most enterprises can't afford to follow up and manage these charity projects. Therefore, funders can donate their charity funds to Rice Donate, where their funds can be made full use of, and they just needs to supervise and evaluate. Funders can achieve the maximum effect with the minimum time and effort.

Public welfare organizations on Rice Donate platform must pass their qualification examination and verification. When these organizations have a charity project, such as donating infrastructure to primary schools in mountainous areas, they can

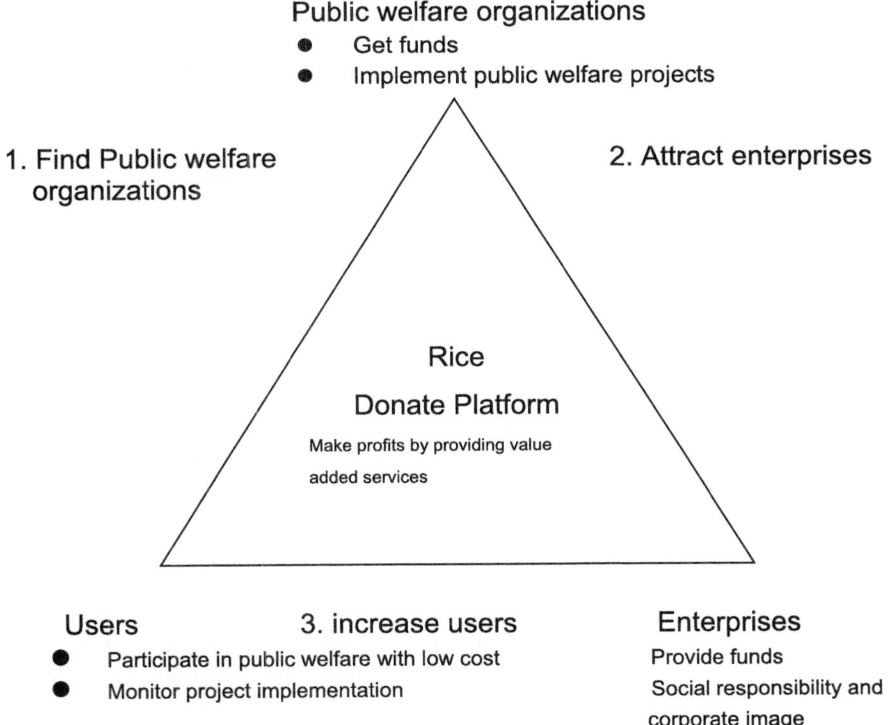

Fig. 3 Rice Donate's business model—"users support, enterprises sponsor, and public welfare organizations implement"

simply launch the project on the Rice Donate platform. These Public welfare organizations can obtain sufficient funds and resources from the platform to implement their projects. Public welfare organizations can obtain funds in this way. Of course, the ranking of the projects on Rice Donate platform is not simple based on the organization's credibility, but also on the comprehensive evaluation of the projects' quality and popularity.

Individual users can earn Rice by doing simple tasks in Rice stretching and Rice aerobic on Rice Donate app, as well as realizing their self-growth. Then, they can choose the public welfare projects they like on the platform, and spend the Rice they earned to buy materials donated by enterprises. There are a lot of projects on the platform, including those of environmental protection, education support, elderly and disabled support, community service, health care, poverty alleviation and disaster relief. The ranking of the projects on the platform is determined by the public welfare organization's credibility, projects' online popularity, and project features. Individual users have the freedom to make their own choices. They can view the description of the projects, number of participants, donation amount, current progress and other details about the project through their mobile. The app also allows users to rate the projects, and helps other users to make better choices on the project, which can guide Rice go to better and more efficient projects, and encourage public welfare organization to improve their performance. All the projects on the platform are executed in transparent mode. The flow and use of all the funds and materials in the whole process are open to the users.

The mobile app allows users to participate in public welfare with low cost and high sense of achievement. They can decide which public welfare project can be granted with funds. At the same time, they also know which enterprises are donating the funds, which helps to increase the influence of the enterprises. In this process, the users actually play the role of supervisors. By reviewing the implementation of the public welfare projects, they can help to improve the effectiveness of public welfare projects.

Rice Donate makes profits by providing additional value-added services for the funders. That is, Rice Donate's main profit comes from its value-added services for enterprises and foundations. It charges consulting fees for activity planning, communication, technical support and other services, rather than charging commissions fees or management fees. At present, Rice Donate mainly provides four services, including public donation, brand communication, technical development and employee involvement, trying to cover all the public welfare needs of the funders (Figs. 4 and 5).

Rice Donate replaced the old chain operation model of public welfare industry with the new triangle model, where the connection between the funders and public welfare organizations will not end when their donation projects end. Instead, their projects will remain on Rice Donate platform for users' supervision and evaluation. Users are not just one-time participants for a certain public welfare activity, but an indispensable part of the whole public welfare platform, making their contributions to all the public welfare projects on the platform. This is a platform where all the three parties win. With the development of Rice Donate platform, as well as the whole

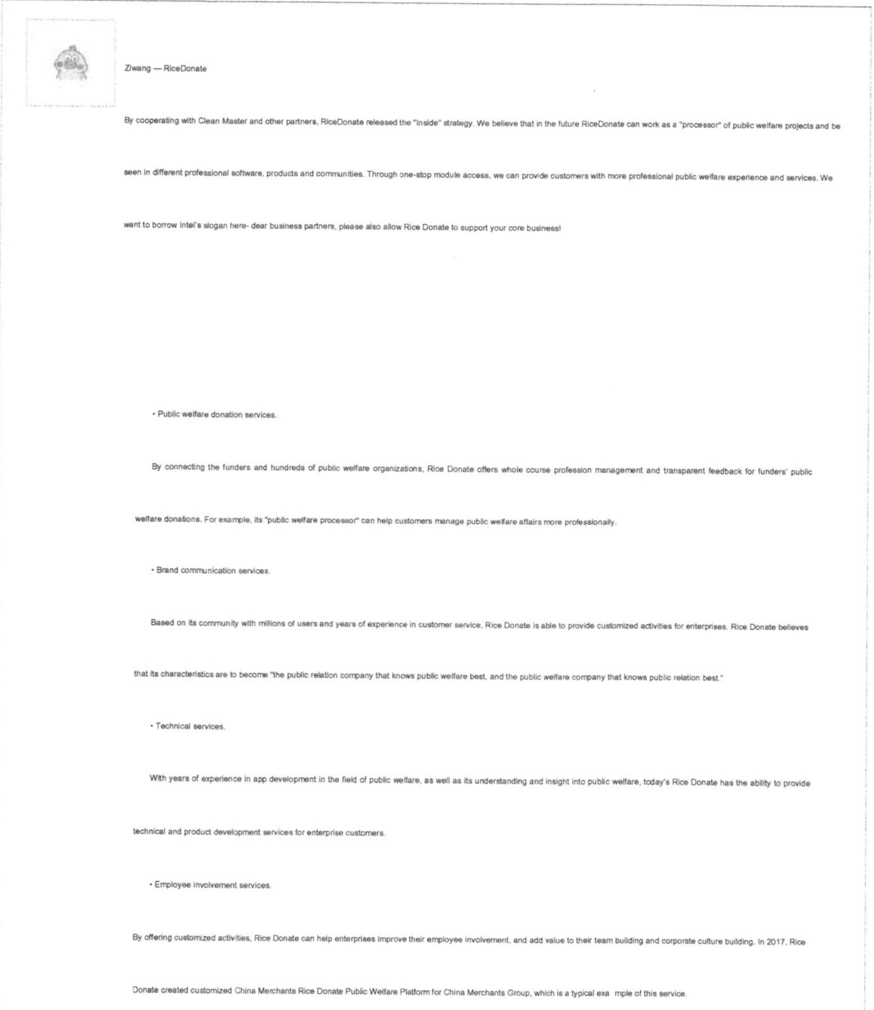

Ziwang — RiceDonate

By cooperating with Clean Master and other partners, RiceDonate released the "Inside" strategy. We believe that in the future RiceDonate can work as a "processor" of public welfare projects and be seen in different professional software, products and communities. Through one-stop module access, we can provide customers with more professional public welfare experience and services. We want to borrow Intel's slogan here- dear business partners, please also allow Rice Donate to support your core business!

• Public welfare donation services.

By connecting the funders and hundreds of public welfare organizations, Rice Donate offers whole course profession management and transparent feedback for funders' public welfare donations. For example, its "public welfare processor" can help customers manage public welfare affairs more professionally.

• Brand communication services.

Based on its community with millions of users and years of experience in customer service, Rice Donate is able to provide customized activities for enterprises. Rice Donate believes that its characteristics are to become "the public relation company that knows public welfare best, and the public welfare company that knows public relation best."

• Technical services.

With years of experience in app development in the field of public welfare, as well as its understanding and insight into public welfare, today's Rice Donate has the ability to provide technical and product development services for enterprise customers.

• Employee involvement services.

By offering customized activities, Rice Donate can help enterprises improve their employee involvement, and add value to their team building and corporate culture building. In 2017, Rice Donate created customized China Merchants Rice Donate Public Welfare Platform for China Merchants Group, which is a typical exa mple of this service.

Fig. 4 In September 2017, Rice Donate was connected to customers as the "public welfare processor"

public welfare cause, enterprise can lift their image, public welfare organizations can improve their executive power, and individual users can achieve self-growth.

2. **"Three steps" strategy**

However, how to implement the three-in-one business model? How to attract enterprise users and public welfare organizations? These are the tactical issues that Rice Donate needs to think about next. It is very difficult to attract a large number of users from all these three groups into one public welfare platform, especially

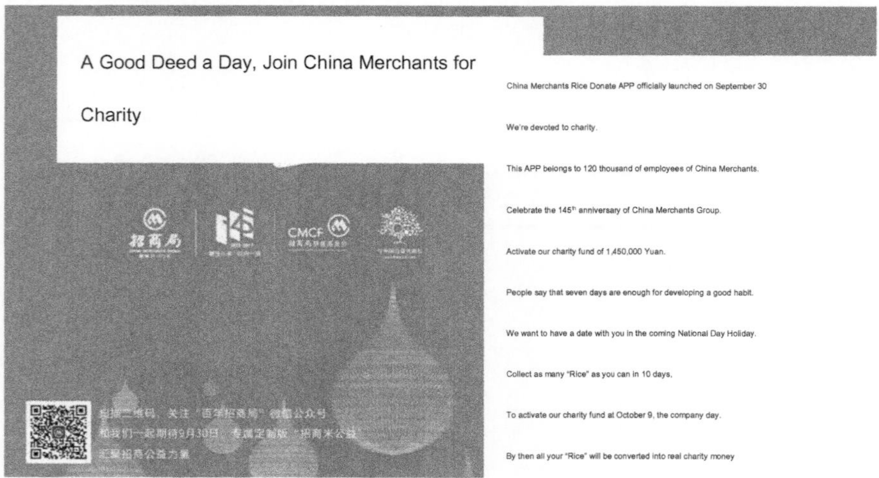

Fig. 5 At the end of September 2017, "China Merchants Rice Donate Public Welfare Platform" went online

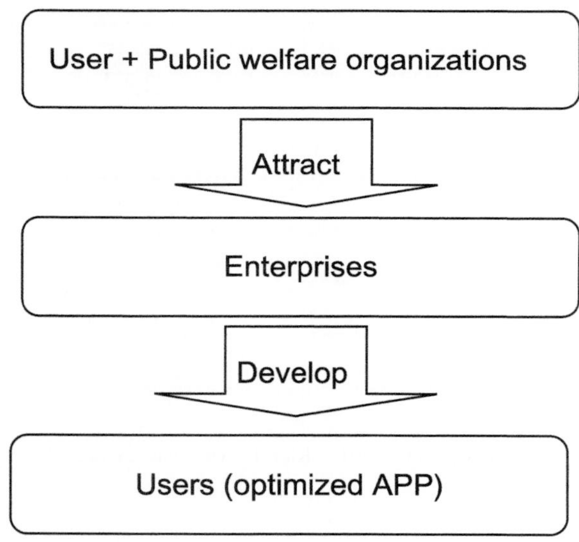

Fig. 6 Rice Donate's "three steps" strategy

for start-up companies. The three parties of enterprises, individual users and public welfare organizations are interrelated: enterprises will join the platform when there are enough active individual users and public welfare organizations resources on it; public welfare organizations will choose the platform as their partner when it has the ability to attract funders; and users will participate in public welfare activities on the platform if they think it's efficient and useful (Fig. 6).

In order to build its business model, Rice Donate adopted a "three-step" development strategy (see Fig. 3), which means to focus on the development of one or two parties at a time in different stages. Therefore, Rice Donate established a three-step development strategy for individual users, enterprises and public welfare organizations. At the same time, it kept on optimizing its mobile app to make it suit users' habits better.

Its first step is to develop public welfare organizations and individual users. It is difficult to attract enterprises to join the platform, and even more so to persuade funders, if there are no active users and public welfare resources on it. From another aspect, developing users and sellers on the platform first is also one of the common practices in the field of Internet in the past years. Rice Donate just applied this idea in the field of public welfare.

In order to increase the number of users, Rice Donate team has made a lot of efforts. Because public welfare demand is not a rigid demand for everyone, it won't be possible to apply Internet thinking here and attract users by advertising. Rice Donate came up with this idea that may be applicable and can retain users for a long time, which is to turn public welfare into something simple, changeable, and interesting, so that user can participate with minimum cost and achieve personal growth and self-management at the same time. Thus the earliest idea of "Rice aerobic" and the concept of Rice which can be used to vote for public welfare projects were invented. It has been proved that these measures that have been adopted since the foundation of the company at the beginning of 2013 aimed to attract users are quite successful. Rice Donate quickly accumulated a large number of users simply by word of mouth.

In the aspect of finding public welfare organization partners, Rice Donate team carried out professional screening of public welfare organizations to ensure the reliability and efficiency of the public welfare activities. The assessment on public welfare organizations mainly concerns two parts. One is to review the qualification of the public welfare organizations, including their registration certificate, major funders and organization of the team. And the other part is to review the specific public welfare projects to be launched on the platform by the organization, including project plans, documents, etc. During real assessment, there will be a comprehensive evaluation system used to evaluate the public welfare organization which involves three evaluators: Rice Donate, enterprises and individual users. The main dimensions of evaluation include the public welfare organization's qualification, credibility (such as its ability to implement projects according to the plan) and user interaction. Excellent organizations and projects will get more resources. This supervision and evaluation system can effectively avoid the problem of black box operation in traditional public welfare industry.

After accumulating a certain amount of users and organization resources, the second step is to focus on attracting enterprises to join. The challenge faced by enterprises is how to make efficient and valuable use of their social welfare funds. Rice Donate provides four services, including public donation, brand communication, technical development and employee involvement, which can fully cover the public welfare needs of the enterprises. At the same time, they also realized that their enterprise users are different from public welfare organizations, as well as enterprise users in other industries. These enterprise users pay more attention to execution and credibility, rather than prices. Zi Wang said, "In public welfare industry, low price does not mean competitive advantage. Funders want to ensure nothing goes wrong. That is what they value the most. They want to 'make it simple' and make sure 'nothing goes wrong.' Competing with low price is not working. The most valuable things in this industry are reputation and credibility."

When the resources of enterprises and public welfare organizations are stable, the last step is to strengthen its hold on individual users. Therefore, Rice Donate made constant adjustments in its client app to better suit user's habits, while keeping its core concept unchanged.

3. **Continuous optimization of the app**

In order to provide better experience to the users and let them achieve self-growth and satisfaction while doing public welfare, Rice Donate kept on improving and optimizing their mobile app. Currently, the mobile app includes four parts, which are "projects," "earn Rice," "latest" and "mine."

In "Project" (beautiful encounter), you can view the public welfare projects that are raising Rice or finish raising, and the selected projects. In "earn Rice" (better self), users can earn Rice from "Rice Aerobic," "Rice Early Rising," "Rice Chat" and "Rice Knowledge." In "Latest," you can see the latest news of your Rice partners and the progress of the public welfare projects. In "Mine," you can view your personal account information (Fig. 7).

Compared with the mobile client in 2013, the new app made the following major changes:

(1) Added more public welfare projects

In the early days, restrained by the limitation in the resources of cooperative public welfare organization, as well as in its capacity, capital and popularity, Rice Donate could not launch so many public welfare projects online. But now, the projects on app are one of the main factors to attract users, enterprises and public welfare organizations.

(2) Adjusted the way of earning Rice

In the old version, there were five ways to earn Rice including Rice Stretch, Rice Aerobic, Rice Twist, Rice Knowledge, and Rice Mom. Now, "Rice Stretch" and "Rice Twist" were deleted, "Rice Mom" was changed to "Rice Chat," and "Rice Early Rising" was added. These changes of one deletion, one change and one addition were all made based on users' daily habits in recent years. Rice Stretch and Rice Twist were deleted because their functions were overlapping with other ways, and the cost-benefit ratio of user participation was slightly lower than other ways. The new module of Rice Early Rising mainly caters to the needs of college students.

(3) Improved social function

Compared with the previous version, the new version added social functions. Users can invite Rice Partners to join Rice Donate, and can see their latest changes.

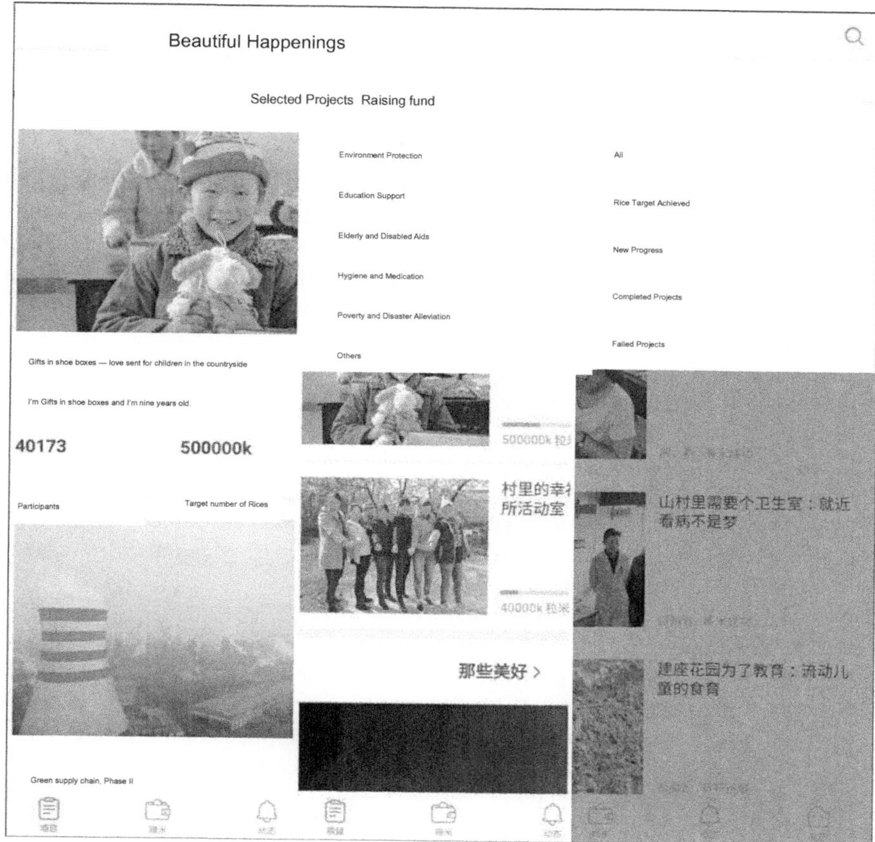

Fig. 7 Interface of Rice Donate app

The new function caught the social demands of young people, and is quite effective to increase the influence of Rice Donate.

After five years of development, the three-in-one business model is getting more and more mature. By the end of 2017, Rice Donate had more than three million registered users, cooperated with more than 150 enterprises, who donated more than 30 million yuan, and 700 public welfare organizations, which had launched more than 1500 public welfare projects with Rice Donate jointly, among which 1,000 has been implemented or got feedback.

Never Forget the Original Mission: Not Just Making a Better Self

1. **User's voices**

Traditional public welfare projects often call for people to donate materials and get love in return. While Rice Donate's model allows users to develop good habits of rising early, exercising and keeping in touch with family and friends, while doing charity. "Those who help others help themselves." Users help themselves to meet a better self when they help the people in need to encounter beauty.

One the homepage of Rice Donate's website, there is a word saying: "Making a better self, and making a better world." This new concept provides a positive incentive for the users to participate in public welfare, and allows them to do charity when forming good habits. It fits the busy lifestyle of modern people, and allows users to make better use of their fragmented time while giving out their love to the society. All these purposes can be achieved at one stroke.

Consequently, Rice Donate app is doing quite well in every app store. For example, in Apple's app store, it has got an average score of 4.9. Many users sincerely recommended it in their comments.

A user named "Magu00" commented on September 15, 2017 that: "I knew about Rice Donate from one of my friends' WeChat Circle of friends. He shared a Rice Donate link. I was interested, so I download it too. I can't believe I've been using it for one year since then. I get up early, walk, answer questions, participate in all kinds of meaningful activities, and donate Rice. Although I stopped for a few days once, now these things have become my habits. It's really amazing and wonderful. It feels good when everyone works together to donate for their favorite projects. Thank you, Rice Donate. I'd like to grow together with you" (Fig. 8).

From these user comments, we can see that user loyalty of Rice Donate is very high. Many users are very happy with Rice Donate's commitment to public welfare, as well as the way they can participate in public welfare by doing small things in daily life. This harmonious relationship depends on Rice Donate's strong sense of

A very good APP. I will recommend it.

The interface looks even better after several rounds of optimization. The administrator has always been

there to help solve the problems for me. I can see that the team behind this APP really works hard for it.

Bravo!

Fig. 8 Some of the user comments on Rice Donate on App Store

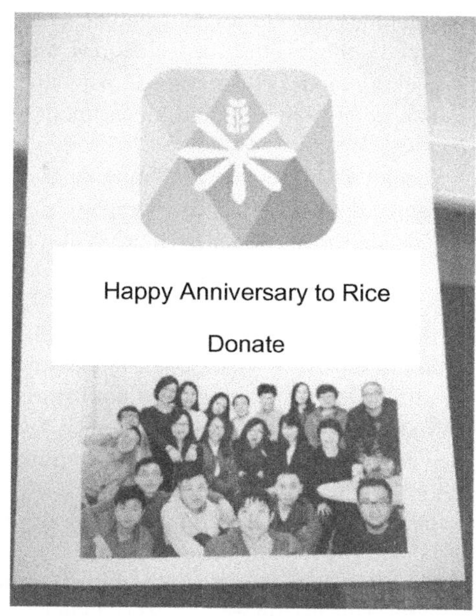

Fig. 9 A pamphlet of users' birthday wishes for Rice Donate

responsibility and excellent service to its users. Another user commented: "Whenever I meet a problem with the app, the administrator can listen to me carefully and help me solve it. I can feel the team is working hard on the app" (Fig. 9).

2. Balance and reflections

During its development in the past, Rice Donate kept on finding solutions to improve the efficiency of the whole public welfare industry, while struggling to achieve financial balance. It has made a lot of efforts to maintain the balance between its sociality and commerciality.

First of all, the organizational structure of Rice Donate represented its commitment to the public welfare goal.

Rice Donate in Beijing is responsible for business and the development and maintenance the app, including the operation of online public welfare projects. In order to obtain more resources and opportunities, Rice Donate set up a non-profit organization in Guangzhou to handle public welfare donation business. It is led by an early founder of Rice Donate in Guangzhou. For donation business, Beijing company, Guangzhou NPO and funders usually need to work together.

Rice Donate in Beijing has a special department for public welfare business. Their employees are responsible for contacting public welfare organizations, learning about public welfare projects, and implement cooperation between public welfare organizations and Rice Donate. In addition, they also maintain the public welfare projects on Rice Donate's platform, including the design and editing of the copywriting and pictures on the interface of each project. They need to find ways to demonstrate the features of each project to get more attention and recognition. Their scope of work also includes supervision and feedback on project implementation, co-hosting activities with public welfare organizations, and creating more value for the beneficiaries. Its working model of Beijing company and Guangzhou NPO in cooperation, as well as its special public welfare department, embodies Rice Donate's commitment to sociality.

Secondly, the founder Zi Wang's passion for sociality and his entrepreneurship guarantee the stability of the company's organizational goals.

This idea he had when he was a senior college student has supported him all these years to build his team to optimize the entire process of public welfare. This road has been full of ups and downs, but Zi Wang didn't give up. The motivation behind this is the initial intension to improve public welfare. It is just his persistence that brings the chance to survive to Rice Donate and ensures the stability of its social goals. Although the articles of association does not clearly define the ratio of profit distribution, it does stipulates the leading position of the two founders in the decision-making of Rice Donate, which guarantees the continuity of the company's decision-making to a large extent.

Thirdly, the team culture and corporate culture of Rice Donate ensure the stability of its organizational goals.

Each company has its own unique corporate culture. The same is true of Rice Donate. The key words of Rice Donate's core culture are "public welfare" and "learning." Public welfare is Zi Wang's initial purpose to establish Rice Donate. He wants to make public welfare easier so that everyone can participate. Therefore, Zi Wang has always been clear about the mission of his company and always takes a positive attitude to do public welfare.

Zi Wang thinks that learning is an important element to help the company grow. The worst thing is not that there are things you don't know, but you don't want to learn them. Therefore, Zi Wang set a regular meeting, where every employee has two or three opportunities every month to share what they have learned. They can share anything, from the use of expression packs, their experience of reading Jin Yong's martial arts novels, to the analysis of copycat behavior of similar enterprises. This meeting is very effective to encourage employees' willingness to learn and improve their ability of learning. It also helps to create a good working atmosphere. Zi Wang said, "I made it clear to our employees from the beginning that if making money is the only thing they care about, and then they may not belong here. Our company's culture focuses on public welfare and learning. I don't mind if there are a lot of things you can't do when you are new here, as long as you are sincere enough and really want to do something, and you are willing to learn… This job is the first job for many of our employees after their graduation. For us, it is our responsibility to help them improve their learning ability. And for them, it is also very useful and can help them grow. After all, we don't want to mess up their first job."

Finally, Rice Donate reflects on social enterprises.

"Social enterprise" is a popular concept in recent years. The core of its definition is that the enterprise can solve social problems continuously and ensure its commercial goals never surpass its social goals. To some extent, an enterprise must have strong ability, as well as strong sense of social responsibility to be a social enterprise. Rice

Donate is an enterprise committed to making public welfare simpler. So apparently, it complies with the definition of social enterprise.

But Zi Wang has different opinions. He thinks that Rice Donate is still a commercial enterprise. It's just that it serves the public welfare. Public welfare service is its product. Moreover, Zi Wang suspects that this may not be so effective for the promotion of public welfare activities in the society. On the contrary, it may seem like a "gimmick" and make some good behaviors look like a show. In his opinion, Rice Donate just wants to do public welfare, and it does not need the label of social enterprise.

"For any enterprise, its most important responsibility is to support all its employees and produce valuable and environmental friendly products. As long as an enterprise is running well and is achieving progress and development, then it will give back to the society eventually. So I think it may be confusing to have a special concept of 'social enterprise.' It may give the public the wrong idea that a social enterprise must have low profit target, and it doesn't need to worry about the issues like commercial enterprises do. It is not the case actually."

Although Zi Wang doesn't think that Rice Donate is a social enterprise, in the eyes of most people, Rice Donate has become a representative of social enterprises. Zi Wang is also happy about this. After all, it represents the popular recognition of Rice Donate and its features. Never the less, Zi Wang thinks that the concept of "social enterprise" and the notion it contains are positive. It shows that social goals and commercial goals are becoming integrated and balanced. As a business graduate, Zi Wang tended to establish a social enterprise in the early years of business practice. But during years of management and operation, he felt that the model of commercial operation is indispensable. This is also the reason why he calls Rice Donate "an enterprise serving the public welfare."

"Historically, the concept of social enterprise promoted a sense of balance. It is standardizing and guiding some enterprises to become social enterprises."

More Challenges

In four years, Rice Donate has grown from this new born company in Guangzhou into a company in its prime based in the capital city of Beijing, which has won wide recognition and many honors (see Table 1).

1. Growing Pain

Although it has overcome the difficulties in moving from the south to the north, as a start-up company, Rice Donate is still toiling forward. It is constantly experiencing growing pains as side effects.

Princes in fairy tales will grow into kings and undertake heavy responsibilities. The same is true for Zi Wang (which means Prince in Chinese) of Rice Donate. As the founder, he has worked on many problems over the years, some of which have been tackled down and become the dust under his feet or the memory in his brain;

Table 1 Major honors Rice Donate won in recent years

1. The founder was selected into "30 under 3 Asia" of Forbes
2. Annual Team award of Nandu weekly
3. Bronze award of the 2nd Tsinghua University president's cup innovation challenge
4. Zhongguancun high tech enterprise
5. Tsinghua X-lab social innovation star 2015
6. Finalist award of Anping and PKU Public Welfare Communication Award 2015
7. Winning award of "CITIC & Guoan Maker Cup" capital youth entrepreneurship and innovation competition
8. Public welfare award of global well-being technology innovation challenge
9. Beijing excellent entrepreneurship project 2015
10. Action pioneer gold award of orion public welfare practitioner competition
11. Gold award and best business model award of the 7th "Northern Lights Cup" Tsinghua University public welfare entrepreneurship practice competition

while the rest are emerging now and then in the daily operation of Rice Donate, requiring his constant attention.

In the early years, Zi Wang had to worry about funds, because even the best cook can't make a dish without food. But now, he's facing different problems. If they introduce external finance, are they going to lose control of the enterprise to investors, or will the commercial interests outweigh their initial commitment to public welfare? The founder of Mobike once said "If we fail in the end, just think of what we did as public welfare." But that is obviously just something he said on a whim. Zi Wang started Rice Donate for public welfare from the beginning. He can't think like that. After the company introduces external capital, if it put too much focus on commercial interests, it will be definitely shift away from it original commitment; but if it pays no attention to commercial interests, it will fail the investors. Moderation is a traditional Chinese wisdom, but it's not so easy to implement.

Although Rice Donate now has more than three million users, Zi Wang still believes that another big challenge is to develop new users and maintain user viscosity. Zi Wang knows that, although it has been developed with some scale, Rice Donate is still spreading by word-of-mouth among users. During an interview in 2015, Zihao Mo, the co-founder, mentioned that as early as 2013, Rice Donate was widely reported by major media in Guangzhou, but these reports had hardly brought any user traffic to the app. Its public welfare attribute determines that Rice Donate can only attract users by long-term accumulation and qualified service. Advertisements won't help.

2. **Plagiarism and copycat**

In the public welfare industry, Rice Donate can certainly be regarded as a pioneer, for creating the innovative platform that brings users, public welfare organizations and enterprises together. In 2012, Rice Donate had the idea of entering the field of public welfare through mobile Internet. In recent years, the success of Rice Donate let many people see the opportunity to enter this field in the same way. Competitors emerged one after another, and reached a peak in 2014, when there were more than 40 similar apps in Apple app Store alone. Even some big companies launched apps with similar functions. During this competition, many creative ideas and models of Rice Donate were copied. This may not be a challenge for the whole public welfare industry, but it definitely is one for Rice Donate.

Zi Wang said that this was actually what he expected to see. The competition in the public welfare industry would increase the social influence of this industry as a whole and enhance its recognition and identity. He thinks that the public welfare industry is still at primitive and immature stage. The entry of competitors can improve the development of the whole industry, which is a good thing. The progress of the industry cannot be achieved by one company. What Rice Donate needs to do is to maintain its good reputation and brand name in the industry. As for being plagiarized, Zi Wang is very optimistic, because it just proves the strength of Rice Donate.

"Our goal is just to maintain our leading position in this industry. Others are copying us because what we are doing is valuable."

3. **The challenge of simplification**

After all these years of development, Rice Donate's app has been upgrading and adding many creative functions. But recently, Zi Wang began to worry about this change, because this is the era of "less is more." This is why WeChat has been so successful. Exquisite and creative design will naturally increase user's learning cost. For example, users have to understand how each public welfare project on the platform operates; how enterprises donate money and materials; how users earn Rice; and how public welfare organizations implement and feed back to the society and users. On the one hand, the logic of public welfare includes the complex process of capital funding to implementation to supervision. While on the other hand, Rice Donate has to simplify its app and reduce users' learning cost in order to promote it.

Despite of all these challenges, the young Rice Donate has been sticking to the idealistic of its founders of Zi Wang and Zihao Mo. It's increasing its influence continuously in the public welfare industry, not just because it is the first, but because it is the strongest.

Further Reading

Ming W, Xiaohong Z (2010) Social enterprise outline. *China's Non Profit Review*, 2010 (2)

Ming W (2016) China's public charity: development, reform and trend. *National People's Congress of China*, 2016 (7)

Xianzhong Y (2004) Market failure and government failure. *Academic Forum*, 2004 (6)

Xiufeng C, Li L (2008) The rise of corporate social responsibility and the development of China's public welfare foundations. *Comparison of Economic and Social Systems*, 2008 (3)

Zhenyao W (2017) "Internet + public welfare" brings a revolution to China's public welfare industry. *Hong Yan Chun Qiu*, 2017 (2)

Company Information

Rice Donate official website. www.ricedonate.com

Tencent Foundation (2013) Rice Donate: how to turn mobile Internet into the promoter of public welfare. http://gongyi.qq.com/a/20130807/015508.htm. Accessed 7 Aug 2013

Zi W (2014). Zi Wang, the post-90s founder of Rice Donate: Charity is flat, and it is also a kind of consumption. huxiu.com. https://www.huxiu.com/article/42796/1.html. Accessed 18 September 2014

123langlang: Help People with Dyslexia to Read Freely

Wei Wu, Jiwen Song, and Yanfang Xu

> When a child who can read grows up, he won't lose himself when he's in a crowd, nor feels lonely when he's alone. That is our mission.
>
> –Lanzi Huang, founder of 123langlang

123langlang is a commercial chain education and training institution that's dedicated to the correction and treatment of children's reading and writing difficulties and the improvement of students' reading and writing abilities. It is a social enterprise with entrepreneurial spirit and runs in commercial means. Ms. Lanzi Huang is the founder. As a leading brand in the field of dyslexia correction and treatment in China, 123langlang also focuses on the improvement of reading and writing ability of primary school students. As the first learning ability (reading ability) intelligent teaching provider in China, 123langlang has been focusing on the field of dyslexia and learning ability improvement training. Since its establishment, 123langlang has been cooperating with Hong Kong experts in reading and writing ability training, and developed an advanced curriculum package algorithm based on the mechanism of matching curriculum package with trigger score range. This algorithm can automatically allocate synchronous and self-adaptive classroom teaching to each student according to their classroom scores, as well as a high-quality and easy-to-operate teaching scheme, to realize personalized and customized teaching for each student. 123langlang hopes to solve the social problem of dyslexia through commercial means.

On May 18, 2009, a young woman who loved literature and art, and published Sicheng Liang's *Twenty Lectures on Chinese Architecture and Art* gave up her publishing career of more than a decade, and founded the first professional education and training institution focusing on dyslexia of primary school students in Beijing. This was a major turning point in her life and career. Since then, Teacher Lanzi Huang became a new member of the education industry dedicated to the solution

W. Wu · J. Song · Y. Xu (✉)
Business School, Renmin University of China, Beijing, China
e-mail: xuyanfang@rmbs.ruc.edu.cn

M. Zhao and J. Mao (eds.), *Social Entrepreneurship*,
https://doi.org/10.1007/978-981-15-9881-4_10

of dyslexia. Her career shifted from publishing books to solving primary school students' dyslexia problems. Around 2009, when people in China still knew very little about dyslexia, 123langlang, led by Lanzi Huang, began to call for changes in the environment of dyslexia students, hoping that parents, schools and the society could understand and help this special group, who was mistakenly called "intelligent but slow children."

In the classroom of 123langlang's Shuang'an campus, Lanzi Huang had a lot to say when asked about her career transformation and entrepreneurship experience. "Actually I was almost famous in the publishing industry at that time. I was living an easy life. I enjoyed it when people told me at parties that "Lanzi, I have read that book you published!" But to help the children troubled with dyslexia, she chose to turn over a new leaf. When talking about "her children," her eyes are always full of tenderness and affection. She has high expectation for the future development of dyslexia and the improvement of reading and writing ability of school-age children in China. She was dedicated to help Chinese teenagers with her own effort.

However, the road to her dream was not always smooth. There were ups and downs. 123langlang started from experimental teaching in Leifeng Primary School in Chaoyang District, Beijing before it was founded, and now it has two direct campuses in Beijing and dozens of chain stores nationwide. It introduced advanced teaching materials from Hong Kong and localized teaching materials to better suitable for the students in mainland. It changed from traditional one-to-one teaching to online teaching software system and "PDA school," an upgraded intelligent teaching system. From its initial social mission of dyslexia correction education and training to the greater social responsibility of improving young people's learning ability, 123langlang keeps forging ahead and never forgets its original intention for establish dyslexia correction education.

"We know the pain points of the market, which helps our new teacher to catch up with experienced. We hope to demonstrate that a social enterprise with commercial value can also make profit it deserves, and set a good example for children. We hope to influence purchase and win the favor of capital by the power of market. We hope to deepen such influence until legislation is in place." This is the corporate Manifesto of 123langlang (Fig. 1).

"I'm Not Stupid; I'm Just a Slow Reader"

Different from western countries, as well as Hong Kong and Macao regions, who have in-depth understanding of dyslexia, mainland China know every little about this issue. A lot needs to be done by the society to educate the public to learn more about it and pay attention to it. Generally speaking, dyslexia is a common learning disorder. Children with dyslexia can't process verbal or written information very well. They have great difficulties in reading and writing.

The World Health Organization in its international classification of diseases (ICD-10) defines "Dyslexia can be divided into acquired dyslexia and developmental

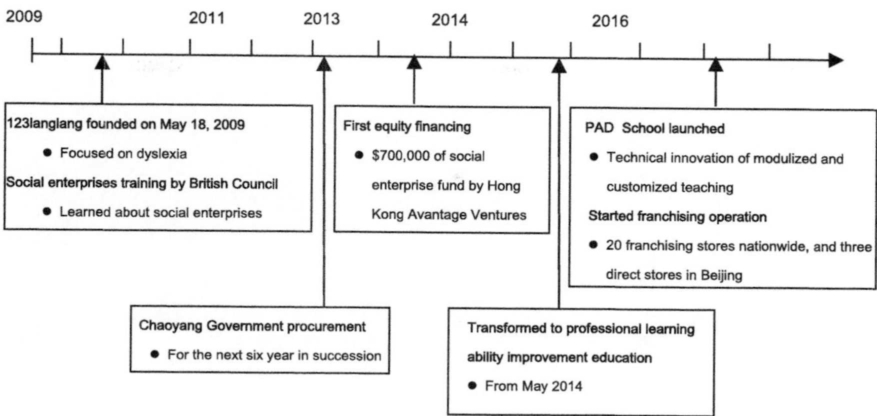

Fig. 1 The development of 123langlang

dyslexia. The former refers to the reading difficulty caused by acquired brain injury or disease; the latter refers to the state of reading difficulty in which the individual has no difference with other individuals in general intelligence, motivation, living environment and educational conditions, nor obvious visual, hearing and nervous disabilities, but the reading performance is obviously lower than the average level of corresponding age. "Developmental dyslexia is the major study object of psychology and education. Reading and writing disorder or difficulties mentioned in this book refer to developmental dyslexia. Studies show that dyslexia is not caused by intellectual factors. The intellectual level of many people with dyslexia is even higher than that of the average persons. However, their brain area processing reading and spelling is different from the ordinary person. Children with dyslexia are often called "intelligent but slow children" (Fig. 2).

"At present, Hong Kong has established national census mechanism of reading and writing disorders. All the children of school age go through a scale screening half a year after they enter school. The census covers all population. The school of education of Hong Kong University also developed special teaching materials. Statistics of Hong Kong in 2012 shows 12% of the respondents have dyslexia. There is no existing screening mechanism for dyslexia in the mainland now. In 2014, we made a survey on more than 10,000 people, showing a 10% incidence rate. Statistics of recent years shows that the proportion of persons with dyslexia is increasing. Dyslexia has become the No. 1 disease that hinders children's physical and psychological development."

According to the result of the screening survey of more than 2,000 primary school students in Beijing, Wuhan, Jinan and other places in 2014 by the task force of "survey of current situation of Chinese dyslexia" of the Institute of psychology of the Chinese Academy of Sciences, the suspected incidence of dyslexia was up to about 11%. It can be estimated that more than 10 million primary school students are affected by dyslexia. However, social awareness of the problem of dyslexia was limited. Researchers knew very little about it, let alone the general public. In addition,

Fig. 2 "I'm not stupid; I'm just a slow reader"

many parents couldn't accept that their children had dyslexia. They thought of it as a denial of their children's IQ or an insulting treatment.

Generally speaking, dyslexia includes three types. The first one is reading and language difficulties, including difficulties in pronunciation, reading speed, rhythm, vocabulary and word understanding. The second one is writing difficulties, including poor handwriting, inconstant writing spacing, large gap between oral expression and written expression. And the third one is movement coordination problems, including poor balance, and uncoordinated gesture of holding the pen. If a child has 6 out of the 12 problems shown in Table 1 for six months, he or she has 70% chance to have dyslexia.

Teaching Experiment in Leifeng Primary School

Lanzi Huang's original intention was to establish a publishing organization like Random House to change and influence generations of Chinese people and become an excellent book publisher. When making entrepreneurial decisions, Lanzi Huang started from efficiency logic to analyze the current situation and existing solutions of dyslexia, and went on to figure out which efforts and achievements she could make. Through her social network and active interactions, she obtained professional support from industry experts, teaching and research project support from the government educational departments, equity investment from Hong Kong Avantage Ventures, a professional social institution, and understanding and support from the parents. With continuous and increasing investment and commitment of these stakeholders,

Table 1 Characteristics of students with dyslexia

Items	Characteristics of students with dyslexia
1	Read hardly or wrongly
2	Cannot understand after reading
3	Poor fluency in reading; skipping words or lines
4	Refuse to write; write with difficulties; poor or wrong handwriting
5	Write slowly; write one stroke at one time
6	Short attention period
7	Low efficiency in learning; hyperactivity
8	Poor sports ability; poor sense of balance
9	Poor gesture of holding pen; clumsy when tying shoes or using chopsticks
10	Bad interpersonal relationship; shy or impatient
11	Low self-confidence; easy to give up
12	Smart, but not for learning

Source of information 123langlang

123langlang kept on upgrading its teaching technology platform and expanding its business scale, so as to realize continuous expansion and rapid growth.

Lanzi Huang knew about the concept of dyslexia from her publishing career. Her original plan was to publish related books to help people with dyslexia to improve their reading and writing ability, and eventually increase reading volumes of such books and boost publishing. This is the typical ideal of a book publisher. So she went to Hong Kong to seek advice from some experts and scholars in the field of dyslexia correction and treatment. Professor Xijin Xie, vice president of the school of education of Hong Kong University, as well as other experts, provided related materials for her to read free of charge. Her interaction with the academic circle of dyslexia in Hong Kong has also attracted a group of Hong Kong professionals to join 123langlang's expert team, which now include Professor and vice president Xie Xijin of the school of education of Hong Kong University, Assistant Professor Fuquan He and Dr. Weizhi Pan of the same school, and Associate Professor Chengzhengjia Li of the department of nursing and medical science of Hong Kong Polytechnic University. At that time, Lanzi Huang discovered a set of teaching materials on the cultivation of reading and writing ability of primary school students in Hong Kong, and realized the great value of it at first glance. "When mainland was still obsessed with cramming education, Hong Kong has begun to improve students' learning ability by improving their reading and writing ability."

Lanzi Huang began her work on the introduction of the teaching materials to the mainland. In order to localize the teaching materials, Chinese Language Teaching Professional Committee of the Chinese Education Society incorporated it as one of the academic research topics of the task force of "recognition, intervention and correction of reading and writing difficulties," and initiated experimental teaching and textbook development in Beijing Leifeng Primary School. They worked together with educational experts to localize this set of teaching materials introduced from Hong Kong and make them suitable for the actual situation in the mainland. The success of the experimental teaching in Lei Feng Primary School gave Lanzi Huang great confidence in this set of teaching materials (Fig. 3).

At the end of the experimental teaching, a student's parents asked her, "Teacher LAN Zi, are you leaving us?" Huang said, "Yes, my dream is to become an excellent publisher." For her, it was just an experimental teaching for the development of the teaching materials. She certainly would continue her beloved publishing career. However, teachers and parents kept on contacting her, hoping that she can continue with dyslexia correction. At that time, she began to hesitate between the choices of continuing her publishing career and becoming an excellent publisher, or shifting to the new field of dyslexia correction? At first, she was still inclined to continuing with her publishing career, although dyslexia correction also meant a lot to her.

Just then, a student named Yingying touched her and changed her. Yingying was a student of Leifeng Primary School in Chaoyang District, Beijing, who was identified with serious dyslexia. She was one of Lanzi Huang's first students. After two weeks of teaching, Lanzi Huang was surprised to find that there were many pleasant changes to Yingying, such as saying some short sentences and even whole sentences, and using prepositions. One day, Yingying's grandmother found Lanzi Huang in the classroom and expressed her gratitude to her. She said, "Yingying has changed! In the past she could only say single words. But now she can talk freely like a bird. She also loves reading now. She opens a book and starts reading once she get home now. She never

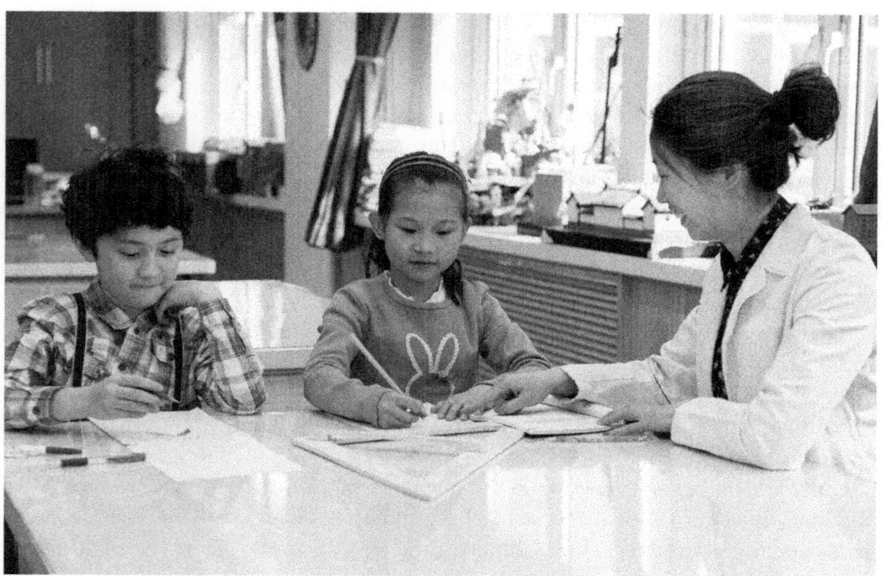

Fig. 3 Giving lessons

opened a book before." These changes happened to Yingying deeply touched Lanzi Huang. She began to think about the significance of dyslexia correction.

"I know that Yingying would never be lonely once she started to enjoy reading. I led her into the world of reading before it was too late. This was like changing her whole life. Nothing is more significant and attractive to me. When I was still hesitating, the words "before it was too late" helped me made the decision.

Once, Lanzi Huang went to the Juvenile Detention Center to hold an intervention and treatment activity for dyslexia. A banner saying "before it was too late" on the wall of the detention center deeply touched Lanzi Huang. Lanzi Huang said, "there is a rule about the intervention treatment of dyslexia globally, that is, the effect of intervention treatment is the best before the age of 12, and will decline dramatically afterwards." It is believed that age 7 to 8 is the golden age of training, 9 to 10 is the critical age, and 11 to 12 is the remedy age. Before the age of 12, intervention is completely in time and effective. My work as a publisher mostly affects the adult population. While intervention therapy for dyslexia is more significant for children before it's too late" (Fig. 4).

Translation of the letter:

Dear Teacher Lanzi,

How are you?

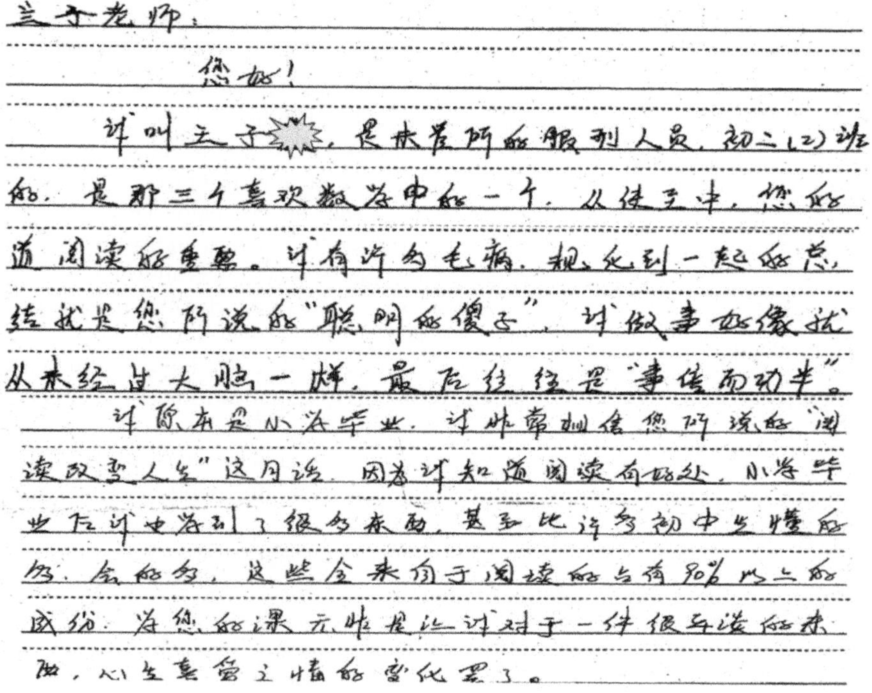

兰子老师：

您好！

我叫王子，是未管所的服刑人员，初二(2)班的，是那三个喜欢数学中的一个。从体王中，您的道阅读的重要。我有许多毛病，想了想到一起的总结就是您所说的"聪明的傻子"，我做事的像就从未经过大脑一样，最后往往是"事倍而功半"。

我原本是小学毕业，我非常相信您所说的"阅读改变人生"这句话，因为我知道阅读有好处，小学毕业后我也学到了很多东西，甚至比许多初中生懂的多，会的多，这些全来自于阅读的占有80%以上的成份。听您的课更是让我对于一件很平淡的东西，心生喜爱之情的变化罢了。

Fig. 4 A letter from Beijing Juvenile Detention Center

> I'm Wang, a prisoner serving my sentences, from class 2 grade 2 of the middle school. I'm one of the three students who are interested in math. You have been teaching us the importance of reading. I have many shortcomings. I think I'm just that kind of person that you called "a smart fool". I seldom think before I do things, so that result is usually disappointing.
>
> I only finished primary school before. I have faith in what you said, that is "Reading can change a person's life". I know it from my own experience. I have been reading since I graduated from primary school, and now I know things that some middle school graduates don't know. 90% of my knowledge, I believe, come from my reading.

At first, Lanzi Huang had never heard about social enterprise. In her mind, traditional social public welfare organizations were not encouraged to make profits or charge for its services. They could only provide free services. But what she was about to do was education and training business that needed to charge. Lanzi Huang felt confused. After receiving a training on social entrepreneur of the British Council in 2009, Lanzi Huang began to understand the concept of "social enterprise." "From the social practices in UK, social enterprises must have both business attributes and social problem-solving oriented attributes. Social enterprises in UK and India are all operated by entrepreneurs, instead of public welfare organizations. Social enterprises transformed from public welfare organizations can hardly survive. Social enterprises will consider and solve the problems from commercial views, which determine they can solve the problems more efficiently and effectively. From this perspective, the value of social enterprises is significant." This timely training of social entrepreneurs gave Lanzi Huang's confidence to run 123langlang as a social enterprise. "The number of Baidu search results for dyslexia in 2008 or 2009 was only about 1500, compared with 2.8 million in 2017. Social awareness of dyslexia has been improving. This is the social change made by 123langlang."

On May 18, 2009, 123langlang was founded in Haidian District, Beijing as a registered company. Since then, Lanzi Huang began to devote all her efforts to dyslexia correction. Huang hopes to teach children to read before it's too late. But the road was not smooth for them as a start-up company. Different from entrepreneurship in other fields, dyslexia correction training is a highly professional field which requires high investment in teaching and research. It is almost impossible for 123langlang to verify the feasibility of its products or development direction by experimenting with minimum viable products for its product development, which increases 123langlang's entrepreneurial risk substantially. The huge investment in curriculum development and no profits in the early stage lead to serious financial problem. Lanzi Huang's spent almost all of her savings "There was this time when I had to sell eight tons of books I published before as garbage, in exchange for tens of thousands of yuan to pay my employees. As a former book publisher, I was really sad that I had to treat books like this."

Despite of all these difficulties, 123langlang achieved great success. First of all, it signed government procurement service contract with Chaoyang District, Beijing. As early as 2011, Social Construction Office of Chaoyang District Government established "Chaoyang District Social Organization Cultivation Base." 123langlang was one of the first eight organizations. Meanwhile, Chaoyang District Government also purchased 123langlang's public welfare project "Dandelion Seed Lecturer Plan," to popularize the concept of dyslexia and promote parent-child reading methods to primary schools and communities in Chaoyang District. By now, Chaoyang District Government has included 123langlang's "Helping Program for Children with Dyslexia" into its government purchase service project for five consecutive years, and awarded 123langlang the title of "Excellent Social Service Brand," to provide correction training for more children with dyslexia. Primary school students aged 6-12 with dyslexia in Chaoyang District will be granted with a government subsidy of up to 3000 yuan. These students will receive professional and continuous training on reading and writing ability, as well as comprehensive and personalized training tracking. From 2016 to 2017, 123langlang carried out "Plan to Help Young Talents Overcome Dyslexia." They went into schools, communities and enterprises, hold more than 30 activities, including "Family Education at School," "Parents' Club," "Primary School Teacher Salon" and "Community Class," and influenced tens of thousands of people.

Secondly, 123langlang was invested with $700,000 by Hong Kong Avantage Ventures for social enterprises at the beginning of 2013, which allowed 123langlang to get rid of its financial pressure, and began its explosion for transformation. "This has been one of the largest single investments in China's social enterprises even until now," Yiran Li, a partner from the investor Hong Kong Avantage Ventures said in an interview. When asked about the reason for this investment, Li said, "We had met many founders of social enterprises, but Lanzi Huang was more like a teacher. She was dedicated to solve the social problem of dyslexia."

After being financing, 123langlang began to think about the essential problems in dyslexia correction and the fundamental solutions to them.

Technological Innovation and Business Transformation

The transformation of 123langlang was the common product of technology transformation and business model transformation. The key for its success lies in its "double helix innovation" ability and continuous evolutionary ability. As define by "double helix innovation," technological innovation and business transformation are interrelated in some kind of structure like "double helix." Technological innovation and market demand are the two driving forces for the development of the business model of social enterprises, and also interact with each other actively. The relationship between technological innovation and market demand innovation are just like "double helix." Driven by the interaction of the "double helix," 123langlang kept on the exploration for its business model transformation as a social enterprise. 123langlang's continuous technological innovation and the increasing market demand for dyslexia correction and reading and writing ability training are the two driving forces for the continuous and rapid development of 123langlang. They interacted and grew together like a "double helix," and strengthened the core competitiveness of 123langlang.

Technological Innovation: Improving Education Equity with Technological Means

In 2009, Lanzi Huang received a call from a volunteer teacher in mountain area in Chongqing Province. He introduced himself, and asked Lanzi Huang if she could provide technical support to improve reading and writing ability of the children in the mountain area. Lanzi Huang considered for a long time, and finally came up with several possible solutions: one was to send a teacher to teach in the mountain area for one year; and the other was to invite the volunteer teacher to study in Beijing for one year. Unfortunately, neither of these solutions was implemented in the end due to time cost and limited technical means. Nobody followed it up or fed back any more.

After receiving the equity investment of $700,000 from Avantage Ventures, an investment organization of social enterprises in Hong Kong, 123langlang no longer need to worry about its financial situation. When the pressure of survival was relieved, the company was able to shift its focus to the transformation of its business model. 123langlang made two major business decisions: one was to realize the modularization and customization of its teaching models; and the other was to realize large-scale training of teachers through technical means. The realization of these two business decisions both depended on 123langlang's forward-looking notion of improving efficiency through technical means. From then on, 123langlang started its exploration for technical solution to education. It began with the pain points of teachers, students and parents in dyslexia education, and tried to reconstruct dyslexia education by technical means. Currently, its PDA teaching platform has realized self-adaptive learning.

In Lanzi Huang's view, the biggest constraint to the development of the industry lies in the cultivation of professional teachers. 123langlang tried to solve this problem by improving training and teaching models through technical measures. According to 123langlang's analysis, mainland area needs more than 20,000 teachers in dyslexia correction, and there is still a big gap in professional teachers now. "With all of its current training capacity, Hong Kong can only cultivate 30 dyslexia correction trainers a year at most. If we want to train 10,000 professional teachers, it will take more than 300 years by this conventional training model. This is obviously unacceptable. Tens of thousands of children with dyslexia in the mainland can't afford to wait for so many years either."

Conventional education relays on teachers' ability to carry out personalized education. Excellent teachers differentiate their teaching methods based on individual students' characteristics, so that students can develop in the best suited ways. This personalized education model has very high requirement on the teachers' knowledge and ability level. Conventional school teaching today is teacher-centered. Teachers should not only teach the whole class, but also give individualized guidance to each student. But in reality, there are usually several dozens of students in a class. Teachers can hardly pay equal attention to each student, which directly affects the quality of teaching and the individualized development of students.

Internet technology makes it possible to implement large-scale teacher cultivation through modular replication. In Lanzi Huang's assumption, "professional teaching platform + professional trainers" makes "excellent" teachers. Lanzi Huang made a metaphor: "It's just like cultivating doctors of traditional Chinese medicine. In the past, cultivating a good doctor of traditional Chinese medicine would take a long time, because it's difficult to make personalized prescriptions in traditional Chinese medicine. The same is true for the cultivation of excellent teachers. But now, software can generate personalized learning plans to each child based on their characteristics, just like the doctors making personalized prescriptions. This function can greatly ease the burden of the teachers, and shorten the time spent on training."

Its innovative teaching software allowed 123Langlang to match personalized teaching programs to different students intelligently. This was a breakthrough in the training of teachers in the field of dyslexia correction, and freed dyslexia correction trainings from the restriction of the shortage in professional teachers. "It used to take at least half a year to train a teacher. By this new teaching system, it only takes one week."

Meanwhile, 123langlang also computerized all the paper-based teaching materials. Inspired by the modules using in movable type printing, 123langlang divided its dyslexia correction teaching materials into several modules. 123langlang reorganized all the teaching materials and input them into the software system as separate modules. At the same time, it conducted personalized analysis on the students with the big data and intelligent evaluation functions of the system. Then it could provide different teaching programs for different students. Through technological innovation, 123langlang standardized and modularized the contents of its education projects. This was the technical support for its future expansion through franchise chain, which allowed 123langlang to quickly duplicate ordinary or franchise stores nationwide. It also broke the bottleneck of insufficient teachers. On this basis, 123langlang proposed standardized intelligent teaching.

On September 8, 2013, 123langlang's online teaching software system was officially launched. Through its online teaching platform, 123langlang realized small class teaching and even individualized teaching within the same class. Teachers could assign homework through the online platform during class. And after class, teachers could send students' learning data to their parents' mobile clients for them to help their children, so as to realize effective interaction between teachers, students and parents. However, 123langlang wouldn't stop there. It planned to develop a more intelligent teaching system, not just automatic teaching software.

The joint of Junyi Bai, CTO of Beijing Beisen Cloud Computing Co., Ltd., turned this plan into reality in short time In July 2016, "PDA School" was officially launched online, which included the functions of intelligent matching of teaching/learning tasks and automatic evaluation. As a fully intelligent teaching management system, PDA School included intelligent teaching function, as well as comprehensive management, maintenance and service functions for all the students and teachers. With PDA School, students could finish exercises on PDAs during class, and their learning data would be recorded by the system. After class, teachers could push the training results analyzed by the system to the parents on their computers

. And then parents could receive children's training and testing result charts and after-school training programs on their mobile phones in real time.

PDA school has four terminals, for students, teachers, principals and agents respectively. By automatically collecting the learning data of each student, the system can dynamically record, feedback and evaluate their learning progress, and automatically match the best learning tasks for them. Thus, it achieved personalized teaching and intelligent teaching, as well as mixed age teaching for primary school period. Teachers could learn each student's learning progress and status through teacher's terminal, so as to provide personalized guidance to the students. They could also evaluate and improve the content and quality of their teaching in real time based on the system evaluation results. Through principal's terminal, administrators could learn about the learning data of each student in each class of each school in time, collect the teaching data of each teacher and carry out effective evaluation, and control the overall teaching progress and make timely adjustments when necessity. The agent's terminal enabled 123langlang to expand its business by franchise chain and freed it from reliance on famous teachers. At the same time, the intelligent teaching system allowed the agents to control its operation in real time, and also allowed 123langlang to supervise and evaluate its franchisees. In addition, parents could also interact with school and their children through mobile phone platform and realize real-time home-school communication. The teaching system was complete visualized, so that parents could supervise the teaching quality. Technology equalizes education. Through technology, 123langlang made the dream come true, where "children in mountain areas and children in Beijing can enjoy the same education."

Through its innovative teaching platform and technical and model innovation of its teacher training, 123langlang has accumulated a large pool of data of students' learning behavior and habits. Its curriculum package and algorithm have been patented, providing technical and data supports for its future upgrading to machine learning and intelligent teaching. This system had neat design and user-friendly interface. Through franchise chain model, it could also quickly popularize learning ability improvement training across the nation.

"If the volunteer teacher in the mountain area of Chongqing Province comes to us now, we will be able to help him. We can give him a short training and an account to our system. We can help with his teaching by our technology. This is the transformation brought by technology and education equity. It makes personalized education duplicable. This is the direction of our future exploration."

Business Transformation: Undertaking Greater Social Mission

When Lanzi Huan was giving dyslexia correction trainings in Beijing, she noticed an interesting phenomenon. In Beijing, many mothers formed teams and took turns to drop off and pick up their children to schools. Therefore, a child with dyslexia was usually accompanied by two normal children in the same class. There were about 10 such children who didn't have dyslexia, but these children had made surprisingly huge progress in their reading and writing ability. Lanzi Huang shared this phenomenon during her exchange in Hong Kong, and attracted wide attention. Experts in Hong Kong told her that reading and writing improvement training was needed for all children.

Montessori education method is very popular in special children's education across the world. This education method was originally designed for disabled children, but it's also very effective in teaching normal and healthy children in practice. Normal children could also improve their reading and writing abilities by using their teaching materials, and even make greater achievements.

Therefore, Lanzi Huang began to think about the possibility of business transformation—from focusing only on dyslexia correction education to including learning ability improvement education as well; from serving only the children with dyslexia, to covering other students who need to improve their learning ability as well. If dyslexia correction training was to be applied to normal children, 123langlang's original operation model needed to be modified. The business area that 123langlang had been engaged in was more about serving the social value. Should it introduce more commercial operation elements and transform the enterprise into a professional training institution that not only provides correction treatments for children with dyslexia, but also reading and writing learning ability improvement trainings, or learning ability improvement trainings, for normal children?

123Langlang held a plenary meeting on this issue, and the resolution of business transformation got passed with the approval rate of 8 out of 10. From then on, 123langlang began to shift its business focus to a wider area of reading and writing learning ability improvement. This transformation not only gave 123langlang opportunities to create more commercial value, but also greater social value.

After the transformation, 123langlang aimed to improving the ten major learning abilities of school-age children and cultivating their comprehensive learning abilities (see Table 2). 123langlang hopes to change parents' purchase behavior through market forces, win the favor of capital by commercial operation, and make profound social influence.

Profit Repays Public Welfare

Business Model

At present, the whole society still knows very little about dyslexia. It is urgent to educate the public and improve their awareness on dyslexia. Enterprises and public welfare organizations engaged in dyslexia are in serious shortage. As a social enterprise, 123langlang has been making contributions to public welfare with its profits from commercial business. It has been subsidizing the training for children with dyslexia in poor families with its commercial profits. Its property as a social enterprise determines that 123langlang does not need to relay on donations like conventional

Table 2 Ten major learning abilities

No.	Abilities	Targets
1	Reading	Improve children's reading speed and accuracy; help them understand the meaning of the article more accurately; let them love reading
2	Writing	Help children to master the structure of Chinese characters more accurately; improve their speed, accuracy, and neatness of their handwriting
3	Concentration	Improve the degree and length of children's concentration of hearing and vision; help them improve their learning efficiency
4	Memorization	Improve the speed and accuracy of children's memorization; teach them how to use various memorization methods, such as association and visualization, to memorize the knowledge
5	Interpersonal skills	Improve children's ability to get along with others in harmony; help them to understand fairness, sharing, courtesy and cooperation; tell them not to be self-centered
6	Communication	Improve children's communication ability; let them express themselves more fluently and with larger vocabulary; train them to give public speaking with confidence
7	Self-Reflection	Improve children's ability to recognize, insight and reflect on their own behavior; help them to recognize and evaluate themselves correctly; help them build sense of rules
8	Imagination	Help children to expand their minds and relate knowledge of different fields; guide them to make sentences with rich, creative and interesting words
9	Logic	Help children to think correctly and reasonably; guide them to observe, compare, analyze and reason things; encourage them to express themselves more accurately and orderly
10	Observation	Cultivate children's ability to observe carefully and discover; encourage them to think and solve problems by themselves

Source of information 123langlang

public welfare organizations. Through commercial operation, it's capable of making market profits to support its development, which frees it from reliance on external financial supports, and allows it to develop faster and more sustainably. "Establish a professional dyslexia correction training institution, and provide free or discounted services for children from low-income families by means of cross subsidy. Solving social problems by commercial approaches is our biggest innovation."

Currently, 123langlang's major sources of revenue include students' tuition fees, service fees of government procurement (mostly from the government of Chaoyang District, Beijing), donations, subsidies and investments from various foundations, and franchise income. 123langlang can obtain stable cash inflow to improve its ability of sustainable operation, without harming its property as a social enterprise.

According to the characteristics of the business models of social enterprises, 123langlang's business model can be identified as the subcategory of cross subsidy model under the category of integrated model, that is, to solve the social problem of dyslexia of children in school age with the profits made from it commercial operation of direct and franchised schools. The main social goal of 123langlang is to improve the reading and writing ability of children with or without dyslexia. Its main customers are students with or without dyslexia. It has a large variety of directly stakeholders, including governments, public welfare organizations, investment organizations, primary schools, students and their parents. For different customers, 123langlang adopts three different charging policies: (1) For students with dyslexia from rich or ordinary families, the charging standard is 3,000 yuan/person/term; (2) For government service procurement projects, the charging fees are subsidized partly by the government, and covered partly by 123langlang. Students only pay the rest; (3) For students with dyslexia from poor families, 123langlang cross subsides them with 3–5% of its annual revenue, following the usual practice of international social enterprises.

123langlang has two product series: professional reading and writing ability improvement products and dyslexia correction treatment products. Since its business transformation in 2014 from focusing solely on dyslexia treatment to also covering professional reading and writing ability training. Using its original teaching materials for dyslexia treatment, it expanded its business scope to reading and writing ability improvement for normal children, and began to focus on the social problem of how to improve Chinese young people's reading ability. Although it expanded the scope of the social problems it focuses on greatly, 123langlang never forgets its original mission of education for children with dyslexia, and keeps on its exploration in dyslexia treatment.

The basic resources of 123langlang include its key partners, essential resources and business activities. Its key partners include experts in dyslexia (such as academic connections in Hong Kong, Institute of Psychology of the Chinese Academy of Sciences, Beijing Academy of Education and Science, etc.), various public welfare foundations (such as Narada Foundation, China Social Entrepreneur Foundation, HNA Group and Hong Kong Avantage Ventures, etc.), its franchisees, students, parents and primary and secondary school teachers. Its core resources include its teaching system, PDA School, professional reading and writing ability improvement training team and its unique teaching materials. These resources, together with 123langlang's business activities, provides foundation for its development.

The customers of 123langlang can be divided into three categories: target customers, client maintenance and distribution channels. In 123Langlang's current commercial model, its target customer groups include normal children in K12 period, children with dyslexia and government procurement services. The distribution channels of 123langlang include direct stores and franchised stores. Currently, 123langlang has two direct stores in Beijing and 42 franchised stores in the whole country. Franchising has become its main business expansion model. In May 2014, 123langlang officially transformed its major business to professional service provider of customized learning ability training for primary school students. At present, in all the direct stores in Beijing, the proportion of children enrolled for dyslexia correction and those for learning ability improvement is 50% respectively. While in the chain stores outside Beijing, 95% of the students are normal children receiving learning ability improvement trainings. As for client maintenance, 123langlang uses both online and off line channels, including official website, WeChat official account and public lectures and sharing sessions.

Thanks to its commercial and technological power, 123langlang achieved rapid development in recent years. First of all, its financial situation has greatly improved after it was invested 700,000 USD by Avantage Ventures Hong Kong. And then, its successful transformation into a professional training provider of children's reading and writing ability improvement brought in a continuous and stable cash flow, which improved its ability for sustainable development. Meanwhile, the online platform "PDA School" realized the replication of its classroom teaching. Its business scale has been growing rapidly with the help of franchising since then. "As I estimated, I would be able to open 20 training centers by the age of 60. But now, with the help of the software system, this goal was achieved last year. It just took one year. By the age of 60, I may be able to open thousands of training centers." Lanzi Huang was very confident about the future of 123langlang.

In the future, 123langlang plans to transform its profit-making model from the conventional way of charging tuition fees to charging commission fees to franchise stores. By breaking the technical barriers and bringing equal education to wider regions in China, 123langlang hopes to serve more school-age children (Fig. 5).

Mission, Vision and Value

When the company was just founded, 123Langlang set its objectives, mission, vision and values. This guaranteed the company always sticks to its original social commitment of improving the surrounding environment of children with dyslexia and providing effective teaching intervention to them (see Table 3).

123langlang always adhere to its value of "reading changes life," and is determined to "help more children to read and free their minds." It believes that "every child should be able to read." It works hard to help children improve their reading and learning ability before it's too late, and "gives them the keys to their own lives." It demonstrates its mission of "attracting public attention to children with dyslexia; improving their situation by providing specialized education and realizing education equity, and letting them fall in love with reading."

The corporate goals of 123langlang is to keep on drawing the attention of the government and common people to children's dyslexia, promote legislation of related laws, realize education equity, so as to improve the situation of children with dyslexia, give them access to individualized learning and scientific corrective treatment, and ensure them to grow up healthily both physically and mentally.

"Establish a professional dyslexia correction training institution, and provide free or discounted services for children from low-income families by means of cross subsidy." Explore solutions to the social problem of children's dyslexia with the spirit of entrepreneurship and by commercial means.

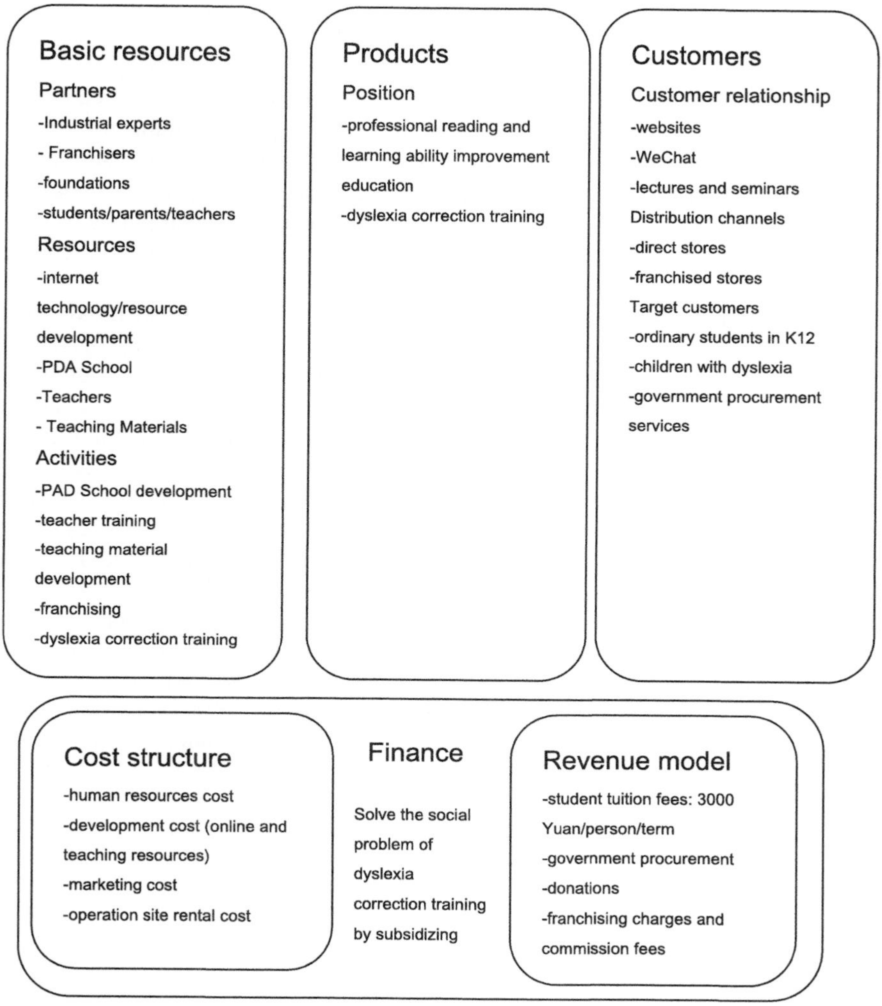

Basic resources
Partners
-Industrial experts
- Franchisers
-foundations
-students/parents/teachers
Resources
-internet
technology/resource
development
-PDA School
-Teachers
- Teaching Materials
Activities
-PAD School development
-teacher training
-teaching material
development
-franchising
-dyslexia correction training
Products
Position
-professional reading and
learning ability improvement
education
-dyslexia correction training
Customers
Customer relationship
-websites
-WeChat
-lectures and seminars
Distribution channels
-direct stores
-franchised stores
Target customers
-ordinary students in K12
-children with dyslexia
-government procurement
services
Cost structure
-human resources cost
-development cost (online and
teaching resources)
-marketing cost
-operation site rental cost
Finance
Solve the social
problem of
dyslexia
correction training
by subsidizing
Revenue model
-student tuition fees: 3000
Yuan/person/term
-government procurement
-donations
-franchising charges and
commission fees

Fig. 5 The business model of 123langlang

Table 3 Mission, vision and value of 123langlang

Mission	Attract public attention to children with dyslexia; Improve their situation by providing specialized education and realizing education equity, and let them fall in love with reading
Vision	Every child should be able to read
Value	Reading changes life

Guarantee by Governance System and Management System

Since its establishment, 123langlang has established a relatively complete corporate governance system. Lanzi Huang, the founder of the company, accounts for 51% of the company's total equity, while Hong Kong Avantage Ventures, its investor, holds 49% of the company's equity. Among the five board seats of 123langlang's board of directors, Lanzi Huang takes one, the investor takes two, and social public welfare workers take two. These measures ensure 123langlang's property of social enterprise unchanged.

As the actual controller of the company, Lanzi Huang never forgets her original intention. The management team and the teacher team have been working together to improve the learning environment of children with dyslexia, as well as the reading and writing ability of school-age children. Meanwhile, the company also uses a certain proportion of its profits to subside children with dyslexia from poor families by giving them free or discounted corrective treatments. Providing corrective treatment for children with dyslexia and improving their reading and writing ability have been integrated into 123langlang's corporate culture, and became the common cause of the whole team. In Lanzi Huang's view, 123langlang is a social enterprise. A social enterprise has its missions. It cannot just pursue economic interests.

"Social enterprises are not common enterprises, nor ordinary social service providers. Social enterprises operate commercially, make market profits and contribute to the society with its profits. Their profits should be used on helping the vulnerable groups, promoting community development and investing on themselves. They attach more importance to social value than to the pursuit of maximum corporate profits."

Conflicts and Challenges

Improving Public Awareness of "Dyslexia"

The issue of "dyslexia" has been widely concerned among the public in western countries and Hong Kong and Macao regions in China. Hong Kong has established a screening and assistance system for children with dyslexia. According to Hong Kong Education and Manpower Bureau, primary school students are required to finish special learning difficulty screen scale charts in school within the first four months after they enter school. Students who are identified with dyslexia can receive a subsidy of 20,000 HK dollars per year from the Bureau. In 2004, the federal government of the United States promulgated *Individuals with Disabilities Education Improvement Act*, which added dyslexia in the definition of learning disabilities. However, in the mainland, dyslexia has not been widely recognized by the society.

From 2008 to 2016, 123langlang carried out the project of "Public Education of Dyslexia" in Beijing, holding nearly 200 lectures on dyslexia to up to 50,000 school teachers, including how to identify, deal with and correct dyslexia. Through these activities, teachers and parents realized that dyslexia is innate. The problem does not lie in the children's intellectual ability, or their attitudes. People should fully understand their situation and provide timely assistance. But compared with Chinese population of more than one billion, 50,000 people is far from enough. There is a long way to go for the improvement of social awareness of dyslexia and even legislation. How to make use of the power of government, society and enterprises to bring more public attention to dyslexia is still pending to be explored.

Potential Conflict Between Social Value and Commercial Value

As a social enterprise, 123langlang combines both social public welfare attribute and commercial attribute. Conflicts between these two attributes happen from time to time during the development of social enterprises. The same is true for 123langlang. How to build a strong team and an efficient business model, while maintaining the balance between the public welfare and commercial businesses?

The first conflict happened during its business transformation in 2014, when it shifted its focus of social problem from dyslexia correction education to reading and writing ability improvement education. Although 123langlang had been subsidizing dyslexia correction education with its commercial profits, there happened some unavoidable neglects during its business expansion. While the original operation model focusing solely on dyslexia might compromise its commercial value.

The second conflict lied between its commercial property as a franchising business and its social property as a social enterprise after the adopting franchising model. On the one hand, franchising model was very effective in expanding 123langlang's business scale and improving its influence. But on the other hand, it also caused the conflict between franchisees' demands for market profits and 123langlang's social mission, because franchisees prioritized commercial value, or profitability, over social value. Currently, in the two direct stores in Beijing, the proportion of children enrolled for dyslexia correction and those for learning ability improvement is 50% respectively. While in the chain stores outside Beijing, 95% of the students are normal children receiving learning ability improvement trainings. Franchisees are more focused on profitability and business value, which challenges 123langlang's social mission of dyslexia correction to some extent.

Financing Difficulties

123langlang has been expecting to attract external capital to accelerate its development. This is also part of its development plan. Lanzi Huang hopes that investors can give enough time to 123langlang, instead of focusing only on development speed or financial indicators. "In fact, we welcome investors who can be patient, or some large investors for social enterprises." However, in reality, it is the general public welfare foundations that pay more attention to social issues and oppose commercialization. Investment organizations for social enterprises can only make small investments—several millions at most, and no precedent for that of over ten millions. Market-based professional investment organizations often expect rapid growth of the invested enterprises. This obviously contradicts with 123langlang's development concept. The financing difficulty has become a challenge for 123langlang's further development.

As the first social enterprise dedicated in the field of dyslexia correction and learning ability improvement for primary school students, 123langlang has made remarkable achievements in the past nine years. It has been committed to providing professional teaching and training for students with dyslexia, changing their environment, improving social awareness on dyslexia to an unprecedented level. Meanwhile, it has also expanded its business to learning ability improvement of primary school students, and shoulders a greater social responsibility. With its online teaching software system and the intelligent teaching platform "PDA School," 123langlang transformed the conventional models o teacher training and teaching through technology, greatly improved the quality of teacher training and teaching in the field of dyslexia, enhanced education equity, and laid the foundation for its transformation to the new business model of franchising operation across the nation. The innovations both in technology and business model have contributed to the success of 123langlang. Today, 123Langlang is undertaking greater social responsibility, while pursuing bigger business success at the same time.

Looking forward to the future, 123langlang is faced with many new challenges. Some are unique for it, and some are general for all the domestic social enterprises, such as how to improve the social cognitive level of dyslexia effectively? How to deal with the potential conflicts between the companies' social value and business value? How to use the capital effectively to achieve fast development? We hope that 123langlang can achieve greater achievements in dyslexia correction education of Chinese primary school students, help more children with dyslexia, and improve the overall learning ability of Chinese primary school students.

Further Reading

China Development Brief (2012) Recruitment of volunteers of Children's Dyslexia Program of Chaoyang District Government. https://gongyi.qq.com/a/20121212/000018.htm. Accessed 12 Dec 2012

The International Dyslexia Association. Definition of Dyslexia. https://dyslexiaida.org/definition-of-dyslexia. Accessed 12 Nov 2002

Peng D (2012) Children with dyslexia need our attention. Soc Welf (12)

Wang M, Zhu X (2010) Social enterprise outline. China's Nonprof Rev (2)

Yangg X, Zhou H (2010) A review of Chinese developmental dyslexia. B Soc Sci (z2)

Zhongshan Wenming Online (2014) "City of love" called on everybody to do "public welfare". http://gdzs.wenming.cn/wmzsjj/201405/t20140512_1158449.html. Accessed 12 May 2014

Company Information

123llanglang official website. www.123langlang.com

123langlang official website. She used seven years and developed standardized teaching materials for children with dyslexia. http://www.123langlang.com/media/2288.html. Accessed 17 May 2016

Carbonstop: Carbon Management Innovation with Information Technology

Yuyu Liu and Yujia Zhai

> As two major driving forces of social innovation today, Internet and low-carbon should go hand-in-hand for better development. A low-carbon Internet industry and an Internet-based low-carbon industry are two major goals of our society and can both bring business opportunities.
>
> —Luhui Yan, founder of Carbonstop

Founded in 2011 by Luhui Yan, who got a master's degree from Oxford University, Carbonstop is China's first carbon management software and consulting service provider. Since its establishment seven years ago, Carbonstop has been dedicated to providing products and services of consulting, training, software, and carbon neutralization to enterprises and organizations. Its core product is the self-developed "Carbon Accounting and Management Platform." It is the first carbon management software designed for organization users in China. Currently, three of its software has been patented. It has been shortlisted in the "Climate Change Software Competition" of World Bank as the only contestant from China, and the top six "Green Life Action" winners of the British Council.

As its name implies, Carbonstop aims to stop the carbon footprint (carbon emissions) of enterprises. In short, Carbonstop means to stop carbon. At UN Climate Change Conference 2015, Chinese government promised the world to reduce carbon emission per unit of GDP by 40–45% over the 2005 level by 2020. This is a mandatory carbon emission reduction index. As for the construction of domestic carbon emission trading system, since 2013, Chinese government has selected seven provinces for carbon emission pilots trading, and a trading market is being shaped gradually. On December 19, 2017, the National Development and Reform Commission organized a teleconference and press conference on the launch of the national carbon emission trading system, interpreting the "National Carbon Emission Trading Market Construction Plan (power industry)" issued previously. This represented the overall

Y. Liu (✉) · Y. Zhai
Business School, Renmin University of China, Beijing, China
e-mail: liuyuyu@rmbs.ruc.edu.cn

M. Zhao and J. Mao (eds.), *Social Entrepreneurship*,
https://doi.org/10.1007/978-981-15-9881-4_11

design of the national carbon emission trading system was completed and the system was officially launched.

The enterprises included in this trading system were the most directly affected by this launch. This means enterprises need to learn the knowledge and current situation of carbon emission, and evaluate the impact of their manufacture and operation made on the environment. However, governments of all levels and many enterprises still know very little about carbon emission. Some enterprises know nothing about carbon emission management, and therefore pay no attention. As a software and consulting solution provider specializing in environment, it is Carbonstop's mission to provide professional guidance to enterprises in carbon management. It has become a driving force to promote energy-saving and emission reduction, realize a low-carbon society.

Market Opportunity for Carbon Trade

What is carbon trade? What is carbon trading market? What is the current status of China's carbon trading market? In order to understand the business of Carbonstop and its role in carbon trading market, we must introduce carbon trade and carbon trading market first.

Mature Carbon Trading Market in Europe

In order to encourage enterprise to reduce their carbon emission, Europe has established a mature carbon trading market, namely the European Union Emissions Trading Scheme (EU-ETS). Carbon trade refers to an artificial market for carbon dioxide emission trading which is promoted by the governments by controlling the carbon emissions of energy consuming enterprises. Europe's carbon trading market is very mature. Back in June 1992, the United Nations Conference on Environment and Development held in Rio de Janeiro, Brazil, issued its Framework Convention on Climate Change in response to global warming. And in December 1997, Kyoto Protocol was formulated in Kyoto, Japan, which led to the formation of carbon trading market scheme, centered on carbon dioxide emissions. The EU-ETS was put into trial operation in early 2005 and official operation in early 2008.

In the carbon trading market scheme, carbon consists of two parts - carbon quota and carbon emission reduction target. The purpose of establishing carbon trading market is to promote the emission reduction of the whole society, and the subject of emission reduction is the enterprises. Thousands of enterprises in Europe are allocated with a quota. They cannot exceed their quota, or they will be punished. When its carbon emission exceeds the quota, the enterprise has two choices: It can purchase local quota which is very expensive. Or, it can invest in emission reduction projects in developing countries through Clean Development Mechanism. Clean Development Mechanism (CDM) is a mechanism recognized by the United Nations to encourage developing countries to reduce emissions. It allows developing countries to develop energy-saving and emission reduction projects, such as wind power projects, and sell the emission reduction credits to enterprises within EU-ETS. However, the proportion of the emission reduction credits traded outside the EU is under strict control. "For example, an enterprise exceeds its emission quota by one million tons. It can choose to buy credits of one million tons locally, but the price is very high. So many enterprises choose to buy carbon emission reduction credits from countries like China to meet the requirement of ETS. One ton of carbon emission reduction credits and one ton of carbon quota have the same effect under EU-ETS, but their prices are quite different." Therefore, CDM is a win-win mechanism. It helps enterprises within EU-ETS to reduce its cost for emission reduction. On the other hand, it encourages developing countries to develop energy saving and emission reduction projects and promote sustainable development.

China's New-Born Carbon Trading Market

In the past decade, the European carbon trading market has gone through a process from rise to maturity and then to decline. While in China, the market was just born and has a bright future.

Carbon trading market is not fully established yet. At the 2009 Copenhagen Climate Change Conference, Chinese government proposed its emission reduction target for the first time, and has been gradually establishing its carbon emission trading market since then. Before 2011, China did not have its own carbon trading market yet. It was involved in carbon trading simply through the Clean Development Mechanism under the Kyoto Protocol. Since then, economic crisis happened in Europe. Carbon emissions dropped rapidly for most of the enterprises, so the demand for purchasing carbon emission reduction credits disappeared. Clean Development Mechanism was not in actual use any more. In order to promote energy-saving and emission reduction, China needs its own carbon trading market urgently. In 2011, Chinese government selected seven provinces or big cities as carbon emission trading pilots, including Beijing, Tianjin, Shanghai, Chongqing, Hubei, Guangdong and Shenzhen. In June 2013, Shenzhen first established its trading market in China, and followed by other pilot provinces and cities later on. These seven carbon emission trading pilot projects cover more than 3000 enterprises with a total annual carbon dioxide emission of about 1.4 billion tons. By November 2017, the total trading value has reached 4.6 billion yuan. On December 19, 2017, the National Development and Reform Commission organized a teleconference and press conference on the launch of the national carbon emission trading system, interpreting the "National Carbon Emission Trading Market Construction Plan (power industry)" issued previously. This represented the overall design of the national carbon emission trading system was completed and the system was officially launched.

This plan put forward the principle of "addressing easier issues before difficult ones, and progressing on a step-by-step basis." It initialized national carbon emission trading system in power generation industry first, and gradually expanded its coverage, as well as trading items and trading methods. Participants of this market include enterprises or other economic organizations whose annual emissions reach 26,000 tons of carbon dioxide equivalent or above, including those in power generation industry as well as self-owned power plants in other industries. More than 1700 enterprises were first included in the carbon emission trading system, with a total emission of more than three billion tons of carbon dioxide equivalent.

As for the national administrative mechanism, National Development and Reform Commission play a leading role for the promotion of the carbon trading market. It works with authorities of relevant industries to formulate the quota allocation scheme, verify the technical specifications, and supervise the implementation. Relevant departments shall supervise the third-party verification and trading organizations according to their respective responsibilities. The authorities of provinces and municipalities with independent planning status responsible for climate change shall supervise the data verification, quota allocation, key allocation, and performance of major emission units within their respective jurisdictions. The quota allocated to each enterprise is based on the government's tracking and investigation on the historical carbon emissions, as well as the size of the enterprise. "The quota allocated to the enterprise is based on how much it emitted. Large enterprises would be allocated with more quota, and small enterprises less." Luhui Yan explained.

There is also another important participant in the carbon trading market - verification agencies. Qualified verification agencies verify carbon emission data and issue independent verification reports in accordance with relevant regulations and technical specifications. Currently, domestic verification agencies include some official institutions like China Quality Certification Center, as well as many qualified private enterprises approved by the National Development and Reform Commission. As for the charging policies of the verification agencies, Luhui Yan said, "considering that carbon itself is an asset, verification agencies cannot charge the enterprises directly, otherwise there will be conflict of interests. So they are basically paid by the governments according to their workload. It also varies between different industries. For example, verification of chemical industry is more complicated so the cost will be a little higher."

Currently, China's carbon trading market is still in trail stage. Misoperations on carbon emission data have been found in some of the pilot regions—Some verification agencies seek benefits from carbon trading by making up and modifying data; and some provide consultation service at the same time. These problems are commonly seen today, but they must be solved. Luhui Yan believes these problems are inevitable in the early stage. With the development of carbon trading market, these verification agencies must be put under strict administration and supervision.

Footprints of Carbonstop

The carbon trading market is essentially a policy market. From data verification, quota allocation, verification specifications, to trade supervision, each step should be strictly controlled by the government authorities. Enterprises provide data to verification agencies; then verification agencies verify data in accordance with regulations and technical specifications; and finally quota is allocated to enterprise based on the verification results. Then what is Carbonstop's role in this process?

What Does Carbonstop Do

In carbon trade, the major role of Carbonstop is to help the enterprises to evaluate their data they will submit to the verification agencies and win more quotas for them. For example, Luhui Yan explained, enterprises have several different sets of data. The responsibility of Carbonstop is to evaluate which data should be provided to the verification agencies to help the enterprises obtain more quotas. "That is not cheating about data. What we do is to evaluate data through technical means and then provide the best solutions to the enterprises." Luhui Yan believes that in the field of data verification and evaluation, Carbonstop has richer experience and more advanced technology than other consulting companies and verification agencies.

Carbonstop also has rich experience in low-carbon training, carbon asset development and management, and low-carbon technical support. In addition to enterprises mentioned above, Carbonstop's clients also include governments, exchange agencies, verification agencies and other carbon asset management companies like itself. Its business scope includes providing solutions for emission control enterprises, offering training for the governments, developing trading platforms for carbon exchange agencies, developing verification systems for verification institutions, and developing and managing carbon emission reduction projects for carbon asset companies. In the past, Carbonstop focused more on export demands. As suppliers of European and American enterprises, many Chinese enterprises were required to provide carbon emission information to them. Besides, many investors also had carbon information disclosure requirements on the enterprises they plan to invest in. A British non-governmental organization (NGO) once initiated a carbon information disclosure project, which represents the common requests of global investment organizations. Through this project, investment organizations hoped to learn more about the enterprises and find out if they are sustainable. This project motivated enterprises to attach more importance to carbon emission reduction. "For the Fortune Global 500 companies, this was like a mandatory requirement. Because otherwise, it won't get any investment, or maintain good relationship with their investors. This requirement was not only on themselves, but also on their suppliers. Therefore, many Chinese enterprises had been driven to do so." Apparently, Carbonstop has rich experience in carbon information disclosure, carbon accounting, and carbon management consulting. It has been widely recognized, and has been playing an important part in the establishment of national carbon trading market.

With its rich experience in carbon accounting, low-carbon training, and carbon asset development and management, Carbonstop has become a leader in the field. However, the founder Luhui Yan has higher expectations. Ever since its foundation, Carbonstop has been dedicated to improving the public's awareness of carbon emission reduction and encouraging them to take actions. Carbonstop has also been committed to motivating the public to reduce emissions. By using Internet technology it was good at, it promoted the public to learn about carbon emission reduction and take actions.

The Founder's Past Experience in Business Start-Up

Although Carbonstop has grown into a solid company, the road was not smooth when it just started. As a former programmer, how did Luhui Yan become interested in carbon management? He worked in a famous carbon management consulting company in the UK after graduated from college. What made him decide to go back to China and start his own business?

From 2011 to 2013—Returned to China alone and started business with difficulties

Luhui Yan majored in computer science back in college. After graduation, he found a job as a programmer in a bank responsible for developing online banking system. However, he often felt lost. In the first two years after he joined the bank, he kept asking himself what he wanted to be in the future. Would he be satisfied with living such a life forever? When he realized the answer was no, he decided to leave and explore the bigger world. He chose the road seldom could understand back then—he quit his decent and stable job and went abroad for further study. In 2009, he received master's degree in computer science from Oxford University, and jointed a carbon management consulting company called BestFoot Forward in the UK as senior software engineer and product manager, responsible for Chinese market. Luhui Yan confessed that it was the first time he heard about carbon footprint and carbon management when he first worked on the carbon emission management system in BestFoot Forward. At that time, he didn't know much about the company's business yet. After working for half a year, Luhui Yan found carbon management was a promising and significant business, which suited him as well. In order to learn more about the industry and the market back in China, he applied to undertake more consulting jobs. In 2010, Luhui Yan made a lot of trips to China to investigate the market and develop clients. From this experience, Luhui Yan got in touch with many domestic frontier companies and got familiar with domestic market. Based on his judgment of international trend and domestic market, Luhui Yan believed that the Chinese government definitely would attach more importance to carbon trading market. Since 2010, economic downturn in Europe caused the decline in carbon management consulting business. Luhui Yan decided to return to China to start his own business.

Since Luhui Yan had technical background in programming, he started with developing carbon management software first thing after he founded his company in March 2011. This software has been the main product of Carbonstop until today. When Carbonstop was first established in 2011, Luhui Yan was the only staff in the company. He registered the company with a start-up fund of only 500,000 yuan, but the potential market was enormous. In the first year, Luhui Yanla called his former colleagues together and developed the carbon management software. In order to foster the market, Carbonstop provided hundreds of enterprises with the right to use its carbon management software free of charge. Luhui Yan believed it would be rewarding to do so, because these enterprises would want to upgrade, maintain and customize the software later, which would generate revenue. Only from the second year after its establishment, Carbonstop began to have paying clients. According to Luhui Yan, the first paying client was an exchange agency. "In 2012, this exchange agency invited us to give them training. The income was only a few thousand yuan, not even enough to cover the airline tickets. But we must go. It was our first paying client. We need a start to get our business on the track." The first two years was difficult for Carbonstop. Since there was no revenue in the first year, all the colleagues who developed the software left the company. It was Luhui Yan alone who managed the company in the first two years. Lucky, Luhui Yan didn't give up, because he saw the prospect of the industry, and had faith in what he did.

From 2013 to 2017—Kept up with hot spots and expanded business scope

Since the second year when it had paying clients, Carbonstop began to expand its business to meet the requirements of its clients. The company was gradually on the right track. Luhui Yan introduced that they started low-carbon training and carbon management consulting in response to the market demand. Gradually, it became another core business of consulting, in parallel with the original software business. Now these two core businesses are IT department and consulting department. Only from 2013 that Carbonstop officially started its recruitment. Most of the members today joined the team during 2014 to 2015. In the first three years after the foundation, the turnover rate of employees was quite high. This was partly because the company didn't make any profit in the beginning. Another reason was that Luhui Yan had no experience in motivating the employees. In 2014, the company began to make profits. Meanwhile, Luhui Yan realized the adverse impact of high employee turnover. He started to take measures to improve talent cultivation and motivation.

Currently, Carbonstop only has two departments, IT department and consulting department, and 12 employees. There is no independent department for other functions such as marketing or human resources. The company operates in project teams, and adopts a flat structure centered on its business. According to Luhui Yan, most of the employees in consulting department have learning experience in the UK, and all of them have master's degree. They are highly competent and able to undertake projects independently shortly after they joined the company. "Goal management" is one of Luhui Yan's major talent management tools. "Everybody has their own annual goals. They need to reach this goal in their own business. There should be a year-on-year increase, and this increase determines their annual bonus." Of cause, this goal is not set by Luhui Yan alone, but through the discussion between Luhui

Yan and all the members of the project team. In order to stimulate the potential of every employee, Luhui Yan tries to adopt a democratic management style. He always consults with the employees and makes joint decisions in project selection, job assignment and goal setting.

Carbonstop has been sensitive to the social hot spots. It began to operate its WeChat official account since 2013, as the first in low carbon field. It developed some small tools, such as carbon calculator, and posted them on their WeChat for its followers to use freely. In order to popularize low-carbon knowledge and improve public awareness of emission reduction, since 2014 Carbonstop has developed a series of products for the general public to use in their daily lives. It worked together with the United Nations Environment Agency and released "Green Meeting Guide and Action" in 2014. It also launched "Carbon School" in 2016, and "Carbon trading simulator" mini program in early 2017. Obviously, promoting enterprises to reduce their carbon emission is not the only goal of Luhui Yan. He's also dedicated to improve people's awareness of carbon emission reduction and encourage them to take actions.

New Attempt to Promote Carbon Emission Reduction

The main business of Carbonstop is to provide enterprises and organizations with carbon emission management products and services, including consulting, training, software, and carbon neutralization. And later, it made a transformation and incorporated its experience in personal products for the public to use in their daily lives to improve their awareness of carbon emission reduction. Software and consulting services may sound superb, but out of ordinary people's reach. While public carbon emission reduction activities are much easier for them to understand and accept. For Carbonstop, they are equally important. Products and services for enterprises are the foundation of Carbonstop. They are the driving force for Luhui Yan to start the company in the first place. While the carbon emissions reduction products for the general public is Carbonstop's attempts towards a larger dream.

"Carbon Accounting and Management Platform"—Carbon Management Software for Enterprises

In 2011, Carbonstop developed China's first carbon emission management software system independently—Carbon Accounting and Management Platform (CAMP, see Fig. 1). This software was designed for governments and enterprises at all levels to calculate, analysis and manage their carbon emission. Through this platform, enterprises can quantify, analyze, manage and report their carbon emissions. The charts provided by the platform give them a general picture of their carbon emission and

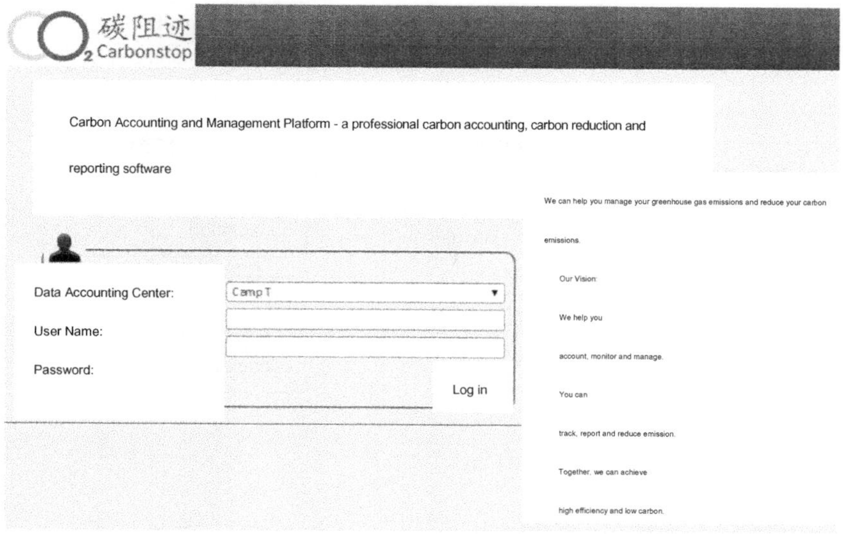

Fig. 1 Carbon accounting and management platform for enterprises (V2012)

help them find the direction to reduce it. According to complexity of client requirements, the software has three different versions: standard, enhanced and customized. Clients can choose the version according to their demands and pay the annual fee.

Currently, CAMP has more than one hundred domestic and overseas clients. Through CAMP, Carbonstop aims to help its enterprise clients reduce 18 million tons of carbon dioxide collectively by 2020. Currently, Carbonstop's clients include multinational enterprises, large state-owned enterprises, private enterprises, international organizations, government agencies and non-governmental organizations, in the industries of communication, steel, chemical, electric power, toys, telecommunications, automobiles, food and beverage, agricultural products, and energy.

Carbon Management Consulting

Carbon management consulting services include carbon accounting, carbon market consulting, carbon information disclosure, and product carbon footprint (see Fig. 2).

Carbonstop can account the carbon emission of a company scientifically and accurately according to carbon accounting standards in China and abroad. The findings can help the company discover its problems and recognize its carbon emission situation. Companies can formulate strategies and implement low-carbon projects based on these findings (see Fig. 3). Moreover, Carbonstop provides comprehensive "carbon market consulting" services for emission control enterprises, including

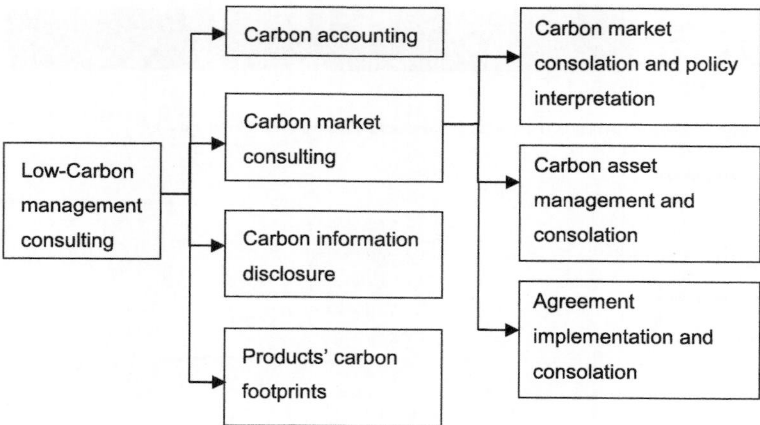

Fig. 2 Carbon management consulting services

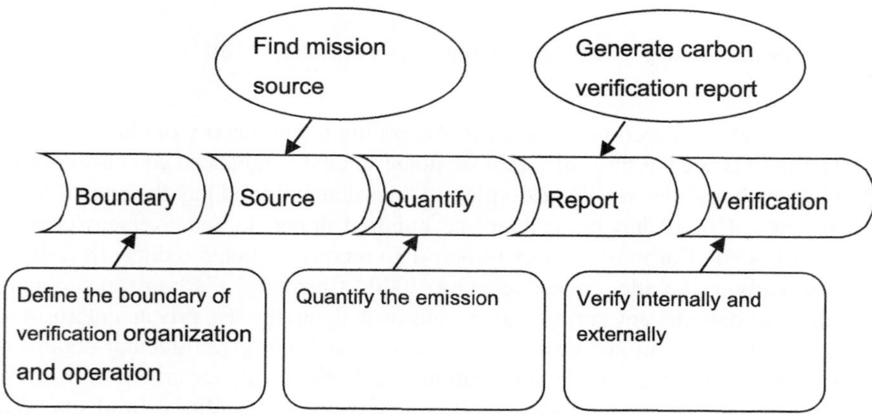

Fig. 3 Carbon accounting process

carbon market consulting and policy interpretation, carbon asset management and consulting, agreement performance management and consulting.

In addition, Carbonstop cooperates with Carbon Disclosure Project (CDP) to provide enterprises with consultation on carbon emission accounting and CDP questionnaire. This project encourages enterprises to disclose their strategies to cope with climate change and greenhouse gas emission data. It helps them to understand carbon emission management, so that they can quantify their carbon emission information and formulate effective carbon emission reduction strategies. Apparently, carbon accounting and carbon management knowledge are the foundation for corporate carbon disclosure. So far, Carbonstop has guided dozens of domestic enterprises to accomplish carbon emission information disclosure. All of them had outstanding performance in their CDP questionnaire.

Carbonstop has partners both in china and abroad in the field of environmental consulting, and they can jointly provide the best consulting and software services. For example, Carbonstop is the partner of United Nations Environment Programme (UNEP) in the field of sustainable development. World Resources Institution (WRI) is Carbonstop's partner in the field of carbon emission calculation tools. While in carbon verification consulting field, Carbonstop has BestFoot Forward as its partner.

Carbonstop enables enterprises with three advantages in carbon management. First, for export enterprises, they can meet foreign customers' requirements on carbon emission disclosure.

Second, through carbon accounting, enterprises can identify the carbon emissions of each production stage, and then formulate targeted emission reduction measures and implement low-carbon projects to reduce costs. Third, fulfilling environmental responsibilities can help the enterprises improve its corporate image and win the recognition of consumers. Carbonstop calculates carbon emissions through scientific methods and accurate data. It provides customized carbon management programs for enterprises from a commercial perspective, so that enterprises can take active responds to risks, seize market opportunities, and maintain leading position in market competition.

Low carbon + Internet: A New Attempt to Promote Public Emission Reduction

In addition to carbon management software and consulting services for enterprises, Carbonstop also applies its experience and products to the daily use of the general public. This is an important transformation for Carbonstop. The purpose is to popularize low-carbon knowledge to the public, improve public awareness of emission reduction, and educate the public that purchasing products or services also impacts the environment.

In 2014, Carbonstop and the United Nations Environment Programme released the Green Meeting Guide and Action, which aims to call on people to give priority to environmental and ecological impacts when organizing meetings. The core concept of "Green Meeting" is to incorporate the priority position of resource utilization and environment into the planning and preparation of meetings as early as possible. That is to give priority to environmental and ecological impacts in every stage of the meeting (Fig. 4).

This is a good way for Carbonstop to promote public carbon emission reduction. For a large conference, transportation, accommodation and other activities of the participants, as well as conference materials and consumptions, all produce a lot of carbon emissions. Through WeChat official account, Green Meeting provides

Fig. 4 Example of green meeting: carbon market trading strategy workshop

participants with online meeting registration channels, online conference materials and conference news, and real-time carbon emission queries.

Green Meeting aims to achieve three goals. The first goal is paperless conference—by cutting down paper use, reduce cost and carbon emission, and improve participants' environmental protection awareness. The second goal is efficient registration—register through WeChat applications, to reduce the manual cost and realized efficient meeting. And the third goal is carbon emission quantification and carbon neutralization—account the carbon emissions generated by the meeting, offset them through carbon sink or emission reduction projects and achieve a real green low-carbon meeting.

In order to promote the concept and practice of Green Meeting, Carbonstop team can provide Green Meeting services for institutions. It also helps institutions to develop their own Green Meeting platforms. Through these services, Green Meeting can be adopted in more fields. Since its launch in 2014, nearly 200 Green Meetings have been implemented by many institutions. Through Green Meeting, Carbonstop is expected to help its clients reduce three million tons of carbon emissions by 2020.

November 4, 2016 was the date when Paris Climate Agreement came into force. That day, Carbonstop launched Carbon School, the first online low-carbon learning platform in China. Carbon School makes use of carbon trading market and public participation. It covers every aspect of low-carbon fields, including climate change science, climate change negotiations, international and domestic low-carbon policies, carbon trade, carbon accounting, carbon disclosure, carbon finance, carbon sink, and carbon asset development. It is committed to making more people learn about green and low-carbon topics such as climate change and carbon market construction in a green and low-carbon way. Carbonstop invites top experts in different segments of the industry to share their carbon market expertise with people interested in low carbon. People can watch videos, interact with each other, and adopt low-carbon services to realize low-carbon transformation and prepare for climate change. Audiences can pay carbon currency to watch the lessons. Carbon currency is weighted by the carbon price of the seven pilot carbon markets in China (calculation may vary after the national carbon market is officially launched). The exchange rate of carbon currency to Chinese yuan is updated once a month. The system will calculate the carbon emission reduced by online courses compared to offline courses. This online platform communication mode is featured by wide coverage, low cost and high efficiency, and can attract the public. Carbonstop aims to give trainings to about 2,000 learners through Carbon School and popularize low-carbon knowledge to people from different industries (Fig. 5).

In January 2017, Carbonstop launched the mini program "Carbon trading simulator." People can learn and practice carbon trading by simulating on this platform. Since its launch, this WeChat mini program has held three phases of online activities. The first phase was participated by more than 2000 people in just five days and was widely recognized in the carbon field. The second phase made a huge breakthrough with more than 20,000 participants and two million visits in the same period of time (Fig. 6).

As for the third phase, the total number of users reached 34,000, and the number of visitors exceeded three million. The number of active users was nearly 7000, increased by 64% over the second quarter. More and more enterprises and ordinary people were getting interest in the carbon market and were eager to learn.

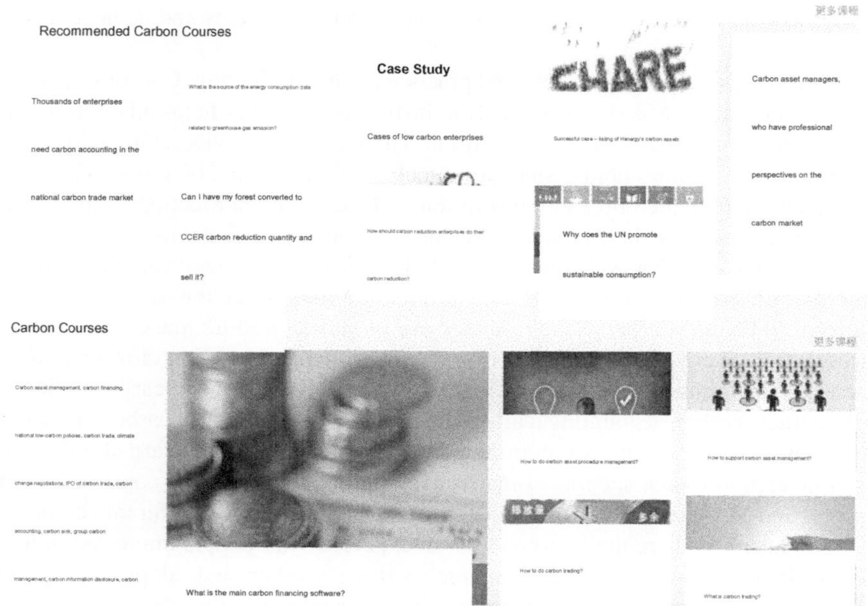

Fig. 5 Carbon School website

Carbonstop's Core Competence

Since its foundation in 2011, Carbonstop has gone through business depression and loss of talents. What were the reasons for Carbonstop to overcome these difficulties and keep on developing its business and new products and become a leader in the field?

Apply Advanced Ideas Learned from Europe and Guide Management with Data

Carbonstop focuses on carbon markets and provides carbon accounting and carbon management consulting services for emission control enterprises. This business mode was borrowed from European excellent carbon management consulting companies. Luhui Yan was frank about the influence of his former employer. "A lot of ideas are similar. We have learned a lot from the companies in UK, such as carbon accounting. And the most important concept is to guide management with data." Even so, Chinese market is distinctively different from European market. Carbonstop must adjust carbon management consulting services before entering the Chinese market. "International and domestic accounting standards are different. At least we

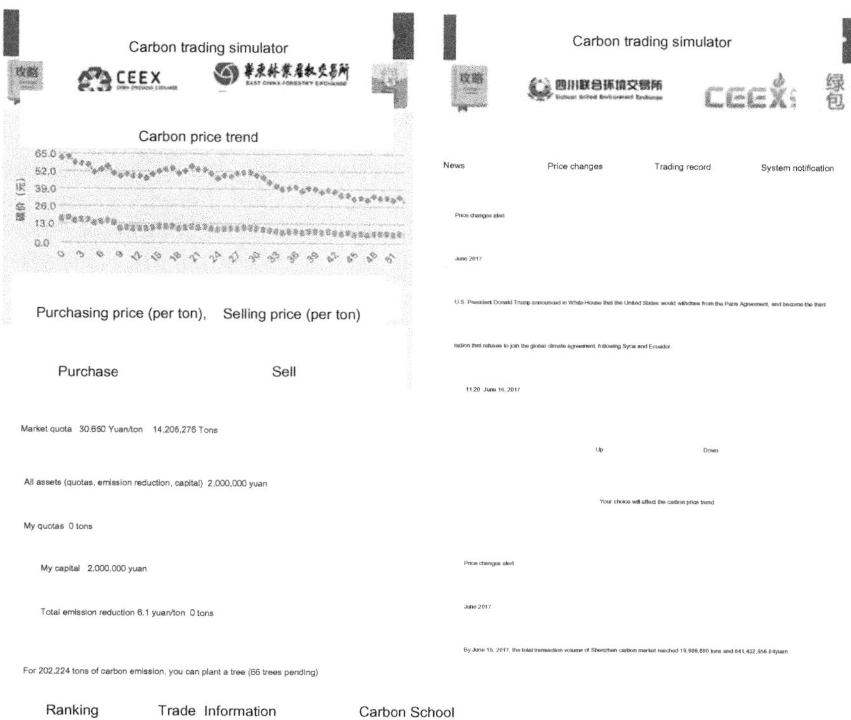

Fig. 6 "Carbon trading simulator" mini program page

need to localize and use domestic data. Take the carbon emission of electric power for example. The difference between domestic and international standards is very large, because the source is very different. The source is comparatively cleaner in UK. In China, the carbon emission of thermal power generation is much higher. The emission formulas are also different."

His two years of work experience in the UK made Luhui Yan interested in carbon industry, and taught him a lot of technologies and ideas about carbon accounting and carbon management. This experience has laid a solid foundation for his later business for sure. But none the less, to take one piece of the big pie in Chinese market, one has to make innovative attempts based on the reality of this market. These unique thoughts and attempts are the keys for Carbonstop's achievements and reputation today in the field of carbon.

Plan in Advance and Create a Comprehensive Solution of Software and Consulting

Talking about the position of Carbonstop in the industry, Luhui Yan was very confident. "Our biggest advantage in the industry is that we can offer a comprehensive solution combining both software and consulting, instead of just one of them. Our competitors either have software or consulting services, but none of them can provide a comprehensive solution." This solution is the result of Carbonstop's rich experience and strong team.

In fact, back when Carbonstop was just founded, it aimed to focus on carbon management software development, which was Luhui Yan's technical expertise. In order to promote its software, Carbonstop provided the Chinese version of carbon management software to clients for free trial. And further services for system upgrading, maintenance and customization would bring in revenue. Meanwhile, clients began to ask them for trainings, consulting and other services. "At the beginning, when we provided software services to clients, we found that they also had demands in training and consulting. So we created a combined solution. This solution also made it harder for other competitors to copy." Thus, Carbonstop expanded its business to low-carbon training and carbon management consulting.

On the other hand, this software plus consulting solution that gives them advantage in the market was actually a result of their strong team. Currently, Carbonstop has 12 members in two departments, IT and consulting. The former is responsible for software business, and the latter for consulting business. Most of the employees in consulting department have learning experience in the UK, and all of them have master's degree. They are highly competent. According to Luhui Yan, most employees joined Carbonstop because they are passionate about carbon reduction and recognize the company's value. This is also why Carbonstop excels in consulting services.

Keep up with the Hot Spot and Seize the Opportunity

Carbonstop is good at keeping up with the hot spots. A typical example is its use of mobile Internet. In low-carbon area, Carbonstop is the first company that has its WeChat public official account and WeChat mini program. This is also an innovation that European carbon management consulting companies don't have. Luhui Yan introduced, "we use the mobile terminal a lot. One example is Carbon Calculator used on mobile terminals. Companies in the UK don't have this kind of product for sure. Another example is Green Meeting. It is the first product of its kind all around the world, and it's available only in China. "In Luhui Yan's opinion, as two major driving forces of social innovation today, Internet and low-carbon should go hand-in-hand for better development." The Internet industry needs low-carbon, because Internet companies face the consumers directly and good customer experience, reputation and social responsibility are the driving forces for its growth in the new consumption era. While for low-carbon industry, everything is based on data, and the most efficient and transparent way to obtain data is through the Internet. Internet can avoid subjectivity and manipulation, carbon emission reporting system is an example."

Internet can easily attract the public, which is the natural advantage of this emerging new technology in China. No matter its WeChat official account or WeChat mini program, all these mobile Internet applications enable Carbonstop to interact with the general public directly and effectively, so that it can convey its concept, improve public awareness of emission reduction. And this is exactly what Luhui Yan wished for in the first place. When talking about the history of Carbonstop, Luhui Yan said, "We focused more on B2B in the beginning, to provide software, consultation and solutions for enterprises and institutions. But gradually, we realized that public participation is the key to our success. And it has become our mission too. The name of our company is Carbonstop, which means to stop carbon emission and reduce Carbon footprints." For Carbonstop, the best thing is to attract people, as well as institutions, to participate in carbon emission reduction, because institutions are just some cold names, while people are the core to make changes.

Therefore, Carbonstop has been applying its experience and products to people's daily lives. Green Meet, Carbon Schools, and Carbon Trading Simulator are all such attempts to encourage the public to care about environmental protect and low-carbon and make changes in their daily lives. Taking Carbon School as an example, as the first online low-carbon training platform in China, it aims to accelerate the capacity-building of low-carbon industry through the Internet, so that China can get ready for climate change as soon as possible. It offers online videos on carbon market knowledge to people interested in low carbon. People can watch videos, interact with each other, and adopt low-carbon services to realize low-carbon transformation and prepare for climate change. This online communication mode is featured by wide coverage, low cost and high efficiency, and can motivate as many people as possible. In recent years, Carbonstop kept on developing activities to the general public on the Internet, to encourage more public participation. For example, it cooperated with the government and carried out activities on low-carbon general rewards. In the future, it plans to carry out carbon emission reduction activities in universities.

Form an "Ecosystem" of Enterprises and Individual Users

Currently, carbon management software and carbon management consulting services are still Carbonstop's main sources of revenue. However, its attempts for the general public are significant, though there haven't been any financial returns so far. In addition to promote enterprises to pay more attention to carbon emission reduction, Carbonstop also aims to encourage the general public to participate in it. When the whole society care about carbon emission reduction, enterprises will be pushed to implement low-carbon transformation. Meanwhile, the attempts for the general public also help to attract corporate clients. Thus, an ecosystem can be formed—"individuals or institutions interested in low-carbon or green development will be attracted, and then they might become our potential clients. Potential client is a more practical way of saying. They are actually part of this ecosystem." Take Carbon School as an example, "many people attended the training not just to learn specific knowledge, but to get in touch with the experts. Because in low-carbon industry, those who are interested in these trainings usually have a clear goal – to make money in carbon trading. So they are willing to enter the market at a very low cost. They can connect with the real experts in the industry and obtain a lot of resources. This is the real value of these trainings."

Public participation, on the one hand, helps to create an ecosystem, where individuals and institutions can interact and communicate with each other, which is helpful for Carbonstop's long-term development. On the other hand, public's interest in low-carbon and related products can force enterprises to accelerate its transformation to low-carbon operation. Luhui Yan believes that forcing or enticing enterprises to reduce their carbon emissions by external factors is not a sustainable solution. On the contrary, if consumers value low-carbon performance of the enterprises or their products and are willing to pay for it, they can effectively push the enterprises to implement low-carbon transformation. This is also the goal of Carbonstop.

Developments and Challenges

Currently, Carbonstop has become a leader of its industry, and Luhui Yan, the founder, has also become famous in the field. However, Luhui Yan has bigger "ambition." China's carbon trading market construction still has a long way to go. Public awareness of carbon emission reduction is still low. Carbonstop has a lot to do. In the next few years, Carbonstop is faced with both opportunities and challenges. Luhui Yan must seize the opportunities and lead the company to a new level.

Business Expansion and Product Development

Carbonstop has rich experience in carbon information disclosure, carbon accounting, and carbon management consulting, and has been widely recognized in the field. For Carbonstop, carbon management software and carbon management consulting services are its main sources of revenue. Businesses facing the general public, such as Green Meeting and Carbon School, bring very little or no revenue. But Carbonstop's goal is not just to reduce the carbon footprint of enterprises in the carbon market. It also has a bigger "ambition" to encourage the ordinary people to reduce the footprint of their daily lives. In the future, Luhui Yan will stick to his idea of reducing carbon footprints from every possible aspect. From the business end, Carbonstop should seize the opportunities brought by the upcoming national carbon trading market, to expand its resources and deepen cooperation with all parties. From the customer end, it will develop more products and functions to promote public participation. Concerning the growth and expansion of the company, Luhui Yan also has his own ideas. "In the long run, we all agree that we don't need many branches or employees. Instead, we still need to refine our business."

Luhui Yan is optimistic and ambitious about the future of his company. "Globalization might be a big opportunity, because China has great advantages in it. China has become the biggest carbon emission country in the world. And China's carbon market is also the largest in the world. With the construction of "one belt and one road," China's experiences in carbon emissions reduction have been exported to other countries. This is also an opportunity for us. Chinese market is not our only target, but it certainly has its uncompetitive advantages, such as its enormous size, as well as the rising of new technologies, such as the Internet applications, which are not available in other countries. We will try to integrate these advantages into a comprehensive product or a complete service solution. That will be our advantage in the competition with the United States and European countries. At that time, we will be ready to go public." In terms of going public, Luhui Yan does not count on it to make profits. He weighs more on the opportunities it brings to Carbonstop and carbon emission reduction industry.

As a company with rich experience and resources in low-carbon field, it certainly is favored by many investors. But so far, Carbonstop has not accepted any investments. As for the reason, Luhui Yan explained, "investors always expect for fast returns. But we are not a pure Internet company, so the return period will be longer. In the early stage of this market, everyone is still exploring, even the administrator, National Development and Reform Commission. So Carbonstop must get down to earth and grow steadily for a while. "Currently, Carbonstop's products and services can form an ecosystem by themselves. Our own businesses can support each other. For example, our software and consulting businesses make revenues, which can support us to develop customer end services. And then in return these customer end services will bring us more clients. A virtuous circle is formed."

Challenges

As an enterprise with seven years of experience in the field of low-carbon, Carbonstop has discovered its own developing mode with Chinese characteristics. As for the future, Luhui Yan has his own plans. The data and experiences Carbonstop accumulated in the past seven years have become its core competitiveness today. "Carbonstop" has also become a well-known brand in the low-carbon field. In 2017, national carbon trading market was launched, which was a precious and critical opportunity for Carbonstop to upgrade to a higher level. However, opportunities usually come hand-in-hand with challenges. How to win in the fierce competition? How to make full use of resources? How to expand the market? And how to attract and retain talents? These are some of the challenges for Carbonstop among others.

Luhui Yan is frank about the difficulties faced by Carbonstop, among which the lack of connections with the government is the biggest one. "We tried to get well connected with the government, but we failed. If we had those resources, things would have been much easier. But we were on ourselves. We didn't have such resource. Many other competitors added National Development and Reform Commission as their shareholders. In order to compete with them, we could only count on our products. We are doing things bottom-up, and they are top-down. This is the reality we face. To put it in an optimistic way, we are like fighting a battle from conquering the outskirts first and then the whole town. If we can succeed, we will make a positive example." The positive side of the lack of connection with the government, according to Luhui Yan, is that Carbonstop was forced to adopt a special business mode with its own advantages. "Those companies (with government background) can't develop product like Carbon Trading Simulator. They don't need to do it of cause. So this is a disadvantage and an advantage at the same time. We are just a grass root company, struggling to survive on our own."

Besides the lack of government resources, which makes it difficult for Carbonstop to have in-depth communication and cooperation with the government, another weakness lies in its marketing. As Luhui Yan said, they developed their first clients by themselves. Later, clients found them, thanks to their advanced technology and good reputation. Carbonstop seldom maintains customer relationship. It relies more on its products and services to retain their clients. However, as national carbon market unveils, marketing and customer maintenance become inevitable tasks for CarbonStop.

Currently, except for occasional cash flow issues, Carbonstop is operating well. Luhui Yan, the founder of Carbonstop, is very satisfied with the company's current development pace and direction. "There are a lot of opportunities before us. The only challenge for us is how to seize them."

Further Reading

Gong H (2015). Carbonstop: stop the carbon footprints. http://www.chinatoday.com.cn/chinese/economy/ls/201510/t20151021_800040858.html. Accessed 21 October 2015

Company Information

Carbonstop official website, www.carbonstop.net

Carbonstop WeChat official account, carbonstop

Carbonstop WeChat subscription account, carbonstop_dingyue

Printed by Books on Demand, Germany